A Sound So Very Loud

ALSO BY TED KESSLER

To Ease My Troubled Mind: The Authorized Unauthorized History of Billy Childish

Paper Cuts: How I Destroyed the British Music Press and Other Misadventures

My Old Man: Tales of our Fathers

A Sound So Very Loud

The Inside Story of Every Song Oasis Recorded

Ted Kessler & Hamish MacBain

MACMILLAN

First published 2025 by Macmillan
an imprint of Pan Macmillan
The Smithson, 6 Briset Street, London EC1M 5NR
EU representative: Macmillan Publishers Ireland Ltd, 1st Floor,
The Liffey Trust Centre, 117–126 Sheriff Street Upper,
Dublin 1 D01 YC43
Associated companies throughout the world

ISBN 978-1-0350-7825-7 HB
ISBN 978-1-0350-7826-4 TPB

9 8 7 6 5 4 3 2 1

A CIP catalogue record for this book is available from the British Library.

Typeset in Warnock Pro by Palimpsest Book Production Limited, Falkirk, Stirlingshire
Printed and bound in the UK using 100% Renewable Electricity by CPI Group (UK) Ltd

Visit **www.panmacmillan.com** to read more about all our books and to buy them.

To O.A. and all who sail in her . . .

Contents

A Sound So Very Loud

A WhatsApp conversation between the authors, summer 2024

HAMISH: You missed out tonight . . . watching Noel up on the hill by Ally Pally, whole of London skyline in the background. Beautiful.
20 July, 11.13 p.m.

HAMISH: Was surrounded by loads of teenagers all singing every word of 'Going Nowhere' . . .
20 July, 11.14 p.m.

TED: Amazing
20 July, 11.20 p.m.

TED: Remember all those kids on the way to the O2 for LG's Def Maybe show?
20 July, 11.20 p.m.

TED: can't think of another band whose music has travelled through generations like this. It's like Star Wars or something
20 July, 11.21 p.m.

HAMISH: hahaha
20 July, 11.22 p.m.

TED: Should definitely do this book idea. Meet in Coach & Horses in next week or so?
20 July, 11.24 p.m.

HAMISH: Def
20 July, 11.25 p.m.

HAMISH: Good seeing you this eve, think this book idea could be really great. Need to flesh out what it is . . . no big rush I guess
6 Aug, 11.30 p.m.

TED: do think that song-by-song thing would be good
6 Aug, 11.32 p.m.

TED: sort of tell the story of Oasis via the music rather than the arguments
6 Aug, 11.34 p.m.

HAMISH: yeah
6 Aug, 11.35 p.m.

HAMISH: er, was out and about last night. Bumped into [NAME REDACTED], she said she's heard an announcement is imminent!
15 Aug, 10.23 p.m.

TED: What announcement?
15 Aug, 10.24 p.m.

HAMISH: THE announcement!
15 Aug, 10.27 p.m.

TED: Surely not. Good on Liam not letting that slip if so
15 Aug, 10.31 p.m.

HAMISH: Yeah. Let's see. We should announce the book just in case, otherwise people will never believe we were talking about it before!!!
15 Aug, 10.33 p.m.

TED: haha
15 Aug, 10.41 p.m.

TED: rumours getting pretty deafening
21 Aug, 3.45 p.m.

HAMISH: 'It was a sound so very loooud . . .'
21 Aug, 3.52 p.m.

TED: Could be a good title
21 Aug, 3.55 p.m.

HAMISH: ha, yeah, maybe
21 Aug, 3.56 p.m.

HAMISH: Can't believe it's happening!
21 Aug, 3.56 p.m.

TED: About time
21 Aug, 3.57 p.m.

TED: Guess we better get on with this book, then
27 Aug, 8.30 a.m.

HAMISH: Yes. We should.
27 Aug, 8.30 a.m.

Introduction

The glorious noise of Oasis

What is the best way to measure the significance of a band? Is it purely down to the number of hit songs they had? The biggest venues they played? The innovations they made? The most complimentary reviews? Is it the extent to which they reshaped popular culture in their own image?

All of these are important factors. Though arguably more important is how they go on to inspire future generations of young people who were not even born when they were doing their best work: people who are connecting with the music without the context of the time in which it was made.

Long after they split in 2009, part of Noel Gallagher's justification for not reuniting the band he led was that everyone who wanted to see Oasis had surely had plenty of chances to see them. Unlike his heroes The Jam or The Smiths – who were in and out within half a decade, never playing stadiums – they had been playing venues that held tens of thousands of people all over the world for fifteen years. When his other key inspiration, the Stone Roses, re-formed in 2012, it gave people who were just too late to the band's original line-up (they disappeared in 1990 having played well under 100 shows ever) the chance to see them play.

But Oasis? They had already done the job of delighting fans who were just toddlers – the likes of Arctic Monkeys, The Killers and many other celebrated noughties bands – when *Definitely Maybe* came out. In their absence, though, something happened.

The 2016 documentary *Supersonic* did a brilliant job of showing just what a unique band this had been: a band that seemed to always be playing by their own rules, who thrived in an atmosphere of barely controlled chaos and who did not care at all what anybody thought of them. They were funny. They were taking full advantage of – rather than cowering at – the fame the more it was bestowed upon them. They triumphed, then fucked up, then triumphed again, the only constant being indescribably great songs and shows that, even just onscreen, could change your life.

When Liam Gallagher went solo the following year and started to play shows that were stuffed full of his former band's songs, he was having every word sung back to him by people who were toddlers when Oasis split up. And not just 'Wonderwall' or 'Champagne Supernova' – the songs that a large proportion of Planet Earth knows – but the likes of 'Rock 'n' Roll Star' and 'Morning Glory'. Similarly, while Noel Gallagher could always expect to have 'Don't Look Back in Anger' bellowed back at him, now he was introducing Oasis B-sides with an 'I appreciate that most of you won't have any idea what this song is', then having them greeted with a similar euphoria.

To go on TikTok or Instagram in the days after 27 August 2024 was to discover a whole new generation of teenagers as desperate to secure a ticket for the reunion shows as the people who had been there the first time around. More so, even. Older-generation fans implying that they had more earned the right to be at the 2025 shows – 'gatekeeping', as this new breed of fan put it – were missing the point. Nothing could be further from the truth. From the word go, Oasis were never an 'I was into them before you' sort of a band. Oasis were, are and always will be for everyone. Even those who came to the band in its earliest days were soon being joined by thousands of others. It's hard to think of many other debut albums that had classic status bestowed upon them as quickly as *Definitely Maybe* did. Within days of its release, Oasis were playing in Japan. When Hamish asked Liam Gallagher, decades later, for his memories of that first trip, he still seemed bamboozled by the reaction. 'It was just hearing people who speak a different language singing your music back,' he said. 'Say if a Japanese band came out now, and they came over here, even if everyone was like, "They sound like fucking God," I'd be like, "You need to do it in English." But we were sounding exactly like that to them, and they were getting it. So that showed me that music is powerful. It was bypassing the language barrier, and just hitting them with the feeling.'

Oasis were transcending the barriers of language, and of genre. Upon release, the dance music magazine *Mixmag* had given *Definitely Maybe* five out of five stars: a reflection of the fact that it was reaching people who previously would have had no interest in guitar music in the UK. When they emerged, guitar music was the preserve of maybe a couple of hundred thousand indie kids. The spectre of Kurt Cobain, who took his own life just a week before 'Supersonic' introduced Oasis to the world, hung over and informed a scene that still deemed itself to be 'alternative'. Kurt Cobain himself had abhorred the idea of connecting with the mainstream. 'I spent all of my life trying to stay away from sports,' he told an arena full of people in December of 1993, 'and here I am in a sporting arena.'

From the word go, Oasis had the opposite attitude.

Friends from the pub and five-a-side football, drummer Tony McCarroll, bass player Paul 'Guigsy' McGuigan and guitarist Paul 'Bonehead' Arthurs – none of them particularly special musicians – had formed The Rain in 1991 in Burnage, Manchester. Their singer at this point was a fellow member of this crowd called Chris Hutton. He was soon to be ousted, however, replaced by a charismatic young man who was one of the few people regularly turning up to their shows.

Liam Gallagher's first suggestion to the band he had now joined as the singer was changing their name. He had a poster on his bedroom wall featuring the tour dates of Inspiral Carpets, a band his older brother was a roadie for. One of the venues they had played was Swindon Oasis. *Oasis*, he thought. *That'll do nicely.*

They got to work, renting a rehearsal room in the Boardwalk, a now-closed gig venue just round the corner from the Haçienda. 'We were rehearsing there every single night of the week, just head down, fucking grafting,' Liam said of this period. 'I loved it, it was mega. We'd rehearse, then go up to the bar in the club afterwards, have a little drink and watch some shit band. There was this band called Puressence next door – they were always telling us to turn it down – and we shared our room with this band Sister Lovers. Everyone was getting gigs except us: you'd see Puressence going off to do a gig, and we'd be like, "Where's our fucking gigs?" We couldn't get a gig anywhere.'

One of the few shows they could get was, inevitably, at the Boardwalk. Liam invited his brother Noel – back from touring with the Inspirals – down to see them. 'He went, "Yeah, you're alright," and I think we just said, "Look, why don't you manage us and get us connections?" I thought maybe he wouldn't want to join the band. He'd messed around with a few lads from round our way before, but he'd never seemed that bothered with being in a band. He wasn't arsed, I don't think. He was quite happy doing his Inspiral Carpets thing. I guess he was making good money and travelling the world, so he was probably looking at us thinking, *I'm not fucking all that off for this dick.* I'd have thought the same thing, to be fair!'

Noel Gallagher had other ideas. Big ideas. By the beginning of 1992, he was installed as lead guitarist in Oasis and – more importantly – writer of all the songs. By the end of that year, 'Rock 'n' Roll Star', 'Bring It on Down', 'Columbia', 'Live Forever' and others were in their set.

What was evident from these songs was that Oasis, unlike all their then-peers, made no bones about the fact that they wanted to gatecrash the mainstream, to take it over, to remake it in their own image. They wanted to have number ones. They wanted to be played on daytime radio. They wanted to play stadiums. They wanted, most of all, to be stars. And even if they had not explicitly stated this in every interview they did, the final, triumphant mix of *Definitely Maybe* – on which producer Owen Morris came in at the last minute, pushed everything into the red, creating a cacophony of swaggering, beautiful noise – would have made it obvious anyway.

Definitely Maybe was advertised, very effectively, in football magazines and programmes. Pretty soon after its release, an entire legion of people who would previously have jeered at someone walking down the street with a Beatles haircut and a guitar had Beatles haircuts and guitars. Before *Definitely Maybe*, it was all but impossible for a straight-up guitar band to top the charts. Not long afterwards, it was the norm and, as with all great albums that incite a huge cultural shift, it became difficult to remember what music looked and sounded like before it arrived. Almost instantly, it spawned legions of copyists, all of whose albums were routinely hyped as 'the best British album since *Definitely Maybe*'. For more than a decade afterwards, this continued to be the case. 'If I see one more advert on the TV for an album that says, "Best guitar album since *Definitely Maybe*"', Noel Gallagher said in 2006, during the last truly fertile period for British guitar bands. 'Fucking hell – I'll shoot whoever writes those fucking things!'

People don't tend to say that any more, not least because barely anyone – especially guitar bands – can afford to advertise their album on television. But, if anything, the modern musical climate has only enhanced the legacy of *Definitely Maybe*. A quarter of a century on from its initial release, stripped of the context of the nineties, the first Oasis album still sounds like the last word in effortless, just-plug-in-and-play garage band immediacy: like the five people involved in it turned up, pressed 'record' and emerged just under an hour later with an album that they all knew, right there and then, would change the course of British music forever.

As wondrous as the songs remain, as peerless as the voice that delivered them was, as much as the swagger was important, what really connected and continues to connect with people is the sentiment of Oasis. The lines like '*Tonight, I'm a rock and roll star*'. Or '*I just want to fly*'. Or '*I'm feeling supersonic, give me gin and tonic*'. The sort of simple, direct, escapist, inclusive lines that might previously have been found in dance music, but which guitar bands would most likely have turned their noses up at.

And that was just the first album.

By the end of 1995, Oasis were a genuine, gold-plated pop-culture phenomenon. *(What's the Story) Morning Glory?* remains the fifth biggest-selling UK album of all time, outstripped only by a pair of greatest hits albums (Queen, ABBA), *Sgt Pepper's . . .* and, most recently, Adele's *21*. It has sold more than 22 million copies worldwide (almost three times as many as either *Definitely Maybe* or *Be Here Now*). But more important than that – more important than any figures – it is the album that contains the songs you and everyone you know can sing every last syllable of, whether a fan of them or not. The songs that will continue to be bellowed by arm-in-arm people of all ages at closing time; murdered by buskers in town squares the world over; and clutched to the hearts of those who have not yet even been born. The songs that, even more so than 'Live Forever', really will live long, long after everyone involved in making them has passed away.

These are the songs that catapulted them to a level of fame across the world that few human beings get to experience. Warring brothers at the heart of a rock 'n' roll band was not an entirely new phenomenon, but something about the dynamic between Noel and Liam Gallagher drew people into their story like nothing before or since. Even when playing to hundreds of thousands – most memorably, of course, across two nights at Knebworth in 1996 – people turned up not knowing exactly what was going to happen. And so it remained, at sell-out nights at New York's Madison Square Garden in 2005 to River Plate Stadium in Buenos Aires in 2009, and right up until the last chord was struck at the final show, at Weston Park, Stafford on 22 August 2009, six days before a fight backstage between the brothers at the Rock en Seine festival near Paris dropped the curtain dramatically upon them for fifteen years.

As much as these shows and hundreds of others may have been unforgettable, the accepted narrative is that Oasis, musically, never matched the heights of the mid-nineties. How could they? Noel Gallagher himself has often expressed a distaste for much of the band's post- *. . . Morning Glory* output. 1997's *Be Here Now* was overblown. 2000's *Standing on the Shoulder of Giants* uninspired.

But to listen to these albums – and *Heathen Chemistry, Don't Believe the Truth* and *Dig Out Your Soul* – without the weight of expectation that greeted them at the time is to find records on which there is much to enjoy, and songs that are a significant part of the story of this most significant of bands.

This book is about telling that story . . .

1993

Bill Clinton is inaugurated as the 42nd president of the United States on 20 January and one month later has an attack on the World Trade Center to deal with. Two weeks before Noel Gallagher's twenty-seventh birthday in May, the Manchester football club that he does not support – United – win the first ever season of the Premier League: their first title in twenty-six years. (The same week, the shadow home secretary and widely assumed next leader of the Labour Party, Tony Blair, turns forty). Jurassic Park *becomes the highest-grossing film of all time soon after its June release. In September, Nirvana release what will be their third album,* In Utero, *the first episode of* The X-Files *is aired and 'I'd Do Anything for Love (But I Won't Do That)' by Meat Loaf goes to number one in twenty-eight countries. The year ends with the gunning down of Pablo Escobar, the withdrawal from public life of Princess Diana, and the recording of the first ever BBC live session – on 22 December at Maida Vale Studios – by Manchester's most promising new band.*

The original Oasis line-up (*left to right*: Noel Gallagher, Tony McCarroll, Liam Gallagher, Paul McGuigan, Paul 'Bonehead' Arthurs) shot at Nomad Studios, Manchester, October 1993, by Jamie Fry. 'I could claim that I saw their success coming, but I'd be a liar,' he said of this photo. 'You could tell they were going to do alright, but . . . fucking hell.'

'Columbia'

WHITE LABEL DEMO

DISTRIBUTED DECEMBER 1993

If you are reading this, it's highly likely you will have seen the 2016 documentary *Supersonic*. If you have not, then spoilers follow.

The film opens with footage of Oasis boarding a helicopter, flying over and then landing in Knebworth Park in August of 1996, before striding onstage in front of 125,000 people and beginning their set with 'Columbia'. It sounds absolutely titanic – 'My guitar was, officially, louder than a rocket,' beamed Noel Gallagher – the crowd in their entirety bellowing along not just to the lyrics, but the riffs, the cyclical three-chord groove of the song taking them higher and higher each time it is repeated.

Until suddenly, just as 'Columbia' is about to reach its euphoric '*come on, come on, come on, come on*' climax, we switch seamlessly to five young men playing the same song in a cramped rehearsal room underneath the Boardwalk venue in Manchester towards the end of 1993: a smart bit of filmmaking that hammers home just how fast the rise of this band was.

In December of 1993, 'Columbia' became Oasis's first release: an extremely limited, one-sided, vinyl-only pressing distributed solely to DJs and journalists in an effort to turn them onto the band. Just over two and a half years later, the same song, with exactly the same arrangement, was serving as the opener to the biggest concerts the UK has ever seen.

'Not wishing to wind everybody up,' read the sticker on the plain black sleeve, 'but OASIS have got everything. Hear for yourself – and this is only the demo! Anyone for any more?'

Creation Records' genial owner Alan McGee was no stranger to making pronouncements of this kind about his signings. His track record meant that people paid attention, with a string of classic albums from the Jesus and Mary Chain, Primal Scream, My Bloody

Valentine, Teenage Fanclub and Ride still fresh in the memory. Helpfully, too, just as the 'Columbia' white label went out, the Boo Radleys' *Giant Steps* album had been named NME's second-best Album of the Year. Creation artists, in other words, were always worth a listen. But surely Alan McGee couldn't be right again? Could he?

'Columbia' was first played in public upstairs at an early show at the Boardwalk, Manchester, on Valentine's Day in 1992. It was the very first song that Noel Gallagher ever wrote for Oasis, having joined his younger brother's band the previous year. (Prior to his arrival, the songs had been composed by Liam Gallagher and Bonehead.)

'One Sunday afternoon, I was at home watching *EastEnders* when our kid rings up and says, "You coming down for a jam?"' Noel remembered. 'I'd never played with anyone else ever. I went, "Alright." We sit there for hours and hours, dead hot and sweaty, and it's great.' A favoured technique in those extremely early days was to, as Noel puts it, 'jam out current acid house favourites and fuck about. "Columbia" derived from one of those nights.'

The riff in 'Columbia' was inspired by a 12-inch by Tortuga called *Axe Corner* that had arrived in 1991. The feel of this very early Oasis song – the swaggering kick drum, the lumbering bassline – owes a lot to a single by Manchester band The Chameleons, 'Swamp Thing', from their final album *Strange Times*.

'I'd forgotten how much this album meant to me,' Noel Gallagher wrote on Instagram in 2018. 'It came out in '86. I was 19! I've been listening to it every day since and I have to say it's blown my mind . . . again! It must have influenced my early years as a songwriter because I can hear ME in it everywhere!!'

The Oasis sound was born. Soon Noel Gallagher was feeding his more sophisticated songwriting through it: the jam-around-three-chords, waiting-for-something-to-happen process confined to history, survived only by 'Columbia'. It joined the likes of 'Rock 'n' Roll Star' and 'Bring It on Down' on an eight-song cassette demo (that would come to be known as 'Live Demonstration') with a cover featuring a Union Jack going down the toilet.

The potential of 'Columbia' was not fully realized until Owen Morris got his hands on it during the making of *Definitely Maybe*. He layered its guitars into a wall of sound, doubled up the drum and bass parts to create a more pulsating rhythm and ended up with 'my favourite mix I've ever done'. There is no question that this is the definitive version. But the demo that Oasis recorded in the spring of 1993 was progressing nicely.

The recording was made at the studio of Liverpool band the Real People, whose singer/songwriter, Tony Griffiths, Noel had met on tour in the US while working as a roadie for Inspiral Carpets. It was produced by Mark Coyle and is, by early demo standards, fairly sophisticated. Buried within its mix are three samples: one at the beginning from a film that to this day no one can identify ('I've seen so much disgust, mother. Take me into your arms. How may I protect you?' it seems to be saying); an almost Hare Krishna-esque chant that appears halfway through then stays until the end; and the voice of Labour MP Tony Benn talking on BBC Radio 3 while the 'Columbia' session was going on.

The version of 'Columbia' was certainly finished enough for Alan McGee – who a couple of months before its recording had made his fateful stumble into Glasgow's tiny, sparsely populated King Tut's Wah Wah Hut and laid eyes on the band – to put out. And the white label, plus accompanying hype note, did its job. On the evening of 6 December 1993, Oasis got their first ever bit of national radio play courtesy of Jo Whiley and Steve Lamacq's influential *Evening Session* on Radio 1. It would go on to be played twenty or so more times on the station. Oasis were on their way.

And the title? It's in honour of the Columbia: the legendary nineties hotel where record labels would have their bands stay when they came to London, due in part to its policy of keeping the bar in the lobby open for as long as anyone staying in the hotel wanted. Noel had enjoyed some late nights there with Inspiral Carpets, and Oasis's time to check in was soon to come . . . until they got a lifetime ban for being – to quote manager Michael Rose – 'more than a tolerant hotel can cope with' having returned from a hard day's recording. This was quite an achievement given what went on behind the hotel's doors most nights of the week. 'We were told, "Get out and don't ever come back,"' Bonehead remembered. 'We were happy to get out as the Columbia is a pit. It's like somewhere your granny would stay.' That night, Oasis were moved next door to a much-more-plush-anyway Hilton Hotel. As a title, 'Columbia' stayed, which was just as well. Because Oasis couldn't very well have gone on to open the biggest rock 'n' roll show of all time with a song called 'Hilton.' **HM**

1994

The same year in which Justin Bieber and Harry Styles are born brings the release of The Shawshank Redemption, Forrest Gump, Pulp Fiction *and, before all of these, in January,* Four Weddings and a Funeral. *Six days before the first ever Oasis single is released on 11 April, Kurt Cobain takes his own life. Nelson Mandela is sworn in as the first Black president of South Africa in May. Two weeks later, Elvis Presley's daughter marries Michael Jackson in the Dominican Republic. In May, Prince changes his name to a symbol. O. J. Simpson's car chase with the police is nationally televised on 17 June and, on the same day, the fifteenth FIFA World Cup begins in the USA – a tournament that England have failed to qualify for and of which Brazil are the eventual winners. The first episode of* Friends *airs in September. Both Pink Floyd and the Rolling Stones are on tour, while The Beatles'* Live at the BBC *is released. A lot of the biggest-selling rock albums in 1994 may be American – Green Day's* Dookie, *The Offspring's* Smash, *Soundgarden's* Superunknown *and Nirvana's posthumous* MTV Unplugged in New York *– but across the Atlantic exciting things are starting to happen in the UK as well.*

Liam stares out the crowd at the 400-capacity Wedgewood Rooms, Portsmouth, May 1994, in this shot by Kevin Cummins. Oasis are delivering 'Up in the Sky' here (you can tell because Bonehead is playing Noel's Hofner S5 PA rather than the Epiphone Riviera he used for every other song in the set at that time).

'Supersonic'

SINGLE

RELEASED 11 APRIL 1994

For a damp little island in the north Atlantic, Britain has an enviable history of culture-defining debut singles recorded by photogenic groups of disaffected youths. 'Anarchy in the UK.' 'Relax.' 'I Can't Explain.' 'Hand in Glove.' 'Transmission.' 'Virginia Plain.' 'Gangsters.' 'I Bet You Look Good on the Dancefloor' was pretty good, too, and as for 'Hong Kong Garden' . . . The list goes on.

Has any debut single ever, though, so accurately predicted the entire decades-long career of an artist quite like the opening fifty seconds of Oasis's 'Supersonic'?

A rudimentary drumbeat. Fingers slide dramatically down the neck of a guitar. A riff circles menacingly twice around the block, then twice more, before a second guitar rhythmically joins forces with it and kicks through the door. We're in.

A voice: true like a vow, hard as a diamond. *'I need to be myself.'* And why is that? *'I can't be no one else.'* Ain't that the truth, as it turns out.

'I'm feeling supersonic, give me gin and tonic.' No more moping, no more navel-gazing. *'You can have it all, but how much do you want it?'* Small time is over. We're shooting for the moon.

'You make me laugh . . .'

Now that's a promise. Give me your autograph, Liam Gallagher, the funniest rock star who's ever been adored, pawed, mimicked, fancied by millions around the world. Just an average lad from Burnage who grew up playing conkers, the lot, not listening to music, not being remotely interested in singing songs or hearing tunes before a hooded-up lad from another school bopped him on the head with a small hammer on the streets of south Manchester, outside St Marks Secondary, aged fifteen.

'I was having a cig when someone came running down saying some lad from another school has slapped a girl,' Liam told me. 'We come out, four of us, about fifteen of them. Bit of a dust-up. I see one coming towards me with a hood up. As I go in for a bit of a ding, he's gone, "Fuck off", pulled out a hammer, bopped me on the head. I woke up in hospital with my head bashed up.'

Bosh. Everything changed.

'Not instantly,' Liam said, but very soon after he got out of hospital. 'Until then I was just into football, smoking weed, getting into scrapes. I wasn't into guitars at all.' Before he'd been whacked on the head with that little hammer, Liam thought 'music was for weirdos'. One week before the hammer attack, he regarded 'Like a Virgin' by Madonna as revolting nonsense. 'It's like when people come out of comas and start speaking Japanese or Russian. All of a sudden, I heard "Like a Virgin" by Madonna and I was going, "That's a fucking tune!" A few weeks after that, he heard the Stone Roses properly for the first time. 'It was like the Bisto kid. Got a whiff of the Roses and that was that. The rest is history.'

'Somebody hammered the music into him, he's got a lot to answer for,' reflected Noel Gallagher. 'I've got the perfect alibi, so it's nowt to do with me.'

What is to do with Noel is the music – the songs, usually – and that's where we initially meet our hero, Liam Gallagher, on 'Supersonic'. Maybe you saw him in the song's video for the first time doing his soon-to-be-famous and much-copied feet-out shuffle through the puddles on a roof by King's Cross St Pancras, followed by the closest he'll ever come to a smile on film.

''Cos my friend said to take you home . . .'

Or maybe you were transfixed by the face, the hair, the suede coat buttoned up to the top. The eyes. 'I looked like a rock star even when I was digging holes in Manchester,' Liam has said. 'I was cool then. People would clock my head even when I was wearing overalls and had a fucking shovel in my hand. Full of shit with a pneumatic drill, I still looked cool.'

It hadn't been long between digging holes, repairing roads in

Manchester, and appearing in the 'Supersonic' video – a couple of years or so. The Liam Gallagher who first sang in Bonehead's house before they formed a band was pretty much the same Liam you meet in 'Supersonic'.

'He looked like Liam's always looked,' remembered Bonehead. 'He had a great topcoat and great haircut, a great walk, a great voice. His voice was just, like, woah . . .'

Girls want to be with him, boys want to be him (apart from those who wish to bop him on the head with little hammers). But without Noel writing songs like 'Supersonic' for Liam to sing, he'd just be the best-looking rock star road digger in Manchester. And where would Noel be without his little brother?

'We wouldn't have been what we were without him, that's for sure,' Noel's admitted. 'As important and as vital as those songs still are, I think the two elements that made Oasis was his thing and them songs. If it wasn't for him, we might just have been another band. I couldn't imagine anybody else being singer.'

So they need each other, they believe in one another. Our introduction to the pair, however, would've been very different if the first official single had been the nihilistic, punky 'Bring It on Down', as suggested by Alan McGee, who'd signed them to his Creation label. 'I love that song, it's like the Pistols, like The Stooges,' says Noel.

But when they booked into Liverpool's Pink Museum studio – owned by Andy McClusky of Orchestral Manoeuvres in the Dark – for three days in December 1993 to record it as their debut single, they discovered they couldn't play 'Bring It on Down' well enough. 'Whatever we had in the rehearsal room and on stage wasn't translating in the studio,' remembers Noel.

Mark Coyle, who was producing alongside Noel, agreed. 'We were all very inexperienced. The first day is horrible and it just gets worse and worse. The whole session starts degenerating.'

Noel identified that Tony McCarroll couldn't keep the beat consistently well enough to record it, and the mood quickly became poisonous. Noting that Noel seemed panicked by the prospect of returning from the session without a first single, Tony and Chris Griffiths suggested they try a different song.

'Noel had a riff, but that's all,' said Coyle. Nevertheless, the band jammed around that riff for a good while, the beat an easy-paced lollop that McCarroll could comfortably nail. After a while, someone in the band complained they were hungry, so a takeaway was sent for. Noel, meanwhile, thought there was something in the jam they'd been having.

'I went in the back room,' Noel told the *Supersonic* filmmakers, 'and, as bizarre as it sounds, wrote "Supersonic" in about however long it takes six other guys to eat a Chinese meal. It was a brilliant moment in time.'

Noel returned to the main room where the band were finishing their food and told them he'd written the first single, then performed it to them. Astonished, they then all played it together in the studio, 'really slow', watching each other for the changes. They recorded and mixed 'Supersonic' within eight to eleven hours of Noel writing it, depending on which eyewitness relates the tale.

'It sounded massive, absolutely massive,' says Bonehead.

Listening on a cassette in Mark Coyle's Renault back to Manchester, Noel agreed. In fact, he thought it at least the equal to 'Bring It on Down' or any of the other songs he had up his sleeve. Everyone's playing was perfect, he noted, but what really set it apart were the layers of backing vocal 'aaahs' that Tony Griffiths had added to the bridge, a hat-tip to The Beatles that elevates 'Supersonic'.

He liked the lyrics, too, which he'd written in just a few moments. In times to come, when the single made its way into the world, the psychedelic declarations contained in 'Supersonic' would be dismissed as nonsense, and there are elements that were just thrown on the page. Like *'a girl called Elsa, she's into Alka-Seltzer'*, whose inclusion was inspired by the massive, flatulent studio Rottweiler called Elsa that Noel could not escape when writing. But within the rhymes and riddles of 'Supersonic' are also declarations of intent that map out Oasis's philosophy, attitude, hidden biography.

'The way I write is the first few lines will form a story,' said Noel of it, 'and then it gets kind of confused and muddled up. I'm not writing novels here, I'm writing pop songs. I like to think all my favourite songs are somehow about me, which is why I love them. I leave it up to others to interpret them. There's a great deal of odd lines that have real, proper relevance to my life, to growing up, but I'm not interested in telling anyone. It's always about the melody. There's something magical going on there.' When the band played Alan McGee 'Supersonic' through speakers at the BBC's Maida Vale studio shortly after, he could hear that magic too. He was quite surprised it wasn't 'Bring It on Down' as agreed, though.

'Noel came in and said, "The recording session was rubbish, it never worked out," McGee told the *Supersonic* documentary makers, '"but I've written a smash." Most people would've gone, wait a minute . . .'

'He went fucking mental,' recalls Noel. 'He loved it.'

Victory snatched from the jaws of humiliating defeat. 'Supersonic' remains Noel Gallagher's favourite Oasis song, for how it came to be, what it represents, the sound and mood it defines. Mine too. **TK**

'Take Me Away'

B-SIDE OF 'SUPERSONIC'

Just two songs into their recorded career, it was apparent that there was much more to Oasis than had initially met the eye. Had their first release comprised 'Supersonic' and then just the live/white label versions of 'I Will Believe' and 'Columbia,' it would have been clear what they were all about. But sandwiched between these two B-sides and their first single was something completely, bafflingly different: a beautiful, melancholic, acoustic guitar-only song sung by another voice entirely.

Noel Gallagher's first ever recorded vocal, on 'Take Me Away,' is maybe his most technically impressive, starting in a baritone and rising so high by the end that his voice is on the point of cracking.

More importantly, though, it immediately showcased another side to his songwriting: as good as he was at producing the up-to-11 rock 'n' roll songs about feeling supersonic and living forever, he could also do downbeat and introspective.

You don't write songs as accomplished and as well structured and as just indisputably great as 'Take Me Away' – or for that matter 'Supersonic' – without first putting in the hours perfecting your craft. And the truth is that, long before the likes of 'Half the World Away' and 'Talk Tonight' were sung back to him by thousands of people, Noel Gallagher had been writing these sort of one-man-and-his-guitar tunes for decades.

The first was called 'Baj', written when he was just a teenager. 'The best line was: "And on your badge, it says, 'Wear a badge'", he recalled. 'I was in my bedroom. Winter time. It went G, E minor, C, D, the basic chords, right, and the chorus was, "And life goes on, but the world will never change". I must have been smoking too much pot at the time. It was, I dunno, just to see if I could do it. After that, I wrote about seventy-five songs no one's ever heard.'

Some of these songs, including 'Baj', featured on a tape that went up for auction in 1998, that dated back to a decade previous when Noel Gallagher was twenty-one (and Liam just sixteen). The sticker attached to the cassette and its case both feature 'Noel's songs' in its creator's handwriting. Another tape of more songs in this vein was later unearthed. In other words, by the time the world heard 'Take Me Away', Noel Gallagher had put in more than the 10,000 hours of practice that author Malcolm Gladwell famously theorizes are the key to mastering any craft, and the key to The Beatles 'becoming the greatest band in history'.

Much of this huge stockpile of material would not have fitted in with the euphoric, celebratory vibe that Oasis presented at their outset. But soon enough, it would become a significant part of what they were all about. In their earliest days, Oasis did not like to do encores. At every show in the first half of 1994, they would play every song from *Definitely Maybe*, plus the frenetic, punky 'Fade Away', then bow out with their cover of The Beatles' 'I Am the

Walrus': Liam then Noel leaving the stage, letting Bonehead, Guigsy and Tony McCarroll blast through its final chords a few more times. The first time they *did* perform an encore came in September 1994 at Club Quattro in Nagoya, Japan. Blown away by the reaction from a crowd who had only just heard their album and would not have understood the lyrics, they re-emerged after much screaming to play 'Rock 'n' Roll Star' one more time.

You could tell this was a spontaneous, unplanned encore because Liam had to ask the audience to throw Tony McCarroll's sticks back onstage, the drummer having tossed them into the crowd at the end of the show. The crowd, in a very Japanese way, obliged.

This, though, could not be a long-term solution. By the end of 1994, Oasis were rising so fast that they were selling out theatre-size venues – around 3,000 or 4,000 people – and needed to play for longer than they had in smaller clubs. By this time, they had 'Whatever', but that still only brought their set's running time up to just over an hour. And so, from September 1994, it became customary for everyone bar Noel to leave the stage after a full-band version of 'Married with Children' and return ten minutes or so later to finish with 'Supersonic' and 'I Am the Walrus'. In between, the man who wrote all of the songs would move to the centre of the stage, sit on a stool and sing accompanied only by an acoustic guitar. This was how, at the first ever Oasis arena show in Sheffield in April 1995, he would debut 'Don't Look Back in Anger'.

The first time he had performed songs in this way in public had been something of a baptism of fire at the Creation Undrugged show (see 'On the frontline with Oasis #1', page 30). Celebrating a decade of the label, it would feature their finest acts playing acoustically. Liam was set to appear, but was ill – though still present, heckling from the balcony – and so Noel, accompanied by Bonehead on twelve-string guitar, sang the vocals. Many people present were not that aware of Oasis at that stage, but the performance was so accomplished that it did not seem at all like it was a best-of-a-bad-situation situation.

The small percentage of audience members who had been playing 'Take Me Away' as much as they had 'Supersonic' for the preceding two months – including me – meanwhile, were already well aware of this side of Oasis. **HM**

'I Will Believe'

B-SIDE OF 'SUPERSONIC'

The atmosphere throughout Liam Gallagher's Definitely Maybe UK arena tour of 2024 was of a riotously religious fervour. This was the thirtieth-anniversary celebration of arguably the nation's favourite debut album, after all, given a new lease of love by its singer, thanks partly to his recent mammoth success as a solo artist helping to lure a new generation of devotees to his brother's earliest creations. Seven songs in to the roll call of classics from Oasis's debut album, though, the first curveball of the evening was thrown into the arena. Right after 'Bring It on Down', a vaguely recognizable guitar riff rang out. Some present looked to friends and partners, attempting to mouth words they didn't really know, instead asking, 'What's this?'

Up on the big screens either side of the stage were two large cassettes rolling with the title scrawled down the sticker: 'I Will Believe'. Like the other early B-side he resurrected later on in those anniversary shows – 'D'Yer Wanna Be a Spaceman' – Liam believed this was the B-side from that era that most deserved its place in this celebration.

Originally, 'I Will Believe' was one of the songs that Oasis had tried to record at the Pink Museum in Liverpool in the aborted 'Bring It on Down' single session.

'We had been trying to get a decent take of "I Will Believe", but it was going nowhere,' remembered engineer Dave Scott. Scott was worried about the band's energy levels playing it and also feared they didn't have a lead song as they couldn't nail 'Bring It on Down'. Instead, Oasis worked on 'Supersonic'.

One problem: they'd run out of spare tape to record 'Supersonic'. Scott suggested they record over at least one of the 'I Will Believe' takes, as it was 'shoegazing shit'. Thus the live studio version appearing as a B-side.

On 2024's arena tour, Liam Gallagher made a convincing case for 'I Will Believe' not, in fact, being 'shoegazing shit', imbuing the vocal with the kind of menace and meaning that thirty years of experience helps lend. In this form, it could easily have appeared on that debut album, each line also memorized by all. **TK**

'Progression is going forwards. Going backwards is regression. Going sideways is just . . . gression.'

On the frontline with Oasis #1

Meet the Gallaghers, May 1994

He was sitting on the floor of a conference room in the basement of King's Reach Tower – the Soviet/Manhattan-style Blackfriars office block that housed *NME* on its twenty-fifth floor – complimentary bottle of Stella Dry lager in one hand, smoke rising from the cigarette in his other. He didn't get up.

'Ted, this is Noel Gallagher,' said his representative from Creation Records, Andy Saunders. 'Noel, Ted Kessler from *NME*.'

A sparkle danced across Noel's eyes. 'Oh alright, yeah, you're the guy who said our kid should stop hanging off the mic stand when he's singing!'

I grimaced in apology. A month earlier, in the week 'Supersonic' was released, I had reviewed Oasis at London's 100 Club, ending a positive *NME* appraisal with the words: 'if Liam Gallagher can just stand up straight every now and then he'll be on *Top of the Pops* by Christmas.'

'Too right, mate!' added Noel approvingly. He jabbed his bottle towards the other side of the room, where Liam was looming over a terrified-looking Mark Gardener, frontman of Ride. 'Slob needs telling. What have you been up to?'

I sat down next to him, explaining I'd just returned from interviewing the Beastie Boys at their G-SON studio in Los Angeles. It was the first and last time I ever impressed Noel Gallagher.

'Love the Beastie Boys,' he said, enthused. 'We have [1992 album] *Check Your Head* on in the van all the time. Is that one of their jackets?'

It was indeed an X-Large-branded Harrington I'd been gifted in the Beasties' new LA boutique, now buying me invaluable credibility with Noel Gallagher in London. 'Nice, that,' he decided, fingering my tan collar with such charm I almost regifted it to him right there.

Noel and Liam Gallagher were in London alongside members of labelmates Ride and the Boo Radleys to publicize Creation Undrugged, a night of acoustic turns at the Royal Albert Hall celebrating the tenth anniversary of Alan McGee's label. As the event's media partner, *NME* had invited two dozen readers to a conference with these representatives from three of the bands: my colleague John Harris was to host the Q&A, while I took notes so that we could write it up for the following Tuesday's edition.

A month earlier, Harris had returned to King's Reach from assignment in Glasgow interviewing the Gallaghers in their hotel room, marched up to the office stereo and immediately inserted his recording of the summit, guffawing. 'You'll want to hear this,' he told the nearest editorial staff, pressing play. It was an interview that focused upon the recently aborted Amsterdam gig where all of Oasis other than an oblivious Noel had been arrested for a drunken punch-up aboard the ferry over. The interview almost ended in a similar bundle between the brothers and was so hilariously fractious that a year later Harris's flatmate, *NME*'s live editor Simon Williams, released it as a 7-inch single titled 'Wibbling Rivalry' on his Fierce Panda label. It reached number fifty-two in the charts, the highest ever placing for a spoken-word single.

'Wish me luck,' said John, picking up the microphone and stepping to the front of the room. We settled down for the question-and-answer session. Ride's Gardener and bassist Steve Queralt were two well-mannered, softly spoken boys from Oxford, and the Boo Radleys' guitarist Martin Carr and singer Simon 'Sice' Rowbottom were sarcastic wags from Merseyside – but none were remotely equipped to keep up with the stream of psychedelic comedy that issued from the two Gallaghers. Noel and Liam took control of the conference.

At one point, a reader asked for the panel's opinion about raving, a music press hot-button topic then. Did they like acid house and the new wave of techno? Everyone was very polite, namechecking recent records and events they'd enjoyed. Nobody wished to appear uncultured or incurious. Then, Liam spoke up.

'I think it's naff, me,' he declared. 'It depends what you call dance music. Sly and the Family Stone is dance music . . .'

Noel: 'Mr Blobby is dance music . . .'

'Sly Stone is good music, right,' continued Liam. 'But all this dance music these days is all that same silly beat going *DANK DANK DANK* and some guy singing *"we're all free"* when you're not. It's shit. You go round someone's house and they put a tune on, and it goes *DANK DANK DANK*, and you sit there and have a cup of tea, and it's going *DANK DANK DANK*.'

At this point, Liam stood and started doing a kind of break-dance, but as if in bowel-distress, while shouting '*DANK DANK DANK*'.

He sat back down as the room tried to compose itself. 'I've got to slag it right off. It's doing my head in.'

After some further back-and-forth, a reader suggested that it was important nonetheless to progress musically – to change, evolve.

'You've got to progress,' agreed Liam. 'But it doesn't mean to say that you've got to go forward.' Time stopped.

'Eh?' said Noel, enjoyably confused.

'You can progress sideways,' insisted Liam. 'Or backwards . . .'

The room started to crack up.

'I'm right!' He looked to his elder brother, deadpan, but his eyes betraying the wind-up. 'Tell me I'm not!'

'Progression,' insisted Noel, contemplatively, 'is going forwards. Going backwards is regression. Going sideways is just . . . gression.'

The conference didn't really recover from that, so soon after the main players headed across the road to the Brunswick for an alcoholic debrief. If we'd known then that we were sitting in our after- (and during-) work pub with the two biggest British music stars of the coming decades we might have loaded up on good future anecdotal quote material. Instead, I just recall Noel lounging in the corner taking the piss out of everyone's football teams for an hour as we demolished his then calamitous Man City in return.

Eventually, the Gallaghers asked if we'd show them around the trendy Camden Town they'd read about in the music mags. 'Can we go to that Good Mixer boozer?' wondered Noel. So we loaded up in two cabs and rode north. Arriving at the Good Mixer, Liam immediately spied Graham Coxon of Blur at a table and marched up to him, bombarding the introverted guitarist with aggressive bonhomie.

'You're him out of Blur!' he boomed. 'Good band, Blur . . . shit clothes, though.'

They met again at the urinal, where Liam jostled the mid-flow Coxon, splashing his strides. An upset Graham complained to the landlord, who foolishly ushered Oasis out of his pub forever.

Later, in the Underworld rock venue, the Gallaghers and various associates became involved in a drunken argument at the bar with several dozen fans of a long-forgotten techno-punk group who had played that night. Confusingly, this dispute became physical and a bundle of goths, record company employees and perhaps some Gallaghers ensued in the Underworld bar area.

Once more, Oasis were shown the door, bringing the curtain down on our evening together. So I wombled off into London's orangey black, swaying at the night bus stop at 2 a.m., wondering hopefully when the next night out with the Gallaghers of Oasis might be . . . TK

'Shakermaker'

SINGLE
RELEASED 20 JUNE 1994

The Liam Gallagher walk was apparent for all to see from the very first glimpse of Oasis. In the opening seconds of the video for 'Supersonic', there striding slowly through puddles on a rooftop in King's Cross, are two soon-to-be-famous suede-moccasined feet, pointed out at ten-to-two. Soon enough this walk would be aped (pun intended) by young people all over the UK, and then the world. For a long time, it would remain the only movement that this singer would make onstage.

'The rule in Oasis was you can do – at the most – a foot-tap,' Liam Gallagher told me. 'Anyone moving around, you'd be getting fucking sacked. A foot-tap is alright, but that's as far as it goes. Maybe do your hair a bit in between songs. But the standing-still thing, I think it started when we were doing bigger gigs. I was like, "Fuck it, I'm gonna take the easy route!" And then everyone was digging it, like, "Fucking hell, man, you look cool as fuck." And I just went, "I can do that again for you tomorrow night, no problem!"'

Why does he think it happened?

'It was just my thing, I guess. For one: I can't fucking dance. For two: it's not for me, all that jumping around shit. Far too energetic. So in my head it was, *Let's go the opposite way*. It was like anti-entertainment: let the music soak everyone up and let *them* go nuts. There were nights when it was all going fucking apeshit, and you'd get in your stance and next thing . . . you're in. Then it just feels like you're controlling the fucking madness. And you can't dance to Oasis music anyway, can you? It isn't danceable music, is it?'

This is true. But one thing you very much can do to Oasis music is swagger. And no song is more custom constructed for this activity than their second single.

'Shakermaker' had served as a set opener for many of their

earliest shows, and so was known to fans (it helped, too, that the melody was already somewhat familiar). In its recorded guise, though, it had been slowed down even more, further accentuating its walking-through-treacle feel, seeming to move almost in slow motion in comparison to other bands' songs. Like 'Supersonic', on record it displayed Noel Gallagher's talent for overdubbing, with all kinds of smart, subtle, melodic hooks that he didn't have enough hands for in a live setting adorning the mix. Like 'Supersonic', too, it takes its sweet time, clocking in at over five minutes, with handclaps coming in as it finishes.

Right up until it was recorded, 'Shakermaker' still contained the original lyrics: a straight-up steal from the New Seekers' 'I'd Like to Teach the World to Sing'. That song originated as the jingle for a 1971 Coca-Cola advert (which the four-to-five-year-old Noel Gallagher would have seen many times), so it can't have been a huge surprise to anyone that the lawyers got involved prior to the June 1994 release of Oasis's second single. 'Now we all drink Pepsi,' deadpanned Noel soon after the matter was resolved.

Not for the first (or last) time, necessity became the mother of some Noel Gallagher invention.

'We'd been picked up and were going to Johnny [Marr]'s house,' he remembered. 'Johnny had a little studio in his basement. We were gonna do this second verse, and of course it was, "Have you written this second verse?" I was like, "Yeah, don't worry about it!" Then ended up going out and getting hammered. Then in the morning it was, "Have you written the second verse?" I was like, "Yes!" We stopped at the traffic lights, and that's where the "*know he stops at traffic lights but only when they're green*" comes from.'

One man who doubtless remains overjoyed at this turn of events is Peter Turner, proprietor of Sifters Records in East Didsbury, visible out of the window when stopping at the above traffic lights. His hasty addition to the song's existing trio of Misters – 'Mr Soft' from the Softmints advert, 'Mr Clean' from the Jam song, 'Mr Benn' from the kids' TV series – meant that to this day he has people from all over the world coming in to gawp at him: the man who sold

Noel – and Liam – songs when he was just sixteen. One of its more recent visitors was Noel Gallagher himself, who was interviewed among its rows of vinyl in 2024 by Manchester legend John Robb to celebrate the thirtieth anniversary of *Definitely Maybe*, in what would be his last interview before the re-formation of Oasis was announced a week later.

In truth, the Mr Sifter-featuring final verse is miles better than the original 'buy the world a Coke' lyric anyway: far more befitting of these drunk-psychedelia stylings. The '*sorry but I just don't know*' middle section, meanwhile – which originated from nowhere other than Noel Gallagher's brain – is Oasis at their soaring, melodic finest. A nice, ironic coda to the legal debacle came in 2011 when, forty years on from the original advert, a new Coca-Cola commercial arrived. In it, rather than 'I'd Like to Teach the World to Sing', the group of children featured this time sang 'Whatever'. The cheque that resulted from this version may even have convinced Noel Gallagher to switch back from Pepsi. **HM**

'D'Yer Wanna Be a Spaceman'

B-SIDE OF 'SHAKERMAKER'

If the 'Mr Clean' who makes an appearance on 'Shakermaker' is an obvious hat-tip to the Jam song of the same name, a much more subtle Jam reference can also be gleaned from the single's flipside.

The Jam's 1979 *Setting Sons* is a concept album, loosely telling the story of three close childhood friends who meet up as adults, only to discover chasms have grown between them. Noel Gallagher became a massive Jam fan the year of its release and spent a lot of time deeply engrossed in its grooves. 'D'Yer Wanna Be a Spaceman', the acoustic ballad he recorded at Mark Coyle's south Manchester house long before Oasis were even signed, employs a very similar narrative to Paul Weller's, but to much more wistful and gentle effect.

Over a sweet guitar melody, the like of which he'd revisit with 'Married with Children' and 'Half the World Away', Noel welcomes an old pal back into his life, wondering if he recalls *'climbing trees and pretending to fly/D'yer still wanna be a spaceman and live in the sky?'* As Weller also found in songs like 'Thick as Thieves' on *Setting Sons,* Noel is disappointed how time has changed his old friend: *'Y'got how many bills and how many kids?/And you've forgot about all the things that we did',* he croons with a deep, true melancholy.

Introspective, mellow and nuanced, 'D'Yer Wanna Be a Spaceman' was about as far away from the belligerent boogie of 'Shakermaker' as it's possible to travel – no doubt Noel's intention in selecting it as its B-side. His songwriting would not be easily typecast.

Despite being one of his most earnestly affecting early ballads, 'D'Yer Wanna Be a Spaceman' led a very sheltered life in Oasis, only being played sixteen times live by the band. The last outing for it was at Maine Road in '96, when Noel started strumming it on his electric guitar before Tony McCarroll selected a beat and Liam leaned into the microphone to sing the first line, but then broke off. 'I can't remember the words,' he told the throng. 'I've never sung it before.'

It lived happily ever after Oasis, though. Noel Gallagher's High Flying Birds made it a live staple for several tours, then, in 2018, Liam unveiled a heartfelt, passionate version (its inclusion perhaps a message to his then estranged big brother?) at his enormous Finsbury Park show. This time, he nailed the words. **TK**

'Alive'

B-SIDE OF 'SHAKERMAKER'

Listening to 'Alive' now, you could almost be hearing another band, one that would've had a very different history. They might well have also been signed by arch indie label Creation Records in 1993 but, now re-formed, would be low on the bill for the Shine On indie revival festival in Butlin's, Minehead, rather than selling out stadiums across the globe in 2025.

Recorded with Tony and Chris Griffiths at the same time as the tracks on the 'Live Demonstration' demo tape, 'Alive' was set aside as it sounded more like an archetypal early 1990s indie band, someone like Adorable, whose debut album was released by Creation in March 1993 but stalled miles outside the top forty as Oasis rolled into view a month later.

'Alive' still has a knock-kneed charm, but in it you can hear a band trying to hone its songwriting identity and personality, both in the guitar sound and with Liam's voice, which is somewhere between Ian Brown and where he himself wound up. Tony Griffiths complained of the demo appearing rather than a finished version when he saw 'Alive' turn up on the other side of 'Shakermaker', but it's just a moment in time. Noel recognized this was the song's final destination. TK

'Live Forever'

SINGLE

RELEASED 8 AUGUST 1994

The first real song Noel Gallagher wrote was 'Live Forever', he revealed in the *Supersonic* documentary. He added that it was also the first good song he wrote. More than that, it was a pivotal moment in both the band's recording history and that of the musical timeline of the 1990s. 'Live Forever' changed everything.

Sometimes, when he writes songs, Noel will play around with chords or a melody on his guitar for weeks, months, for years even, not getting anywhere with it or really paying that much attention to it. Just messing around with things that sound good to him. Other times, the song will fall out from the heavens into his lap fully formed. 'That's what happens with the best songs,' he always says. 'Live Forever', which is unquestionably among his best songs, is one where both of those things happened.

For a while, after leaving school at fifteen, Noel and his brothers worked for their dad, who had a business doing concrete floors. It was, says Noel, 'the worst thing in the world – you can't do anything right working for your dad.' When Oasis became well known, journalists would typically ask him if it was difficult being in a band with his brother. Noel had another perspective, which he described to *Q* magazine in 1996. 'What about being on a building site in January when it's hail-stoning with your dad and your two brothers and two of your cousins and two of your uncles and you fucking hate the lot?'

They spent days on end in the back of a yellow Transit van being ferried from building job to job, bickering, until Noel quit. He then got a job with a building firm who sub-contracted to British Gas, which is where, unbelievably, the future of guitar music was shaped.

One day while working on the British Gas site, a fat steel cap fell off a heavy gas pipe they were laying and landed on Noel's foot, smashing it to bits. He was laid off sick for a good while. When he returned to the site, he was given a job in the storeroom handing out 'bolts and wellies.' It was not taxing work and allowed him lots of solitary Noel-time.

'Nobody turned up for days,' he recalled happily.

After a month or so there, he decided to bring his guitar in, to help pass the time.

'I look at the foot sometimes in the winter when I get chills in it because of the cracked bones and I give it a thumbs-up,' says Noel. 'I wrote four of the songs for the first album in that storeroom.'

The first song he wrote in there was 'Live Forever,' though it wasn't called that – or called anything – then, but he came up with the melody, the outline. 'I have songs that are in cold storage and I know they are great. I know I am going to finish them one day, but I'm not going to rush it. It's going to fall out of the sky. I'm not going to just write it for the sake of it. That's why I have a backlog that need a first verse or a middle eight, but they are essentially fully formed.'

'Live Forever' first entered Noel's consciousness when he was working on the road with Inspiral Carpets. Mark Coyle used to line-check the drums each night playing a lolloping beat on the ride cymbal and the floor tom. 'That's the opening bar of "Live Forever",' said Noel during a 2023 Gibson TV interview. 'I don't know why, but I played the first four chords of "Live Forever" and we played around that endlessly for the front-of-house sound guy. When I wrote "Live Forever", I was, "Oh that's that fucking . . ."'

The tipping point of 'Live Forever' came when Noel was listening to 'Shine a Light' from the Rolling Stones' *Exile on Main Street* album at home. 'You know that line, *"May the good Lord shine a light on me"*? I was on the guitar going, *"Maybe, I don't really wanna know"* . . . It came out of that.' Noel had now worked a word that ran across the two bars convincingly. *Maaay-be* . . . He wrote the rest of the song that night. Soon he took it into rehearsals.

'I remember being in a rehearsal room and we were one kind of band – a shit indie band from Manchester – then the next night going down with "Live Forever" and everything changed. I knew enough about music and about songs to know that that was a great song.'

Bonehead wasn't so sure.

'You didn't write that,' he said to Noel in the rehearsal room upon hearing it for the first time.

'Yeah, I did.'

'No, you didn't.' This went on for a while. 'I wouldn't believe it, you know?' said Bonehead. 'You heard songs like that on the radio, you didn't hear them from someone you knew in the same room, claiming that they had wrote it. So for someone to come in and just go, "I'll play you one of my songs," and play you "Live Forever", fuck off. Wow, what a song.'

'I must have strummed the opening chord sequence for "Live Forever" for weeks and weeks until a melody came,' said Noel. 'I had the music and melody, then I arranged the whole song without any words. The words came later, right at the end.'

The lyrics elevated an already lovely shade of medium-paced, blue-lit mood-rock to a new plane. Or, perhaps, several planes. Noel has dedicated the song to his mother, Peggy. A beautiful tribute. He's also said it's for his nearest pals.

'It's about friendship,' he told *Uncut* magazine. 'Your best friend of that night. The most important line in it is: "*We see things they'll never see.*" When you have a friend and the two of you have a sitcom or a favourite album that everyone else thinks is shit, but you know it's got something special.'

It's also written in direct opposition to the prevailing mood of whiney, cynical self-loathing that had wafted across the Atlantic in the previous two or three years from the grunge bands of the Pacific Northwest – particularly Nirvana's singer/songwriter Kurt Cobain.

'That came out of Nirvana's second album,' said Noel, 'where he had a song called "I Hate Myself and I Want to Die". I was, like, "That cunt is sat in his mansion in Seattle, on smack, he's got everything, he's got the world at his feet. He's in the biggest and most revered band in the world today, and he fucking hates himself and he fucking wants to die." I'm not having that. Bollocks! He might be depressed but there's no need to bring everybody else down.'

The music writer Sylvia Patterson tells a story about the first time she came across Oasis: she was staying at a friend's flat after a night out in London, watching Saturday morning TV, when the video for 'Supersonic' aired for the first time in April 1994. 'WHO IS THIS?!' she excitedly demanded of her host, a fellow music writer called Tom Doyle. Tom, however, had just walked into the room with shocking news: Nirvana's Kurt Cobain had been discovered dead at his home the previous day, a victim of suicide.

Patterson identifies this as the moment the musical eras changed, from grunge to Britpop. It's a convincing argument. It wasn't until four months later, though, that we were presented with a new manifesto, a design for life, an anthem to take to heart. No longer were we to hate ourselves and wish to die. Instead, you and I, we're gonna live forever. TK

'Cloudburst'

B-SIDE OF 'LIVE FOREVER'

Anyone – A&R person, booking agent, whoever – sliding Oasis's 'Live Demonstration' cassette into the tape player back in 1993, while reading the attached note from the young Mancunian hopefuls, may not have got much further than the tape's opening moments and a song called 'Cloudburst'.

A baggy drumbeat lollops out front, followed by a funky guitar riff that sounds suspiciously like John Squire, with a melody that's a dead ringer for the Stone Roses' 'Standing Here', B-side of 1989's ubiquitous 'She Bangs the Drum'. Click! Few genres were viewed in '93 with more distaste in the British music business than the disposed 'Madchester' sound. Happy Mondays had disintegrated messily the year before, Stone Roses were four years into recording a second album without any hint of progression, and all the groups who'd followed in their immediate wake were cooked. And here was a new Manchester band that sounded just like a group from 1989: the beat even perfectly echoed that of the single that rang the final Madchester death knell, the Mock Turtles' 'Can You Dig It?'

However, if the listener had persevered just a few bars, then forty-five seconds in to 'Cloudburst' Liam Gallagher signalled the group's true direction of travel with winning charm, opening by insisting, '*Wake up! There's a new day dawning!*' 'Cloudburst' is an atypical Oasis song: one could conceivably dance to it, and Liam's vocal is so wide-eyed, verbose and sunny it's practically a rap. But even decades later, it's a declaration of intent and positivity, a lust for adventure and life that's wasted as a B-side – unless the A-side is 'Live Forever', of course. TK

Definitely Maybe

(ORIGINAL UK RELEASE: 29 AUGUST 1994)

1.	'Rock 'n' Roll Star'	5:22
2.	'Shakermaker'	5:10
3.	'Live Forever'	4:35
4.	'Up in the Sky'	4:29
5.	'Columbia'	6:08
6.	'Supersonic'	4:42
7.	'Bring It on Down'	4:18
8.	'Cigarettes & Alcohol'	4:49
9.	'Digsy's Dinner'	2:32
10.	'Slide Away'	6:32
11.	'Married with Children'	3:12

All songs by Noel Gallagher

Producer: Tracks 1–9, 11: Mark Coyle & Oasis

Producer: Track 10: Dave Batchelor

Additional production: Owen Morris

Mixed by Owen Morris

Mastered by Owen Morris

Engineers: Anjali Dutt, Dave Scott, Mark Coyle, Roy Spong

Bass guitar: Paul McGuigan

Drums: Tony McCarroll

Lead guitar, backing vocals: Noel Gallagher

Rhythm guitar: Paul Arthurs

Vocals: Liam Gallagher

'Rock 'n' Roll Star'

By the time Oasis reached the point of playing venues without roofs (beginning with Maine Road), 'Rock 'n' Roll Star' had been retired from live performance, not to be played at all from 1996 to 1999. A wise move. It would have seemed crass during this period to sing the *'Look at you now, you're all in my hands tonight'* refrain during this period. 'Don't take that the wrong way,' Liam had in fact commented after he sang those words during Oasis's first Glastonbury headline performance in 1995. Its key line is, *'In my mind, my dreams are real'*. How can you sing that with any authenticity when, all of a sudden, your 'real' exceeds any dream that you or anyone else ever had?

'Rock 'n' Roll Star' is not about being a rock 'n' roll star. It is about having nothing and dreaming of being a rock 'n' roll star.

It is also Liam Gallagher's theme song, as indelibly linked to him, no matter who wrote it, as 'New York, New York' is to Sinatra, 'Hound Dog' is to Elvis Presley or 'What's My Name?' is to Snoop Dogg. The likes of 'Live Forever' or 'Slide Away' would likely have been great no matter who sang them. But not 'Rock 'n' Roll Star'. No song better encapsulates the person he is and probably would have been even if he was still working dead-end jobs in Manchester and living for the weekend. When I interviewed him just prior to the release of his first solo single, I asked whether he would be playing any Oasis songs live (his post-Oasis band, Beady Eye, had not, until very near the end). Of course he would, he said. I asked him which ones.

'I'm gonna start with "Rock 'n' Roll Star",' he replied. 'Because . . . well, you know, I have to.'

There was, too, no other way for the debut Oasis album to start. As a statement of intent, 'Rock 'n' Roll Star' set them apart from all of their contemporaries. Rock stardom was not something that most bands were aiming for in 1994. To the people that Oasis shared a stage with in their earliest days, it felt like both a naff concept and a wholly unobtainable one. Genesis were rock stars.

Guns N' Roses were rock stars. The American grunge bands were embarrassed by success. In the UK, similarly, the biggest bands with guitars prided themselves on being alternative. None of them were dreaming about being rock 'n' roll stars, let alone *singing* about dreaming about being rock 'n' roll stars. 'People say it's a waste of time,' indeed.

And then, suddenly, there they were: five guys from Manchester, barely even moving onstage, so defiant were they in their belief that they were already rock 'n' roll stars. It didn't matter if they were only playing to twelve people. In fact, so far as the sentiment of their perennial set opener in the early days was concerned, it was better if they *were* only playing to twelve people. It takes a certain kind of genius-slash-fantasist to write a song like that, knowing the reality of who you will be playing it in front of. It takes a similar kind of genius-slash-fantasist to think that you deserve to be singing a song like that.

No song more needed to go through the at-times-painful gestation that *Definitely Maybe* went through than 'Rock 'n' Roll Star'. Written at the end of 1992, it was played at every show from there on in. By the time it appeared as the eighth and final song on the 'Live Demonstration' cassette demo, its arrangement, right down to the piledrive crescendo that makes up its final two minutes, is set in stone, never to change. But the guitars sound tinny and Liam Gallagher's vocal, despite being double tracked, is nowhere near what it would become.

The initial sessions for *Definitely Maybe* took place at Monnow Valley in Monmouthshire in January 1994. Production was to be handled by Dave Batchelor, who had worked on seventies albums by the Sensational Alex Harvey Band and who Noel had met while touring with Inspiral Carpets. His recordings were not a success: they lacked the power of Oasis live shows and, having been recorded with all the band playing in cordoned-off spaces, were far too clean. Engineer Anjali Dutt – a veteran of numerous Creation albums, not least My Bloody Valentine's notoriously difficult-to-get-right 'Loveless' – was brought in at Olympic Studios in London to see if anything could be salvaged from the sessions. She quickly concluded that 'no' was the answer to that question.

So back to the studio Oasis went: this time to Sawmills in Cornwall, with long-term live engineer Mark Coyle at the controls and the band set up just as they would be onstage, with the sound from all the amplifiers bleeding into one noise. These recordings were better, but given a short amount of distance from them, Noel Gallagher again concluded that they were not right, were not giving a true representation of the band.

Unwilling to again start afresh, Owen Morris – who was recommended by Johnny Marr, having worked on his and Bernard Sumner's Electronic – was asked to have a go at mixing. He was left alone to do what he wanted: pushing the guitars into the red, making them sound titanic and deafening. Suddenly, it sounded like Oasis. The only new things he recorded were several of the lead vocals, starting with 'Rock 'n' Roll Star'. Responding to the new, more powerful version of the song he was hearing in his headphones, Liam Gallagher roared his way through one take that sounded like an entirely different singer to the one who had featured on the demo, but just like the Liam Gallagher that the world would come to know.

'I often wonder,' said Noel Gallagher, reflecting on the final version of 'Rock 'n' Roll Star' and *Definitely Maybe* twenty-five years on, 'what it must have been like to be, say, fifteen years old and a fan of music, and to buy that record and put that on and to hear it for the first time.' I remember exactly what it was like: where I was, what I was doing, how it changed my life in so many ways, not least that I began living my life for the stars that shine, no matter if people say it's a waste of time. When I first interviewed Noel Gallagher, he asked me as we were finishing up how old I was when I bought *Definitely Maybe.* I told him I was fifteen.

'Bastard!' he said with a smile on his face. **HM**

'Shakermaker'

SINGLE RELEASED 20 JUNE 1994 (SEE PAGE 34)

'Live Forever'

SINGLE RELEASED 8 AUGUST 1994 (SEE PAGE 38)

'Up in the Sky'

The guy who wrote the lyrics for Oasis was always very keen to let people know they shouldn't read too much into them. It's all about the tunes, Noel Gallagher liked to tell anyone reading worlds into his words.

'Usually, it's lyricists that tell you the words are everything,' he said. 'They are not. The words don't mean shit to anybody. It's the melody that you remember. We all whistle tunes. Roger Waters, for example, is very willing to tell you what every single line of his songs mean. When I first heard "The Wall", I was gone . . . then you find out it's about his dad. Don't fucking tell me that. I thought it was about me! I leave it up to people to interpret songs.'

The exception to this rule is 'Up in the Sky'.

'It's basically about people who think they're the voice of a generation,' Noel told *Melody Maker* upon *Definitely Maybe*'s release. 'Or the figurehead of a movement. It's just saying, "Why are you lot down here looking up at him?"'

This could just be seen as Noel restating his position on lyrics. Don't look to Bono or Paul Weller, The Clash or Chuck D for political guidance. Don't look to Noel Gallagher.

'This band is about the music,' he continued. 'It's not about us.' Do not trust musicians who are overtly political, he advised. 'I'd sack anybody in this band who started making political speeches.'

There have been several versions of 'Up in the Sky' in circulation. On the B-side of 'Live Forever' there lives a version filled with slide guitars and sung by Noel. For the thirtieth anniversary of *Definitely Maybe* in 2024, Oasis released the version recorded in Monnow Valley studio with Dave Bachelor. If you spend enough time reading Reddit threads about Oasis (yes, OK), then you'll find a well of fans who prefer this clean, multi-tracked, more typically indie-band-sounding version, actually. There has also been an acoustic version released from the Sawmills session on that same anniversary package, and recording engineer Anjali Dutt fondly recalls a more psychedelic take she worked on with lots of backwards guitars . . .

These all sound great in theory. Then you listen to the original recording on *Definitely Maybe*, as mixed by hidden ingredient Owen Morris, with a four-note motif played by Noel and Bonehead, a cut-and-shut of the paisley button-down mid-sixties Beatles of 'Paperback Writer' and 'Rain', Liam's taunting songbird vocal soaring above the groovy cacophony and, really, it's very hard to imagine how it could be improved. It's an immense tune in this form, a glorious melody on repeat. What more could one need? TK

'Columbia'

(SEE PAGE 15)

'Supersonic'

SINGLE RELEASED 11 APRIL 1994 (SEE PAGE 21)

'Bring It on Down'

There is a moment in the 2004 documentary about *Definitely Maybe* when Liam and Noel Gallagher are taken back to the Pink Museum and encouraged to recall the events of 19 December 1993. Asked precisely why had they binned off 'Bring It on Down', Noel Gallagher looks into the camera and says, with barely disguised contempt, 'Funnily enough, we couldn't get the drumming right.'

Tony McCarroll had been a founding member of The Rain, joining before even Liam Gallagher did. He had met Paul 'Guigsy' McGuigan while playing football, who was friends with Paul 'Bonehead' Arthurs. Soon after they formed in the late 1980s, they had grown dissatisfied with their singer Chris Hutton. He was replaced by Liam Gallagher, and a journey that neither McCarroll, McGuigan nor Arthurs could ever have dreamed of began.

In retrospect, it seems obvious that Tony McCarroll's cards were being marked pretty soon after Oasis started to garner serious attention. It's hard to think he would not have struggled with the more complex, off-kilter rhythms that would characterize 'Wonderwall' and 'Cast No Shadow'. But even by the late 1994 sessions for 'Half the World Away', Noel Gallagher – a more than capable drummer himself – was stepping in and putting down the rhythm track.

The problems with 'Bring It on Down' – one of three *Definitely Maybe* tracks that begin with drums – had continued long after the aborted Pink Museum session. McCarroll had again been unable to nail it at Sawmills in Cornwall, where most of what would become the final versions were recorded. Finally out of options, a session drummer was hired for a last-gasp session at Eden Studios in

Chiswick in an attempt to get it right (which 'must have been awful' for Tony, admitted Noel).

But give Oasis's original drummer his due: wound up by this turn of events, with his back against the wall, he went in and that day got it right in one take. That, if nothing else, shows real character. And so the most aggressive song on *Definitely Maybe* ended up being propelled by the anger of the man playing the titanic drums that powered it, and stands as Tony McCarroll's moment of glory.

As a debut single, 'Bring It on Down' would have been a very different introduction to Oasis. It is much more fiery, more nihilistic than 'Supersonic': tinged, in lines like '*You're the outcast/You're the underclass/But you don't care/Because you're living fast*', with politics. Noel Gallagher spent a lot of his earliest interviews explaining that the lyrics to 'Supersonic' didn't mean very much at all. He would have faced a very different type of questioning had this been the first song people heard.

Drums aside, this is Oasis at their most punk rock. 'The Sex Pistols could have written it, so could The Stooges,' Noel said of 'Bring It on Down'. He was not wrong. **HM**

'Cigarettes & Alcohol'

In between the white label of 'Columbia' being sent out to tastemakers and 'Supersonic' being released as a debut single, the first publicly available Oasis recording was discreetly snuck out. 1994's 12 February issue of *NME* was billed as a celebration of ten years of Creation Records: its cover a collage illustration of the label's biggest artists. Primal Scream's Bobby Gillespie, the Jesus and Mary Chain, Ride's Mark Gardener (no Andy Bell) and others.

For now, the biggest stars the label would ever have would have to settle for a live review of their first ever London show – Liam Gallagher resplendent in Marks & Spencer's finest in the photo – and being tucked away on a five-track cassette that came attached to the cover. 'The Mutha of Creation,' as it was titled, featured songs by the Boo Radleys, Ride, Teenage Fanclub, Sugar . . . and a demo of a song that would go on to become a generation-defining classic.

'"Cigarettes & Alcohol" is a complete rehash of "Get It On", down to a T. Rex,' that review had declared, not unfairly. On the demo featured on the cassette, the theft of Marc Bolan's riff was even more brazen, stripped of the extra guitar part that would introduce the drums on the later version. Noel Gallagher would reflect that ripping off songs in this way (Oasis would be sued for far less obvious steals in the near future) came about because at the time he never imagined they would be heard by anyone bar the small audiences they were being played to. Besides, you don't have to delve too deeply into the catalogue of, say, Led Zeppelin to find evidence that great rock 'n' roll can be as much about reconstituting old riffs as it can be about coming up with new ideas. And, just as few people now listen to 'Whole Lotta Love' and give much thought to the Small Faces' 'You Need Loving,' no one hears the opening bars of 'Cigarettes & Alcohol' and thinks of anything other than 'Cigarettes & Alcohol.'

The vocals on the demo, meanwhile, are angelic: far more informed by Ian Brown's singing on early Stone Roses records than John Lydon's sneer on 'Never Mind the Bollocks'; the opening line's '*imagination*' yet to be gloriously, iconically stretched out. That particular innovation happened when Oasis were playing an early live radio session in Manchester. Alan McGee heard it, rang Noel Gallagher to tell him how amazing it sounded. Noel Gallagher relayed this information to his brother and after that it stayed, forever.

The mix of 'Cigarettes & Alcohol' was one of Owen Morris's most extreme: white noise bleeding from amplifiers before anything had even happened; the opening riff, when it did arrive, pumped up to a deafening, vulgar volume.

Marr was shocked when he heard how in-your-face Morris – who was using his studio – had made it sound. But the moment Oasis played back his version of 'Cigarettes & Alcohol' in the van on the way to a show, they knew they had what they needed. That was the sound of Oasis live, and what would become the sound of their debut album.

A firm live favourite long before *Definitely Maybe* arrived (Noel would regularly tease its opening riff in between songs at early live shows), 'Cigarettes & Alcohol' was always destined to be a single in its own right. Yet even though it came with perhaps the strongest set of B-sides ever to grace an Oasis single, not much was expected of it sales-wise. It was typical for post-album singles, in 1994, to chart much lower than their pre-album predecessors. Especially post-album singles with very radio-unfriendly choruses about white lines.

'And then the call came in,' remembered Noel Gallagher, 'telling us that it had gone in higher than [last single] "Live Forever". At which point it was decided that we should all strap ourselves in, because it was going to get pretty fucking wild from here on in.'

That was certainly true. And no song better indicated what was happening, or how fast it was happening, than 'Cigarettes & Alcohol'. When Noel had written it just a year prior, the lyrics – '*Is it worth the aggravation/To find yourself a job when there's nothing worth working for?*' – had been about being on the dole, having no money, no prospects, no future, and turning to drink and drugs for solutions. By the time it was released as a single, the same song had become an anthem to rock-star hedonism: complete with a sleeve depicting its creators plus two drinking champagne in a hotel room; and a video, filmed at London's Borderline Club, featuring them wearing sunglasses inside and doing similar in a dressing room packed full of . . . well-wishers.

The dressing rooms would get much bigger, and 'Cigarettes & Alcohol' much louder. HM

'Digsy's Dinner'

It's not controversial to describe *Definitely Maybe* as timeless. Yet there is one song that is very much rooted in a particular time and place.

The place is 15 Porter Place, L3, in Liverpool's city centre. That's where Tony and Chris Griffiths of local heroes the Real People had a studio, and where their then friend Noel Gallagher gathered his troops to record Oasis's 'Live Demonstration' tape in 1993, using the Griffithses' studio know-how and eight-track recorder.

Noel would sometimes travel to Liverpool to mess about on songs there, too, and one day he found himself behind the drum kit, bashing away with Guigsy on bass and the Griffithses' cousin Peter 'Digsy' Deary, of another group with a sizeable local cult following, Smaller (formerly Small, but now reduced further), messing around on the guitar.

Digsy had met Noel after his own brother and bandmate Steven Deary was introduced to Gallagher at an Inspiral Carpets gig in Birmingham in '92. Deary and Noel exchanged demo tapes, then met up the following night at Manchester Academy, enthusiastically complimenting each other's bands. Soon enough, both groups were doing home and away supports for the other, with Smaller going on first for Oasis at Manchester's Boardwalk and Oasis reversing the order at Le Bateau in Liverpool.

Noel and Digsy became good friends soon after that first meeting, with Noel delighting in the Scouser's madcap, psychedelic sense of humour. 'Digsy's like a barrel of monkeys,' said Noel. 'He's a funny, funny fella. He's just chaos.'

Noel also recognized the talent in him. 'He's a brilliant songwriter. He sings these songs with the most vicious, offensive lyrics about kids and women, mates, next-door neighbours, everybody. Nobody else does stuff like that. He's one of a kind.' The night that Noel was playing the drums in the studio had begun, as many sessions down there did, with a few looseners. 'We were all off our barnets, having a jam,' Digsy told the Oasis Podcast. 'Then I farted.'

The stench was offensively powerful. To a chorus of groans from all present, Digsy grabbed the mic.

'Guess what I had for dinner?' he bellowed. 'Lasagne! Lasagne!'

The next morning, Noel rang him up with a sore head and a question. 'What was that song you were singing about lasagne?' he asked.

'Oh, I just made it up on the spot,' replied Digsy.

'Well, I've got a song for that bit and I'm going to call it "Digsy's Dinner".'

The song that Noel had written is arguably *Definitely Maybe*'s anomaly, the one number that roots the album in a particular era – and not an era that any member of Oasis has much affection for: that early nineties indie disco scene where a novelty record with silly lyrics by someone like the Sultans of Ping or the Frank and Walters would pack the dancefloor with singing students. It's like a landlocked sea-shanty crossed with an East End pub sing-along.

'It's a shit song that comes from a fart,' declares Digsy, dismissively. 'It's not even a song. It's a ditty. Richard Ashcroft gets "Cast No Shadow" and I get this. It's shite!'

'He was very upset about it,' admitted Noel in 2004 on the tenth-anniversary *Definitely Maybe* documentary. 'He wrote a song in revenge called "Noel's Nose". It's very childish.'

The best thing about 'Digsy's Dinner', a song centred on going round to someone's house for lasagne followed by strawberries and cream, is the line where Liam cautions that '*these could be the best days of our lives . . .*', tapping into a seam of nostalgia for the present day and a sense of living in the moment that runs throughout Oasis's debut.

'That is good, that bit,' allows Digsy. However: 'I think it's the worst song Oasis have ever written. I hate it with a vengeance. It'll haunt me to my grave.'

Nobody else, though, has been directly named in the title of an Oasis song, forever tied to one of the greatest debut albums of all time. Digsy's association continued afterwards as well, with Smaller regularly supporting Oasis in the early years and Noel even playing guitar on their one album, 1996's *Badly Badly*. Noel namechecked him again on the title track to *Be Here Now*: *'Your shit jokes remind me of Digsy's'.* He also gave Digsy his Les Paul Epiphone guitar, the one featured in the 'Supersonic' video, and which, many years later, in straitened circumstances, Digsy sold to Christies for £15,000. So there have been upsides for him.

There is one further redeeming feature about 'Digsy's Dinner' for its subject. 'That song has brought me many rounds,' says Digsy. 'It's got me drunk in so many places.' **TK**

'Slide Away'

The stated intention with 'Slide Away' was to write something in the vein of 'Cortez the Killer' by Neil Young. Young had been a key touchstone for the likes of Nirvana and Pearl Jam – he was called 'the Godfather of grunge' and his lyric '*It's better to burn out than to fade away*' was quoted in Kurt Cobain's suicide note – but he was also a huge influence on the writing of Noel Gallagher, whose band was a direct, upbeat, positive reaction to all of that music.

As early as June 1994, he had guested onstage with Neil Young's long-time/sometime band Crazy Horse at King's College in London, playing on their cover of The Seeds' garage rock classic 'Pushin' Too Hard'. Later, on tour with Oasis, he would sing on a cover of 'Hey Hey, My My (Into the Black)', the song from which Cobain took the above line. He describes Young as 'the only guy I've ever been in awe of meeting'.

Another one of Noel's key heroes played a part in the writing of 'Slide Away'. Oasis were at a residential rehearsal studio during 1993 when a guitar turned up, care of Johnny Marr: the Gibson Les Paul that he had written 'The Queen Is Dead' on, no less. Noel took it upstairs to his room immediately, opened the case and not long after that Oasis had a late but incredibly powerful addition to *Definitely Maybe* ready to go.

As a third single, 'Live Forever' had silenced the dissenting voices that had Oasis pinned as a band who would be remembered as much if not more for their antics offstage than for their music. Liam took the brunt of this: often insisting, most notoriously in an *NME* interview that would end up being released as the 'Wibbling Rivalry' 7-inch single, that it was just as important for a band to have attitude and a sense that something was going to happen.

Noel violently disagreed. 'If you're proud about getting thrown off ferries,' he says as the topic of Oasis's chaotic trip to Amsterdam was brought up, 'then why don't you go and support West Ham and get the fuck out of my band and go and be a football hooligan. 'Cos we're musicians, right? We're not football hooligans.' The argument continues, before Liam concludes: 'I'm in this band to make fucking music, but that thing will come along with it. It always does.' (They're both right, of course.)

He'd done as good a job as anyone ever, up until the release of *Definitely Maybe*, of supplying that thing. ('I don't know what it is,' he told me when I asked him to define what 'that thing' is, 'but I've got it.') But 'Slide Away' is the performance on which Liam Gallagher announced himself as a singer to be taken very, very seriously indeed. Had he been producing vocal takes such as this and gone to bed at 10 p.m. with a cup of cocoa every night, he would still be held up as one of the greats, no question.

Even just the difference between what he's doing here and 'Supersonic' and 'Shakermaker' is extraordinary: the attack is still there, but now, as his voice verges on the point of cracking in the chorus, there is a real, undeniable soulfulness. As well as one of the greatest, most beloved songs, 'Slide Away' is the start of the road that would lead to 'Wonderwall,' 'Champagne Supernova' and beyond. 'Up until the night I wrote "Live Forever",' Noel remembered. 'I was writing a certain kind of music. The night after, I found myself writing a different kind of music. So I always go back to that song as being a pivotal moment in my songwriting.'

'Slide Away' was this in action: a giant leap forward for Oasis and their songwriter. Noel described it at the time as 'the one and only love song I'm ever going to write'. This ended up not being true. But it was a turning point, no question, and a turning point that came with a gorgeously raw guitar solo that was the most Neil Young-esque he would ever sound to boot. HM

'Married with Children'

Neither Oasis nor Alan McGee were meant to be in Glasgow's King Tut's Wah Wah Hut on 31 May 1993. The reason for both parties being present that night went by the name of Debbie Turner, an ex-girlfriend of McGee's, and also a member of Sister Lovers, a band that shared a rehearsal space with Oasis.

'We were asking Debbie what they were up to, and they said, "We're going to Glasgow to do this gig,"' said Noel. For an unsigned Manchester band to announce to another unsigned Manchester band that they were playing in Glasgow was so far-fetched it was like claiming they were sailing across the Atlantic. Turner pressed home her advantage. 'Why don't you play with us?' she wondered.

Noel set the wheels in motion. 'We got a few headcases together,' he told the *Supersonic* filmmakers. 'If we all put £25 in we can hire a splitter van and get up there, kip in the van, do the gig, get back Friday night.'

Oasis and friends arrived at Glasgow's King Tut's in their gold van – 'which was amazing' – before Sister Lovers, or anyone else other than the club's manager. 'We're Oasis,' they told him. 'We're playing tonight.'

No, you are not, he insisted, pointing at the bill of headliners 18 Wheeler and support act Sister Lovers. They pleaded, they begged, they made the point that they'd driven up especially for this, their thirteenth gig, with a crew of mates. They did not, however, threaten the manager with violence, as has been previously reported. Nobody who has ever been on a night out in Glasgow would ever do that to a club owner in the city, no matter how mob-handed they were.

The manager remained unmoved until Sister Lovers arrived, alongside 18 Wheeler, and threatened not to play if Oasis couldn't. The manager eventually relented, telling them they'd have to start earlier and deliver shorter sets. 'That wasn't hard,' said Turner, 'because we only had five songs.'

McGee, meanwhile, hadn't even told Turner he was coming, but as he'd signed 18 Wheeler to Creation, he decided he'd get there early with his kid sister Susan and spook out Debbie before her gig into the bargain.

The McGees were standing at the back when Oasis took to the stage before a crowd estimated to number somewhere between ten and twelve, launching straight into 'Rock 'n' Roll Star'. Never a truer word sung.

Halfway through that first song, Susan leans into her brother's ear. 'You should sign these,' she tells him.

Alan McGee is a bit drunk and a bit high, but yeah. They do sound great. Maybe he's just drunk. Maybe.

Next up is 'Bring It on Down'.

Fuck me, thinks McGee. *This is like Happy Mondays doing The Stooges.*

'I'm signing these,' he shouts into Susan's ear.

The riff to 'Up in the Sky' rings out next, part George Harrison, part Johnny Marr, and Liam Gallagher – still holding the microphone untethered from the mic stand at this early juncture in his stage career – lets the room know exactly where he's at.

'Definitely!' mouths McGee to Susan, eyes wide. By the time, 'I Am the Walrus' rattles the venue's foundations, McGee is checking out each of the other audience members to make sure none are from rival record labels.

Afterwards, Noel is chatting with Mark Coyle by the mixing desk when this tall, wild-eyed ginger Glaswegian marches up to him.

'What's your band called?' asks Alan McGee.

'Oasis.'

'Do you want a record deal?'

'Who with?'

'Creation Records.'

Sounded good to Noel, and if it sounded good to him, it'd sound good to the others too.

'We went back that night,' recalled Noel. 'I don't remember anybody high-fiving in the back of the van. I don't remember us being nonchalant about it either.' This was mainly because nobody really knew much about Alan McGee and Creation Records at that moment, but once they found out he also put out records by Primal Scream, Teenage Fanclub and Ride, it all felt more legit. The money they'd invested in that gold splitter had been worth it.

The van eventually made it back to Manchester around 6 a.m. Noel slipped the key into his flat in India House, Whitworth Street, and announced his return to his girlfriend, Louise Jones, with whom he'd been together for a few years. She was up, getting ready to leave for work.

'Creation Records have offered us a deal,' he told her excitedly.

Louise burst into tears. 'She knew,' Noel reflected later, 'that that was going to be the end of us.'

There comes a point in all cohabiting relationships when the writing on the wall spells out either 'stick' or 'twist'. For Louise, she probably could see that this was Noel's opportunity to twist, something she could no doubt sense in the air between them. Noel's thoughts about the relationship's status were detailed in a gentle, if acerbic, acoustic song he'd written on their sofa while half-watching *Married with Children*, an American sitcom about a deadbeat, miserable family, after which he named the composition, which was lyrically inspired by his own relationship.

'Married with Children': a song recorded in Mark Coyle's home, on John Squire's acoustic (which happened to be there), sung by Liam Gallagher, about Noel Gallagher's relationship, from Louise Jones's point of view. For someone who says he hates to reveal stuff about himself openly in his songwriting, Noel displays a lot of brutal self-reflection in 'Married with Children' *('I hate the way that even though you know you're wrong/You say you're right . . .')*.

'I was sitting in my ex-flat two years ago, with my guitar, being scowled at when *Married with Children* was on the telly,' Noel recalled in 1994. 'I looked at them two in the show, and looked at us two, and I thought, *That's us, that is.* If you live with a girlfriend – or even a flatmate – there are always petty things that you hate about them: that song's about the pettiness. That's why we put it after 'Slide Away', an uplifting song about two people in love. Then comes the cynical one where they've moved in with each other and they fucking hate each other.'

Your music's shite, it keeps me up all night, up all night . . . 'This person came up with that immortal line,' explained Noel. '"I don't know why you sit up all night playing that guitar. Your music's shite and it keeps me up all night." A-ha! I'm having that one!'

Sometimes, when you gotta go – you gotta go. Judging from the song's lyrics, Louise may have felt the same deep down.

'People tell me I'll never get a girl like that again,' said Noel of Jones to the *Observer* magazine, just before *(What's the Story) Morning Glory?* came out. 'But I'd rather be alone and live like this.' **TK**

'Sad Song'

DEFINITELY MAYBE BONUS TRACK

Even just by virtue of its title or its opening line, '*Sing a sad song, in a lonely place*', this extra track does not fit in with the rest of *Definitely Maybe* at all. There is a reason for this. 'When we cut the vinyl of the album on a single disc,' Noel explained, 'the grooves were so close together that it was really quiet. The way round it was to do a double album. But that meant we were a song short, so the record company said, "You've got to come up with another song by tonight." *Piece of piss!* I thought.'

Once again, just as it had with 'Supersonic' and the final verse of 'Shakermaker' and many more times yet to arrive, the last minute proved to be a fertile place for Noel Gallagher. He strummed some chords, they sounded sad, so he wrote a sad song. There was no time to conjure up something and have a full band play it, so acoustic it stayed. Liam recorded a vocal take – he would revisit the song live during his solo period – but it was the Noel version that was included. Shortly after writing it, he had debuted 'Sad Song' on BBC Radio 1's *Evening Session*. It was clear that people were taken with Noel singing it.

Minus 'Sad Song' – absent from all but the vinyl version, where it sat between 'Columbia' and 'Supersonic' – *Definitely Maybe* was a perfect garage rock album in the purest sense. Despite its troubled recording, the finished version sounded like five guys walking into a room, plugging in, turning everything up as far as it would go, and blasting through every song they have in one take. The early Oasis live set, in other words. Added in, not least because it featured a very different lead vocalist, 'Sad Song' showed a band who were capable of much more than that.

Very quickly, it became a mainstay of the mid-set acoustic segment Noel Gallagher started playing at shows. People would sing along, quietly, to its chorus: more people than could possibly have bought the vinyl version of Oasis's debut album. When Oasis made their debut appearance on the BBC's *Later . . . with Jools Holland* – a grown-up live music show, for which all the band wore suits – 'Sad Song' was the second of three songs they played, chosen over anything else off *Definitely Maybe*. Noel Gallagher knew what he was doing. 'Sad Song' would bamboozle an audience beyond Oasis's fanbase: the mums and dads and casual observers who had Oasis in their minds as a loud, riotous rock 'n' roll band would have no choice but to change their opinion. It worked. **HM**

'Cigarettes & Alcohol'

SINGLE RELEASED 10 OCTOBER 1994 (SEE PAGE 50)

'I Am the Walrus'

B-SIDE OF 'CIGARETTES & ALCOHOL'

'We did four songs and finished with "I Am the Walrus",' Liam Gallagher said when I asked him what he remembered about that fateful King Tut's Wah Wah Hut show. 'I Am the Walrus,' he said, was a key part of his sales pitch to the venue manager who was reluctant to let Oasis play. 'That's what I was saying to the guy before,' continued Liam, '"Come on, we do 'I Am the Walrus,' man! Even The Beatles never played 'I Am the Walrus'!"'

We'll never know if this is what tipped the balance for the venue manager. What we know for certain is that the version of 'I Am the Walrus' Oasis closed with that night – the same version that they would close Knebworth and countless other shows, not least their last ever pre-reunion set in 2009 – did play a large part in convincing Alan McGee that he had to sign them to Creation Records. 'The first song was really good,' he recalled of the set. 'Then the second was incredible. By the time they did this fantastic version of "I Am the Walrus", I'd decided, "I've got to sign this group, now."'

It is not breaking news to say that Oasis were inspired by The Beatles. Just visually, there were the haircuts. The round sunglasses they took to wearing during their imperial phase. The hollow-bodied Epiphone Casino guitars, as seen around the necks of the Fab Four from about '65 onwards, that were such a key part of their early sound. The realization that interviews are a chance to entertain rather than just explain. Musically, debut single 'Supersonic,' alone, featured 'Yellow Submarine' in its lyrics and lifted its guitar solo from George Harrison's 'My Sweet Lord.' It was far from the last time Oasis music would directly reference The Beatles.

In terms of straight-up covers, Oasis would at one time or another perform versions of 'Help!,' 'You've Got to Hide Your Love Away,' 'Helter Skelter,' 'Within You, Without You,' 'Tomorrow Never Knows,' 'Day Tripper' (live, with Ocean Colour Scene), 'I'm Only Sleeping' (with Kelly Jones) and excerpts of 'Octopus's Garden.'

From Liam and Noel's solo/post-Oasis periods you can add 'Strawberry Fields Forever', 'All You Need Is Love', 'Across the Universe' and 'Cry Baby Cry'. And then there's the two unreleased tracks Noel came across during lockdown.

'There's a great version of "Eleanor Rigby", a punk version of "Eleanor Rigby",' he said. 'And an amazing version of (1969 George Harrison Beatles track) "It's All Too Much" we did on the day George died. We went to the studio and did it as a tribute, and Johnny Marr's on it. There are two drummers: I was playing with Alan White and Johnny is on guitar. It's fucking amazing.'

That may well be true. But it would have to be pretty fucking amazing to top the first and unquestionably best Oasis Beatles cover of all.

The lyrics of 'I Am the Walrus' were written by John Lennon to deliberately confound the intellectuals who were constantly trying to 'decode' the Beatles' lyrics (right from the start of Oasis, Noel Gallagher was constantly doing something similar: rubbishing theorizing by others as to what his songs were about). It always remained one of his favourite Beatles songs 'because I did it, of course. But, also, because it's one of those that has enough little bitties going to keep you interested even 100 years later.'

The genius of the Oasis version is that it doesn't even try to replicate all this. Instead, it goes to the other extreme: taking maybe the most intricate, layered recording The Beatles ever made and steamrolling over every last one of its 'little bitties' – the strings, the spoken snippet of King Lear, the trombone – with raw, simple guitars. In the process, it becomes an Oasis song, the descending chord sequence at the end just going round and round forever while Noel makes all manner of discordant noise on his guitar. And just as he did with his brother's songs, Liam sings it like he owns it.

The version that became the B-side of 'Cigarettes & Alcohol' – like the version that got Oasis signed – was played in Glasgow, at The Cathouse . . . or at least that was what it said on the single sleeve. It was only five years later that Noel admitted it was actually recorded at a Sony Records seminar in Gleneagles, which he described as 'one of them shit things where all the twats in suits get together and they roll on the new signings.'

'It was an absolutely empty hall,' he remembered. 'At the beginning our kid's going, "Doesn't matter if it's out of tune, because you're cool." I was pissed as an arse.' When it came time to release a version of their set closer, however, it was decided, rightly, 'that it would look shit if you put "Live at Sony Seminar in Gleneagles". We had a version of it from The Cathouse in Glasgow, which sounded quite similar but it was rubbish. So we thought, *Fuck it, no one'll fucking know*.' Some crowd noise from a Faces bootleg was added, and that was that.

In the end it didn't matter. Nothing is real, as a wise man once said. **HM**

'Listen Up'

B-SIDE OF 'CIGARETTES & ALCOHOL'

The era of staggeringly strong Oasis B-sides did not begin immediately. Aside from the Noel-sung solo acoustic songs, their first three singles were filled out with demo and live versions. It was only on 'Cigarettes & Alcohol', their first single post *Definitely Maybe*, that the truly, absurdly good songs began. 'I Am the Walrus' and 'Fade Away' were both live favourites from the word go. But 'Listen Up' was a revelation: the first Oasis song to be much, much too good to throw away on a B-side.

Sounding like a highlights reel of *Definitely Maybe* – the drums and guitar intro from 'Supersonic', the skyscraping chorus from 'Slide Away' – this is an epic that, as its writer said of it, 'is the sort of song that other bands would launch their career on.'

'I don't really sit and write B-sides,' Noel Gallagher said. 'I just write songs in my spare time. Then I kind of pick the best ones for the album and then the things I pick as B-sides aren't necessarily not the best; they are just, you know, maybe I don't like the lyrics, or the lyrics are great but I don't like the tune, or the tune is good but I don't like the singing, or there's just something and they're not perfect. But people hear them and go, "God, I fucking love that."'

'Listen Up' was written the day after Oasis got thrown out and banned for life from the Columbia Hotel. Noel – who had been staying in Chiswick – turned up to record at Maison Rouge studio in Fulham, at the agreed time of midday. Half an hour before, in fact. Due to the events of the previous evening, the rest of the band didn't turn up until 8 p.m. – 'looking like they're still up from the night before' – and so Noel had been sat in the kitchen, writing lyrics for hours. They were good lyrics: some of the best to ever feature on an Oasis song. '*Day by day there's a man in a suit who's gonna make you pay*,' yearns Liam, '*for the thoughts that you think and the words they won't let you say*.'

Aside from the usual majestic one-take vocal, Liam Gallagher did make another important contribution. As the band were listening back to the finished version, he noted that the guitar break was much too long. Noel disagreed, and it went to the pressing plant as it was. But four years later, when 'Listen Up' was presented on *The Masterplan*, its duration had been trimmed by thirty seconds. Liam had been right. Cue an argument. **HM**

'Fade Away'

B-SIDE OF 'CIGARETTES & ALCOHOL'

Liam Gallagher has hailed Buzzcocks as 'the second greatest band to come from Manchester', slotting the quartet in above the likes of Stone Roses, Joy Division, The Fall, Happy Mondays, The Smiths (and 10cc). The lure of Pete Shelley's class of '77 was vivid: Buzzcocks delivered high-energy punk riffs filled with lovelorn melodies and sing-along choruses. It was Motown you could pogo to.

Noel Gallagher saw their appeal too. One of his earliest songs for Oasis, something that they played from the first rehearsals at the Boardwalk, was cut very much from the same cloth as

Buzzcocks. The version of 'Fade Away' located on this B-side is a punky explosion of guitars and clattering drums, much like 'Bring It on Down', but at its core is not the nihilist dark heart of The Stooges or the Sex Pistols. Instead, it's a song that wistfully wonders why '*while we're living, the dreams we have as children fade away*', a sentiment delivered by an indelibly catchy vocal melody.

It didn't take very long for everyone to notice that that melody was in fact Wham!'s 'Freedom', a worldwide hit single ten years earlier. This may have been why a song as sticky as this wasn't included on *Definitely Maybe*, though Noel himself suggested it was simply because he had to choose between 'Slide Away' and 'Fade Away' and (correctly) decided the former would fit better.

For what it's worth, George Michael loved 'Fade Away'. He was, according to Simon Halfon – who designed artwork for both Michael and Oasis – an Oasis fan anyway and laughed in approval when Halfon first played 'Fade Away' to him. 'George was flattered,' said Halfon. 'He took it as a compliment.'

Another reason for Noel not including it on his band's debut album may have also been that he could see its shape-shifting future, that 'Fade Away' still had time to mature.

There was a much slower version delivered for War Child's *Help* benefit album in 1995, with Noel on lead vocal and Liam on backing vocals. Even then, Noel was unsatisfied. 'That ended up wrong,' he told *Melody Maker.* 'I'd like to do it just on a piano. Really slow, sort of an "Imagine".'

Eventually, the song did settle, working at its most potent as a warm, melancholic ballad in Noel's High Flying Birds set long after Oasis had called a hiatus in 2009. This slow and rusty version worked best largely because Noel's voice had attained just the right amount of living to give this song about the passing of time suitable pathos: '*Now I know much about the way I feel . . .*' TK

'Whatever'

STANDALONE SINGLE

RELEASED 18 DECEMBER 1994

Neil Innes was a musician and funny man who came to prominence as a member of psychedelic music hall jesters the Bonzo Dog Doo-Dah Band in the sixties, before unofficially joining Monty Python, contributing music and appearing in much of the comedy superstars' TV and film work. The whistling in 'Always Look on the Bright Side of Life' from *The Life of Brian*? That was Neil Innes.

In the seventies, he joined up with that song's writer, Eric Idle, to form The Rutles, an affectionate pastiche of The Beatles. The duo were encouraged in these endeavours by George Harrison, who liked the idea of a satire of his former band so much that he gave the pair archival material for use. In the quartet, Innes played the John Lennon character, Ron Nasty, while Idle delivered the Paul McCartney-adjacent Dirk McQuickly, appearing in TV shows on both sides of the Atlantic before they released a spoof feature-length documentary in 1978 called *All You Need Is Cash*. Innes wrote all the music for it, which was then released as a surprisingly good album, *The Rutles*. Noel Gallagher and Oasis were such fans that sometimes they'd play the album over the PA before gigs.

One of the reasons *The Rutles* was so convincing – other than Innes's skill as a mimicking songwriter and satirist – was because often the line between pastiche and rip-off was blurred to a confusing degree. They really did sound like The Beatles, but with sillier lyrics.

The Beatles' publisher Sony/ATV Music agreed, and Innes was made to change songwriting credits on several songs to Lennon/McCartney/Innes, despite Lennon apparently having given his personal blessing. Innes was reportedly heartbroken by this development.

'George occasionally attempts to get the rights back,' said Innes in 1996. 'I've stopped sulking about it.'

This may have given Innes an insight into how Oasis felt when his own publishers, EMI, got in touch with Oasis about the similarities contained in their 'Whatever' single to the title track from Neil Innes's 1973 solo album, 'How Sweet to Be an Idiot'. Ironically, it was Paul McCartney's brother Michael who pointed it out to Innes.

Nicky Campbell had played the two songs back-to-back on BBC Radio 1, underlining how close the melodies were, and McCartney got straight on the phone to Innes.

'They're virtually identical at the beginning,' he told him.

This was true, but Innes filed it away in his mind. More people got in touch with him over the coming days, however, so he called up EMI to see what they thought. What they thought had already been communicated legally to Oasis. Oasis subsequently agreed to a songwriting credit for Innes.

'They settled out of court,' Innes said in 2013. 'Put their hands up and gave me a quarter of "Whatever". It goes to EMI, where it's divided 50/50 between EMI and me.'

Noel Gallagher said in 1995 that he had absolutely no knowledge of 'How Sweet to Be an Idiot'. He'd been summoned to his manager's office when the complaint came through from EMI, his 'Whatever' at number three in the charts. 'Honestly, I nearly fell over,' he told *NME*. 'I was pleading with everyone, "I haven't heard it!" They're like, "But it's identical!" "But I've never heard it, I swear to God!"' With the single already a hit, there wasn't much for it other than to offer a credit and royalty. 'We can't very well delete it,' said Noel.

'Whatever' had been in Noel's back pocket for years, from the very earliest Oasis rehearsals. The first time he played it, acoustically, to the others in his band, it garnered a soon-to-be familiar reaction from Bonehead.

'You've not just written that,' he said to Noel, awestruck.

'I have!'

'No . . .'

Later, Bonehead would reflect, 'You just don't expect someone you know to play a song like that in your rehearsal room. It always did my head in.'

For Noel, it must have been very useful to have such a reliable bellwether for all his best songs over those earliest sessions. If Bonehead thinks it's not something you've written, then it's especially good. 'Whatever' was aired in those first rehearsals and gigs alongside other songs he'd sit on for several years, such as 'Hello', 'She's Electric' and 'All Around the World'. In 'Whatever', Noel saw a particular eventuality.

'I've got a song that's gonna be a Christmas number one,' he said to me of it in the summer 1994. 'I've got a Christmas number one and a Eurovision winner ("All Around the World") but I have to pick my moment with both.'

The moment he chose for 'Whatever' was that year, where it eventually lost out on the top two spots for the final UK top forty of 1994 to 'Stay Another Day' by East 17 at number one and second-placed Mariah Carey's 'All I Want for Christmas Is You' – two perennial Christmas hits to this day. Over the years, 'Whatever' has been used to sell everything from Coca-Cola and Asahi beer to mobile phones, so perhaps Noel had simply misjudged its eventual commercial impact. It lives on, too, with both Noel and Liam including it in their solo sets.

Neil Innes, meanwhile, had one final word to say about 'Whatever' when, in 1996, The Rutles re-formed for their *Archaeology* album, a piss-take of The Beatles' *Anthology*. It contained a song titled 'Shangri-La', which Innes had updated from its original 1977 state to open with the 'Whatever' melody and to finish with Innes singing *'we're free to be whatever we are.'*

'These are things you can do for a laugh,' commented Innes when quizzed about it later.

Noel didn't mind, either, even suggesting to Innes that he'd appear in the video for it until it was discovered Oasis were on tour in North America at the time. Unfortunately for Innes, they had bigger fish to fry. TK

'(It's Good) To Be Free'

B-SIDE OF 'WHATEVER'

When Noel Gallagher played the first ever High Flying Birds show on 23 October 2011 at Dublin's Olympia Theatre – the day his first solo album went in at number one – he started with '(It's Good) To Be Free'. Beady Eye had gone out playing only their own material, but Noel immediately made it clear he would be playing Oasis songs as well as new stuff. They were his songs, after all, so why would he not?

As with the version of 'Fade Away' that Oasis recorded for the *Help* charity album in 1995, Noel took one of his band's heaviest songs and rearranged it to better suit his voice rather than Liam's: a softer, acoustic take. He had in fact been playing this arrangement since 2007, when he went out to do some solo sets – one or two attended by Liam – in support of the *Stop the Clocks* 'best of' album, and a few charity shows thereafter. It would remain his set opener for long into his solo career: a song that he always had a huge fondness for, despite the trying circumstances in which it was written.

'(It's Good) To Be Free' came from the period when Noel Gallagher was, briefly, free of Oasis in September 1994 – more of which in 'Talk Tonight' on page 91 – unsure at that point whether he would ever return. In the end he did and, after a few more shows, it became the first thing they recorded together at Congress House in Texas.

The Oasis version is as dark and heavy as they ever got on record: Liam sounding wired and raspy, Noel making all manner of discordant, overdriven noise in the background. In stark contrast to the title, it feels a long way away from the euphoric, upbeat vibes of its A-side or *Definitely Maybe*. Its sound bore similarities to the middle section of Tears for Fears' 'Shout': a song that – like Wham!'s 'Freedom', whose melody had informed 'Fade Away' – its writer would have heard on the radio as a teenager, just as he was starting to experiment with writing his own songs. One of Noel Gallagher's greatest strengths as a writer was the fact that his antenna was always alert, picking up snippets of things that sat far outside his stated influences.

'(It's Good) To Be Free' also marks the start of what would be a long-running love of brackets in song titles: one that encompassed *(What's the Story) Morning Glory?* and stretched right up to '(Stranded On) The Wrong Beach' from the first High Flying Birds album. 'I don't know why "It's Good" is in brackets,' he said, 'Loads of other people used to do it on their records and I could never understand why, so I thought I'd do it, and I don't understand why. If you took that out, "To Be Free" is a shit title. But I suppose I was trying to make myself look intellectual.' **HM**

'Half the World Away'

B-SIDE OF 'WHATEVER'

Like Noel and Liam Gallagher, Caroline Aherne was the product of Irish immigrants who eventually settled on an estate in south Manchester in the 1960s. They had more than just their geographic and ancestral backgrounds in common too. Both the Gallaghers and Aherne were part of a new arts and media class that emerged in the 1990s, a generation of state-educated British artists, musicians, writers, models and actors who came of age in Thatcher's Britain, but, unlike their forebears, were not interested in protest or political moralizing. Instead, their ideology was to make the most of their talents and to reach as many people as possible without compromising the basic proposition.

For Aherne, that meant her work as a once-in-a-generation writer and performer of comedy characters and situations. She forged her reputation principally as Mrs Merton, a slyly prim Mancunian pensioner whose fake BBC chat show featured her interviewing and skewering real celebrities with deliciously deadpan relish. After that success, she and her writing partner Craig

Cash (another Mancunian) could sketch their own TV future. What they chose to make was *The Royle Family*, a situation comedy set entirely in the front room, kitchen and occasionally toilet of a (not often) working-class family in a terraced house somewhere in Manchester.

The Royle Family broke every TV comedy convention. Most of the 'action' centred on the family members, neighbours and associates sitting on a sofa half-watching television and chatting, eating their dinners on trays and smoking. No laugh track, no backstory; everything took place in real time. There was quite a lot of silence. If it didn't take place in that room – and very little physically happened – it didn't exist. It was all about the characters, the kind of dole class Northern family that was entirely absent from all popular culture but no doubt clearly recognizable to the members of Oasis.

'I instantly fell in love with it,' Noel told Matt Morgan for his podcast. 'My dad was a version of Jim Royle, which is like, "Everything on the telly is shit", and me mam was like, "Jesus Christ, shut up!" That was our house. I fell in love with the pregnant pauses more than anything.'

The first episode took place at 10 p.m. on 14 September 1998, on BBC One, and centred on the story of Jim Royle, the irritable patriarch, buying a pair of knock-off jeans from family friend Twiggy, as well as consuming a bag of pork scratchings he makes his son Anthony pick up from the shop on a three-pack cigarette dash. The subplot involved the arrival of a phone bill and the hunt for the perpetrator of a surprising phone call to Aberdeen. Future son-in-law Dave (played by Craig Cash) describes his dinner of corn beef hash and later farts, twice. Daughter Denise – Aherne's character – browses the Y-fronts in a clothing catalogue. That's it. As the credits roll to introduce the show to a grainy time-lapse video of the sofa and its occupants, the only piece of music ever featured floods the screen with emotion: 'Half the World Away', Noel Gallagher at his most plaintive, a melancholic masterpiece of yearning and frustration about one's location-cursed circumstances that he'd inexplicably buried on a B-side four years earlier. The song is repeated over the black-screen end credits to often devastating effect.

Sometime earlier, Mark Coyle had introduced the Oasis tour bus to the wonder of Burt Bacharach and Hal David's 'This Guy's in Love with You,' the 1968 heartbreaker hit they'd provided for Herb Alpert to sing. Upon hearing it, Tony McCarroll claims he suggested to Noel that the shuffling beat (one of his two specialities) could be lifted for a new Oasis song. Noel thought it deserved more than that and sketched out 'Half the World Away' in its image. 'It's exactly the same,' he admitted later. 'I'm surprised he [Bacharach] hasn't sued me.'

That's a harsh self-assessment. The electric piano riff is very similar, as is that shuffling beat, but the vocal melody framing the choruses is noticeably different, as are the sentiments. Hal David is among the greatest lyricists of all time and 'This Guy's in Love' is another lyrical miracle about unrequited love in the same lineage of his 'Walk On By' or 'I Say a Little Prayer,' but would David have been able to capture the desperation to escape the environment you are a product of as poignantly as Noel does on 'Half the World Away'? Arguably not. Noel wasn't signed to a recording contract until he was twenty-seven and would have felt the darkening of one's horizons more keenly than most superstar songwriters. 'Half the World Away' is Noel's wheelhouse, occupying a similar desperation to that frequently mapped by another late-developing Mancunian of Irish parentage, Morrissey. It also reveals a mental vulnerability – *'I can feel the warning signs, running around my mind'* – that Noel wasn't otherwise describing in his 1994 songbook.

'Half the World Away' was recorded on tour in October '94 during the quick-fire, ill-tempered Congress House sessions in Austin, Texas, that also delivered 'Talk Tonight,' 'a second country and western song' as Noel described it. Frustrated by McCarroll's inability to play '(It's Good) To Be Free,' Noel banished the drummer from the studio during recording and put down the beat to

'Half the World Away' himself. Bonehead provides the gentle electric piano.

Over the years, as the show that brought the song to the nation's attention grew across three seasons and five specials into one of Britain's most beloved comedies, even Noel came to think of 'Half the World Away' as the *Royle Family* song. He was, however, initially sceptical about its use.

'I'd known Craig Cash for a while and he explained what *The Royle Family* was about,' Noel said, when discussing the original pitch for a theme. 'I was thinking, *Well, "Married with Children" is perfect.* "Half the World Away" didn't make any sense to me. It's all about desperately trying to leave the situation you're in, dreaming of being somewhere else, leaving the house, leaving the city you're in. When you put it together, it's quite tragic. They're all tied to each other in that little room.'

Four days after Aherne died of cancer at just fifty-two on 2 July 2016, Noel appeared with his High Flying Birds in Nashville's Ryman Auditorium. That night, he dedicated 'Half the World Away' to 'a friend of mine . . . her name was Caroline, and she was a very, very, very funny woman. She used the next song on a very, very, very brilliant sitcom in England called *The Royle Family*.' He's dedicated it to her again at subsequent performances, the song becoming a staple of his post-Oasis live show. It even found its way onto Liam Gallagher's setlist during his 2024 Definitely Maybe Tour, with Liam dedicating it to 'Noel fucking Gallagher' at Reading Festival. In 2015, a soft-focus cover version by Norwegian singer-songwriter AURORA soundtracked the John Lewis TV Christmas advert, reimbursing Noel, as he later joked, for some of the money he'd spent in the department store over previous Christmases.

Where would 'Half the World Away' sit in Noel Gallagher's canon had Caroline Aherne and Craig Cash not chosen it as the theme to *The Royle Family*? Would it have connected so forcibly with so many otherwise? It made its way onto the multimillion-selling *Masterplan* compilation, so perhaps it would have still been described by Noel as his favourite B-side, as he revealed in conversation at a Salford Lads' Club benefit in 2019. Like 'Don't Look Back in Anger', though, it's an Oasis song that had to flee the nest to truly find its place in the universe, and for that it owes its life to *The Royle Family*. TK

'Here comes that twat from Sandhurst in the cowboy hat . . .'

On the frontline with Oasis #2

The Paris match, November 1994

As soon as *NME* got to Paris for the *Les Inrockuptibles* festival, people were keen to let us know just how much they hated Oasis.

'Don't mention Oasis to me,' said Rick Witter, singer with Shed Seven, as we checked into the Amiral Duperre Hotel in Pigalle, where all the groups playing the festival that week were put up. It was a five-minute stroll to the show later at La Cigale, a 2,000-capacity Parisian concert hall. 'I don't know what their problem is. They're so arrogant and rude. They think they're God's gift! We saw them last night and asked Noel how it's going. He's like, "Alright but there's a lot of shit groups playing these gigs." And,' he said with justified paranoia, 'you know who he's talking about.'

Andy Henderson, drummer with Echobelly, also had thoughts about his Mancunian rivals. 'I would love to give one of those brothers – or any of Oasis really – a smack in the mouth,' he announced, with intent.

Justine Frischmann, Elastica's leader (and Damon Albarn's partner at that time), had opinions about the Gallaghers that were so profane she had to stop herself from sharing them. 'I know we're just chatting, and it's all off the record,' she said later that first night in a bar, 'but you're still a journalist on a job and what I think of Oasis really can't be printed . . .'

And yet there was only one British band appearing on the *Les Inrockuptibles* touring French festival who were being supported by chartered coachloads of British fans in town simply to see them. So Oasis were clearly doing something right.

I was there with photographer Roger Sargent to report for *NME* on the Paris leg of *Les Inrockuptibles,* a magazine-sponsored six-band festival on two rotas that revolved across four cities – Lille, Paris, Lyon and Marseille – over four nights. On one bill there was Elastica, Shed Seven and Gene; on the other Oasis, Echobelly and, incongruously, American rap-blues duo G-Love & Special Sauce, the latter booked after the *'L'année Britpop'* posters had been printed, presumably.

On the afternoon of the second day in Paris, we ran into Noel Gallagher in the very spot Rick Witter had described him as arrogant to us twenty-four hours earlier. As a diligent music journalist, I asked Noel what he thought of that.

'Well, we've been doing the same interviews a day after them, and in every interview,' he said, 'we've had journalists go, "Oooh, we spoke to Shed Seven yesterday and they really took the piss out of you." Then we bump into them and they're all dead matey, asking how it's going . . . it's embarrassing. Slag us off, but don't make small talk. It's not as if they're any good.'

Oasis, on the other hand, were supernaturally good by November 1994. I'd seen them play around a dozen times that year, each occasion ferocious, joyous, overpowering: it was no secret why so many had navigated the Channel to catch them. They were unmissable. In just a few months, they'd enlisted a following of passionate supporters the like of which hadn't really been seen since the early eighties, when fans of The Jam, Specials and Smiths would follow their loves across Europe for another glimpse. I was no different. It's why I'd engineered the commission.

In Paris that night, Oasis played the entirety of *Definitely Maybe,* threw in 'Fade Away' three songs deep and ended on an epic 'I Am the Walrus,' by which time the whole of La Cigale was vibrating, as if in communal ecstasy. Liam Gallagher, standing alone in the white-light feedback, was applauding the room, beckoning a fan aboard, smooching with her, and then exiting with a swagger stage left. Most of the other groups over the two nights had been enjoyable, and the audience had donated appropriate applause, a stage diver for Shed Seven, some wolf whistling for Elastica and an exquisitely timed heckle of 'Morrissey!' during the Smiths-In-Their-Eyes Gene's set, but it was all typical gig fayre. Oasis, meanwhile, were received with a devotional fervour and orgiastic mayhem more akin to a religious awakening. Every gig that year felt like the last time you'd see Oasis in a venue that modest – and so it proved.

Afterwards, I bumped into Noel in a backstage corridor, and he conspiratorially suggested going to a bar away from the others, in particular Oasis's plummy-voiced new 'security co-ordinator', a former paratrooper called Iain Robertson. Robertson had been hired to prevent fans jumping on stage to punch either brother, as had happened at Newcastle's Riverside in August, and, perhaps more specifically, to keep an eye on both Gallaghers, making sure they didn't disappear mid-tour, as Noel had after the Whisky a Go Go show five weeks earlier in LA. Noel was both very reluctant and incredibly keen to discuss his American lost weekend.

'One day I will tell you and you will have the story of your life,' he said, before somewhat surprisingly telling me the story (see 'Talk Tonight', page 91) on pain of my legs being broken and my fledgling career ended should a word appear in print about it.

As well as a great songwriter, Noel Gallagher is world-class barroom company, but as we entered our third round of gossip, Robertson's rattled face appeared in the window of the bar. 'Watch out, here comes that twat from Sandhurst in the cowboy hat,' noted Noel with a sigh.

Robertson had a specific task that he'd been given by manager Marcus Russell: keep Oasis together in one place while on manoeuvres. He begged Noel to join his colleagues in the nearby Lily la Tigresse 'world famous topless bar', where a private upstairs room was hosting a drink-up for the band. Reluctantly, we followed him out.

Stopping en route to deposit some of Roger's film at the hotel, I was surprised to find Liam Gallagher sitting in the lobby. 'Have we met before?' he asked quizzically for the first of many times over the years. 'Who you here with?'

NME, I told him, to which he hissed and made the sign of the cross. Suddenly, a frantic Iain Robertson burst through the doors. 'Liam!' he shouted in furious relief. I said we'd see them at the party.

At the doors to Lily la Tigresse, Echobelly's drummer Andy was being refused entrance to the Oasis knees-up. Up the stairs, Oasis's PR Johnny Hopkins made a beckoning motion, so I squeezed in past the bouncers. 'Are you mates with Oasis?!' asked Andy in disgust. 'Yeah, they're a good laugh,' Roger replied.

'They're a good laugh alright,' shouted Andy after us. 'Are they a joke band? You see Bonehead, I could have him. He reckons he's hard? No problem. That bloke from Sandhurst? No problem . . .' The bouncers stood firm.

Inside, the atmosphere was celebratory – though Bonehead had fallen asleep on his stool. Every few minutes, a band member would ask Roger to take a photo of them balancing drinks on his head as he slept. Around 5 a.m., Liam chipped off to bed, telling the room he was homesick. 'I miss my mam, I'm mad for seeing her,' he declared very sweetly, a reminder that despite his ruggedness and notoriety, he was a newly twenty-two-year-old kid who lived at home still.

Noel pressed on, ordering another six bottles of Moët & Chandon. Two nights earlier, FC Barcelona had dismantled Manchester United 4–0 in the Champions League. Having earlier led the room in song to celebrate the happy event, with older brother and fellow Manchester City fan Paul joining in, Noel now proposed a toast.

'To all Welsh bastards, especially our manager, Mr Marcus Russell! Cheers!'

Cheers!

'To my younger brother Elvis, my older brother Paul and to FC Barcelona! Cheers!'

Cheers!

'To Oasis! To Paul Weller! To the French! And to never, ever, ever going to Walsall ever again!'

Cheers!

'To Bonehead for being a fucking Bonehead and to more champagne! Cheers!'

At which point Bonehead – a Manchester United supporter – awoke, grabbed an ice bucket and threw it across the room in the general direction of Noel's voice. Within seconds, every ice bucket in the room had been launched, smashing glasses and drenching all in magnificent anarchy.

Moments later, the bouncers arrived, ushering the party outside into the milky chill of the morning light. I wandered back to the hotel, leaving Noel and friends to negotiate entry to the Le Dépanneur bar next door. 'Good laugh, that,' called Noel after me. 'I'm staying at the Hilton Kensington next week. Give us a ring if you fancy doing it again.'

Around 10 a.m., my hotel phone blew.

'Morning, Ted, sorry to wake you, old chap,' boomed Iain Robertson. 'Noel's not with you, is he?'

I checked the room.

'Fuck,' exhaled Robertson. 'Where is he?'

An hour and a half later, I found a distraught Robertson downstairs in reception. Somewhere between being refused entry to Le Pandora Station bar at 7.30 a.m., saying goodbye to his colleagues in the hotel lobby at 7.34 a.m. and the 8.30 a.m. room call, Noel Gallagher had once more gone AWOL.

'Balls,' summarized Robertson, as he weighed up his chances of finding Noel in time to join the band, who'd left for Lyon three hours earlier. 'I hope you weren't reviewing tonight as well because it's not going to happen. Situation normal: all buggered up.'

He started laughing, somewhat hysterically, pausing suddenly to stare forlornly out of the door at the passing Parisians. 'Oh God, why must it be so difficult?'

Iain Robertson's time in the employ of Oasis would end in that same city six months later, when in the midst of a furious row with Robertson in the back of a cab, Liam threw himself out of the moving vehicle. Robertson was forced to do the same. When they both stood up in the street, Liam punched him, and that was that. Iain Robertson's services were no longer required.

Noel, meanwhile, turned up at the venue in Lyon later that day just in time for soundcheck, claiming that he'd awoken at midday in the right hotel but the wrong room. Nobody batted an eyelid.

Back in London, I moved on to my next week's assignment, which was gathering four *NME* favourites together to analyse the singles of the year for the magazine's annual Jukebox Fury feature for the Christmas issue. I already had Jarvis Cocker from Pulp and Andy Cairns from Therapy? signed up, and while in Paris Justine Frischmann had agreed to join us. I picked up the phone and called the Kensington Hilton.

Incredibly, they put me directly through to Noel Gallagher's room. Even more surprisingly, he answered.

I knew that Oasis were exclusively on the *Melody Maker* Christmas cover, but perhaps if I asked Noel directly I could circumvent that exclusivity . . .

'Oh yeah,' said Noel immediately, when I suggested the line-up and his attendance. 'That sounds good. I'll be with Guigs as he's staying with us.'

Arrangements were made to meet the following Monday morning in the lobby of his hotel with Jarvis, Andy and Justine. I'd supply a full array of refreshments. The hangover from this end-of-year gathering would, however, linger for years . . .

1995

Two weeks after Manchester United break the British transfer record by signing Andy Cole for £7 million, one of their other strikers, Eric Cantona, kung fu kicks a supporter during a game, then justifies it with a bizarre speech about seagulls. Toy Story *becomes the first entirely computer-animated feature film. In July, Robbie Williams quits Take That, two weeks on from drunkenly dancing onstage with Oasis at Glastonbury during their headline set on the Pyramid Stage. On 5 August, a law is passed that allows UK pubs to stay open all day on Sundays, rather than closing for four hours in the afternoon. A company called AuctionWeb – later eBay – is founded in California in September. The day after* (What's the Story) Morning Glory? *is released, O. J. Simpson is declared not guilty. In a strong November for the BBC, Martin Bashir's interview with Princess Diana is aired within twenty-four hours of the first ever major Beatles retrospective,* Anthology. *Soon after, divorce is made legal in Ireland. Michael Jackson's 'Earth Song' is the UK's Christmas number one.*

Portrait taken when Oasis-mania was in full flight.
Shot in Gloucester, June 1995, two weeks before the band headlined Glastonbury for the first time, by Niels van Iperan for *Rolling Stone* magazine.

'Some Might Say'

SINGLE

RELEASED 24 APRIL 1995

There remains, on the internet and perhaps beyond, a consensus among a hardcore band of Oasis fans that Oasis without the drumming of Tony McCarroll is not really proper Oasis, that he added a rudimentary but essential ingredient to the group's sound. This is not an opinion shared by some key figures in Camp Oasis.

McCarroll's big technical problem, as identified early on by the band and producer Owen Morris, was that he could only play two beats. He'd stomp on some songs, shuffle on others: there was nothing in between available to him. 'It wound the band up chronically,' Morris remembered. 'Because they couldn't do anything other than that.'

This wasn't really a problem on *Definitely Maybe*. Though he struggled with the intro to 'Bring It on Down,' he did nail it eventually, as he did the rest of the album.

After *Definitely Maybe*, though, it was decided that McCarroll needed some professional help, because Noel knew that even if McCarroll managed to record 'Champagne Supernova' or 'Wonderwall,' he couldn't be relied on to play them live night after night. 'The last throw of the dice was to get him drumming lessons.'

They teamed McCarroll up with sticks-for-hire Dave Larcombe. Larcombe's slightly kinder opinion was that McCarroll had all the attributes of a great drummer, but his big problem was that he only really used one arm. (This was not an obstacle on Def Leppard drummer Rick Allen's career path; he lost his arm after a car crash in 1985 but nevertheless performed subsequently on several multimillion-selling albums. Maybe his one arm was better than McCarroll's.)

McCarroll was advised by Larcombe to buy a small home practice kit and given some drills to build up his skill set in his own time.

A little while later, Morris met McCarroll at Loco Studios the day before recording started of a new single, 'Some Might Say,' so that they could arrange the drum sound in the room before the rest of the band arrived. 'So,' Morris asked the drummer, as related in Paolo Hewitt's *Getting High*, 'how's the practice been going, Tony?'

'Oh, I haven't done any,' replied McCarroll. 'I've been too busy.'

Hmm, considered Morris sadly to himself, *that probably won't be an issue for you going forward if that's the case.* He felt sure lots of spare time would be appearing on McCarroll's horizon.

Noel had written 'Some Might Say' shortly after first moving to London in the autumn of 1994. He was living in a flat owned by and opposite the now-demolished Eden Studios in Chiswick, on the top floor 'above Mike Oldfield's ex-wife,' though it was a short-term favour while the studio residential was unoccupied and Noel found his feet in the capital.

'I was out sampling the London nightlife,' he said, 'and I wrote it over a couple of nights after coming home at all hours – which is why the lyrics are kind of nonsensical. Dogs itching in the kitchen and all that kind of thing. I was quite hammered when I wrote it.'

Shortly after composing the song, Oasis went back out on tour. When Noel returned, he told Johnny Marr that he was a bit sick of living out of a suitcase as he had to vacate the Eden studio digs. Marr had a surprising solution.

'The Smiths have got a place in Chelsea,' he told Noel. 'I'll get you the keys.'

'Amazing, amazing flat, one of the best places I've lived in my life,' recalls Noel.

Comfortable in his new home, Noel found himself regularly playing this 'Some Might Say' tune that he'd finished on his acoustic. It sounded so great in this place, a kind of old Stones-like riff. It was the sort of thing Richards and co. might have played in their own communal Chelsea flat in the early sixties, or even in the more palatial Cheyne Walk gaffs in the seventies – a slow, circular groove accompanied by a sweet vocal melody. In fact, it was most influenced by something more contemporary: the shaggy-haired Californian soft-rockers Grant Lee Buffalo, in particular their minor 1993 indie hit 'Fuzzy.' The main riff is practically identical.

‘Everything I do is a nod to something,’ said Noel in 2019 about the influence. ‘I’m not a genius. Paul McCartney is a genius. Morrissey, Bob Dylan. I’m just a fan of theirs. I’m not a snob about where it comes from. I’ll tell you where it comes from. Nothing’s original: there’s only twelve notes.

‘Grant Lee Buffalo . . . I’m not a fan, but they had a tune, “Fuzzy”, and you can tell it’s a big influence on “Some Might Say”. I’ll obsess over a song for years and get twelve different songs out of it.’

The first song Noel got out of ‘Fuzzy’ was ‘Some Might Say’. Soon he decided he needed to get it down and demo it. This was unusual for Noel. If he could avoid demos, he would – in fact, this is the only . . . *Morning Glory* demo that he recorded, but he wanted to hear this one back.

So Noel called Owen Morris, asking if he could spare him some demo time. Owen told him he was in luck. He was at Loco in Wales with The Verve recording their second album, *A Northern Soul*, but they’d gone home for the weekend leaving the studio free, along with Owen. Noel hopped on a train immediately. ‘The demo is recorded on all The Verve’s equipment,’ says Noel. ‘That’s me on bass, drums, guitar, but it’s Nick McCabe’s rig and Simon Jones’s bass. Maybe that’s why it all sounded so loud.’

Noel loved this demo so much that he, in fact, demoed it a second time at Maison Rouge, sharing vocals this time with his brother. It had by now grown into what Morris described as ‘a proper slow Stonesy sort of groove’ and was deemed a good enough recording to be aired on Steve Lamacq’s Radio 1 show, but not perhaps for commercial release. The band reconvened at Loco in February 1995 to nail it for good, but things went quickly awry.

‘What happens in the studio,’ Owen Morris told Paolo Hewitt, ‘is that Noel is all hyped up and starts playing double fast. When me and Noel were listening back to the tape, we were like, “This is too fast compared to the demo.”’

The new slight speed increase was not the only issue. ‘The drums were all over the place,’ said Morris. ‘Proper bit of tragic drumming. It just loses it on the first chorus. On the mix we had to try to hide the drums, which is not ideal.'

By the time they'd finished fiddling with everything, the pair were only vaguely happy with the mix. Liam, however, was furious about the new version. They'd lost a psychedelic guitar lick from the demo that he felt was crucial and he told Noel so in his typically blunt fashion. 'You fucking dickhead,' he shouted at his brother. 'Where's the guitar bit?!'

This did not sit well with Oasis's commander-in-chief. A huge, vitriolic row erupted, only ending when Noel demanded everyone other than Owen Morris leave the control room.

As Noel sat there swearing about his brother, Owen listened back to the tape. Maybe, he said quietly after it had ended, Liam was right about that guitar section. Noel glared at him furiously, before warning Morris about his job prospects if he took Liam's side again. He then swung out of the room.

A few hours on, a becalmed Noel returned to the control room. 'Maybe he's right, you know,' he admitted to Morris. He stepped back into the studio and added a slightly altered guitar part to the song, immediately elevating this final version of 'Some Might Say'.

Soon after, at the start of March, Oasis flew to the US for a three-week tour (during which they befriended tennis legend John McEnroe in New York), before returning to the UK for their first arena headline in Sheffield (see: 'Don't Look Back in Anger', page 115). None of this had any bearing upon Tony McCarroll's employment status. Two days after the Sheffield Arena show, manager Marcus Russell informed McCarroll by phone that his services were no longer required in Oasis. He hadn't shaped up, so now he was being shipped out.

'Getting that call was something I never expected,' McCarroll told *Supersonic*. 'We were going to start rehearsing for a second album the next week, but Marcus phoned and he said, "Are you sat down? Listen, I've some bad news for you, the band want you out." I was shocked, shell-shocked.'

'We couldn't take him any further,' explained Noel. 'I showed him the drum fill to "Don't Look Back in Anger" and the look on his face . . . it looked like I gave him a book in Braille and said, "Read this." When most people in your band are better drummers than your drummer, and you're about to become the biggest band in the world, you've got to make that call.'

Did all this – the recording, the speed-change, the drummer being relieved of his duties, the drumming itself – tarnish one of his favourite songs subconsciously for Noel? He says it did not.

'It's still one of my favourite Oasis songs. There's a strange melancholy to "Some Might Say" considering I knew it was going to be number one before I even wrote it. It's about the passing of something, a people's anthem about "one day we'll find a brighter day". I don't know what that was all about. Looking back on it now, instinctively, I may have meant the end of some kind of age of innocence, for us personally, as people about to become real rock stars. But when it actually happens you just think, *Is that it?*'

Oasis were curiously resistant to playing 'Some Might Say' live, removing it entirely from their set from 2002. But this shouldn't distract from one of the great Liam Gallagher vocals, swathed in echo but still imbuing Noel's confessed nonsense lyrics with a real sense of soulful meaning and longing. It's no coincidence that Liam revived the song himself for his own solo shows from 2016 onwards, turning it back into a communal celebration.

For that's how it was born in the public's imagination, straight in at number one on the UK Singles Chart on 28 April 1995, the band's first chart-topper – released almost exactly a year after their debut single. An incredible rise in such a short period, one that put all other British bands signed to independent labels on red alert that the rules of engagement had now changed.

'Creation had never had a number one and were very excited,' remembers Noel. 'Nobody is really doing the conga; it was what we expected. When you see the footage [of hearing the news], me and Marcus just have a quick handshake. You are still the same person, it's just that your record is the most popular that week.'

'Me and Liam went to the pub,' said Bonehead. 'Had a couple of beers, I had my three-month-old daughter with me. It was great.'

A few days before that landmark number one, on 25 April, Tony McCarroll made his final public appearance with Oasis, miming his 'Some Might Say' drum parts on *Top of the Pops,* behind Liam Gallagher looking like a substitute footballer awaiting instruction before entering play in a long Umbro sports coat.

Back home in Manchester on 3 May, a still-shell-shocked Tony McCarroll switched on *Top of the Pops*: he was about to absorb a fresh blow. There were his old colleagues introducing the show themselves with the glee of new chart-toppers, before miming triumphantly along to 'Some Might Say.' In the intervening seven days, Liam appeared to have had a makeover – his hair seemed longer, his poise prouder – but perhaps this was just the instantly rejuvenating effect of overwhelming success. Behind Liam, in a trademark John Smedley shirt, sat new recruit Alan White on Tony's old stool.

'I watched and it was really hard,' McCarroll admitted. 'I've been sacked for apparently not being the best drummer in the world, but our tune's number one. We've got a number-one album. Why am I sat home? What's wrong?'

He noted that this new fella was miming along to McCarroll's part alright, but something was different. Unlike McCarroll's clenched-fist stickwork, White held his sticks like pens, rolling and flicking them around in the jazz mod style. It sounded the same, but it looked very new. The times they were already a-changin'.

Many years later, in 2016, after the out-of-court settlement for £550k he received from Oasis in 1999, after McCarroll had spent the intervening years thinking 'about it every day,' Noel Gallagher delivered a surprising, welcome piece of vindication for McCarroll.

'*Definitely Maybe* wouldn't have sounded as good without him drumming on it,' Noel said to the makers of *Supersonic*. 'He was part of that sound. He was the right man for the job at that time.'

'That's actually a truth,' wrote McCarroll in his autobiography. It's one all can testify to. TK

'Talk Tonight'

B-SIDE OF 'SOME MIGHT SAY'

'One day I will tell you,' Noel Gallagher assured Ted that night in Paris, soon after the release of *Definitely Maybe*, when asked what had happened when he briefly left Oasis after a show at the Whisky a Go Go in Los Angeles that September. 'And you will have the greatest story ever.'

Noel Gallagher was not exaggerating.

Ted was actually told this story a few drinks later, as detailed in the previous 'On the frontline with Oasis' segment. But he was also assured that if he wrote about it then it would be harmful for both his legs and his access to Oasis for future interviews. At the end of 1994, he needed both – the latter more than the former – and so he kept it off the record. It would take twenty-two years until the tale was fully told, in the *Supersonic* documentary.

I extracted my own, expanded version of events from Liam Gallagher around this time.

'We were snorting crystal meth, thinking it was cocaine,' he told me. 'I still don't know if it was crystal meth, but whatever it was it was super fucking strong. I do remember the gig being all over the shop in parts, but I'm sure it was alright. Might have fucked up a couple of tunes, but come on, man. It's fucking LA! If we'd just gone on and done a normal gig, they'd have been like, "We've seen all that before." They want a bit of fucking wonky shit. That's what they're into, innit?'

Into it or not, the few hundred people assembled to gawp at this much-talked-about band from over the Atlantic certainly got 'a bit of wonky shit' that night. Oasis had had to start opener 'Rock 'n' Roll Star' twice, and it didn't get much more coherent from there on in.

'When you listen back to that in the film,' Liam admitted, grinning, 'I swear to God Guigsy is playing a totally different bassline in one of the songs: it's like he's in a different fucking band!'

Given that someone in the crew had put out an old setlist from the previous British tour at Noel's feet, while the others had the newer one, this was not a surprise. Even before you added in the drugs.

'That gear,' Liam continued, 'we were all wired for days after that. The tyres on the tour bus went down, we couldn't pay the hotel because fucking Putin had run off with all the money to go and see some bird he'd met in San Francisco the night before. I remember we were sitting around outside, all we've got is this gear, no fucking money, and I'm walking up and down going into every hotel on Sunset, going, "Is there a Mr Noel Gallagher here?"'

Oasis had flown to America direct from Japan, where they had experienced their first taste of full-blown, screaming-fans-chasing-you-down-the-street, 'A Hard Day's Night'-style mania.

'I loved Japan,' he continued. 'The jetlag and the whiskey and the drinking can send you a bit fucking cuckoo. I've always been absolutely twisted in Japan, never been there sober, so it's always been a bit mad. I remember I was sharing a hotel room with Guigsy and he fucking hated it. I'd be coming back with a shitload of people and he'd be like, "What you doing?" "I'm having a party, you miserable cunt, put your book down and let's fucking go!" I loved it. I remember it being fucking well hot, and loads of kids going mad, but that's what you want, innit? Got some shit-hot clothes as well. Bit small. But one day I'll get into them.'

The flight from Tokyo to Seattle had coincided with Liam Gallagher's twenty-second birthday, the time zones meaning that he got to celebrate it twice. Twenty-two years old, twice, with the world at his feet and Oasis's biggest UK tour to date to look forward to in December. All the shows had instantly sold out. They'd have Christmas Day and Boxing Day at home, but by the 27th would be back out there. Why would anyone want a day off at this point?

In between, there was just the small matter of sixteen shows in the USA. And they were, by comparison, small. The first, Moe's Mo' Rockin' Cafe in Seattle, had a capacity of 800 people. It and the next three similarly sized shows had passed without much incident. But then the Oasis tour bus had pulled into LA, and the crystal meth/

maybe-not-crystal-meth had been snorted. Liam had launched a tambourine that hit his brother in the head. At the end of the show, Noel Gallagher had demanded the tour float from the tour manager, Maggie, and disappeared, off to do what he would later describe as 'my Hunter-S.-fucking-Thompson thing'.

Noel Gallagher had met Melissa Lim after the band's show in San Francisco. He turned up at her house – she a fan of strawberry lemonade, who made sure he'd eat that day and who took him walking to where she played when she was young. Noel was determined to leave the band. Melissa told him this was not a good idea. The phone rang. It was the ever-industrious Maggie, who had been through the bill for Noel's room back in Los Angeles, spied a number in San Francisco and thought it was worth a go. It was. Two weeks on from the Whisky show, Noel Gallagher was back onstage with Oasis.

With their popularity growing by the day, the plan was to release 'Whatever' in late December, to give it a shot at being the UK Christmas number one. So Oasis needed B-sides. Owen Morris flew over to the Congress House studio in Austin, Texas, where on the first night the band recorded their heaviest, darkest song to date in the shape of '(It's Good) To Be Free'. The next morning, with the rest of the band still in bed, Noel finished and recorded a song he had written about his San Fran escapade in just a couple of hours. A bit of Rhodes piano was added, as well as a single, ominous handclap all the way through.

'Talk Tonight' is the most inspired-by-true-events song Noel has ever recorded: a document of what was, as promised, 'the greatest story ever'. Later that day, he would also put down the older 'Half the World Away'. The three extra songs required for the 'Whatever' single were in the bag. But there was a problem. Liam hated 'Talk Tonight' to the extent that he insisted it would never find its way onto an Oasis release. There was no time to record anything else. So the fourth song on the 'Whatever' release would have to be the *Definitely Maybe* version of 'Slide Away'.

But the cat was out of the bag. Noel – and Liam – had talked about 'Talk Tonight' in interviews, so fans were fully aware of its existence. On 15 December, Oasis turned up at Maida Vale Studios in London to play a six-song set for competition winners on BBC Radio 1's *Evening Session*. After the first two, host Jo Whiley asked Noel what he was going to get Liam for Christmas. 'A new personality,' he said. 'To go with his other seven.'

He then played 'Talk Tonight' for the first time ever in public. By the time the first Oasis number-one single came around the following April, fans wanted to own it, Liam had come round to it and so on it went. Thus, sandwiched in between 'Some Might Say' – with Liam and Noel singing in harmony at the end about finding a brighter day – and 'Acquiesce' with its chorus of '*We need each other*', came the tale of the few days that might have been the end. HM

'Acquiesce'

B-SIDE OF 'SOME MIGHT SAY'

It was February 1995 and Noel Gallagher was on a train, heading west. The only member of Oasis who at that time lived in London, he was off to meet his bandmates at Loco Studios in south Wales.

When the train hit the Severn Tunnel, it ground to a halt. *Fucking leaves on the track again,* thought Noel, reaching for his guitar for something to do. It was late at night in the smoking carriage of the last train towards Wales out of Paddington, which Noel was sharing with four or five other stragglers heading towards Newport.

Noel starts to play the A minor barre chord on the fifth fret on his guitar, strums that, then slides his hand along to the top of the neck.

Ooh, that sounds good, he thinks, in the stationary carriage. *Maybe I'll go A minor, D, F, G . . . yeah. Let's do that again.* He starts humming along as he strums, getting ever louder the more the chords gradually knit together as a whole.

Forty minutes later, a fellow traveller finally pipes up a few rows away in long-supressed exasperation. 'DO YOU MIND, MATE?! WE'VE HEARD ENOUGH OF THE GUITAR NOW!'

No matter. By the time the train eventually docks into its final destination, Noel Gallagher has written the arrangement for a new song.

At Loco, the Chief insists the rest of his band gather to record a version of it while it's fresh in his mind, bashing out the lyrics to it swiftly in the control room. He's not sure what it's about, really, just various lines that have been jostling for space in the back of his mind. Nothing dramatically leaps out to him as a title from the chorus, so he decides to call the tune 'Acquiesce', a word he'd recently heard used for the first time by an interviewer.

'I didn't know what it meant,' he told *NME*'s Keith Cameron in 1998. 'The person described it as when the Pied Piper took all the kids out of the city, playing his flute like the geezer out of Jethro Tull: all the kids were experiencing acquiesce.'

That's ridiculous, thought Noel at the time. He'd imagined that acquiesce might be like absinthe or advocaat, a fancy, foreign alcoholic drink to be wary of.

At the top of the lyrics, Noel wrote the word 'Acquiesce', underlining it twice. Then he and Oasis recorded the song swiftly. There was just one problem. Liam couldn't sing the chorus. Perhaps his throat was still affected by the throat infection that had caused the cancellation of their recent Japanese dates.

'I think he was drunk or something,' suggested Noel later, mischievously, 'but he couldn't get the high notes.'

So Noel took care of that, painting in *'because we need each other/we believe in one another'* after Liam's snarled verse with a perfect longing catching in his own voice. Soon after, Oasis returned to the US on tour. After performing on NBC's *The David Letterman Show* and at the Academy in New York City, the band had a rare day off booked in. To celebrate, they decided to indulge in some of Manhattan's fabled nightlife.

The next day in London, Alan McGee hears 'Acquiesce' for the first time, blasting it out just before lunch in the Creation office.

Fucking hell! He can't believe what he's hearing. He sticks it on again and grabs the Oasis tour diary. *Where are they staying tonight?* he wonders. He picks up the phone and dials.

The ringing cracks apart the leaden silence of Noel Gallagher's hotel room. It is just after 7 a.m. and a recently-to-bed Noel reaches in the dark towards the bedside table.

'Hello?' he croaks.

'Och, Noel, I've just heard "Acquiesce"!'

'Alan . . .'

'It sounds fucking amazing, man! It's gotta be the next single!'

'Alan . . .'

Alan McGee starts singing the chorus to 'Acquiesce' down the phone to Noel Gallagher, who leans over and, squinting, clicks on his bedside lamp. It sounds awful at this precise moment to Noel.

'Alan, not now, I've got a really bad head, man. Not now. Let's talk later.'

Alan McGee wants to talk now, though. They begin to debate it, with McGee frequently breaking into song. *Fucking hell,* thinks Noel, *maybe this song is actually shit.* He starts telling McGee that he reckons 'Some Might Say' is a much better song. 'No way,' shouts McGee. 'It's gotta be "Acquiesce"!'

'I suppose I was just being a stubborn cunt,' recalled Noel later. 'Because he was from the record company and I'm from the band. If he wanted it, then I'm going to do the opposite.'

So 'Acquiesce' became the B-side to 'Some Might Say'. What's an 'Acquiesce'? Liam wondered of his brother, looking at the title. 'It's a new car by Volkswagen,' Noel replied. 'You wanna get yourself one.'

Once the song made its way into the outside world, during the glorious spring when it became clear that Oasis would be taking total control of the British listening public upon release of their second album, close analysis of 'Acquiesce' began in the media, as well as in teenage bedrooms across the world. Liam sings the verses, Noel the chorus, a chorus that insists that they need and believe in each other. It's obviously a song about fraternal love, isn't it? Obviously.

'Total bullshit,' insisted the song's author. Nevertheless, he added, 'we went along with it.'

For a couple of years after its release, Oasis opened all their live shows with 'Acquiesce'. It remained an absolute key live staple thereafter.

'We had to drop singles from the set in order to keep that in,' recalled Noel in '98. 'Just because the place would go ballistic when we played it.'

On reflection, admitted Noel, it might have made a good A-side. Talking in 2016 with Keith Cameron, he identified his B-side largesse as a key issue in his dissatisfaction with his next album, *Be Here Now*.

'Giving all those great songs away as B-sides, that is the germ of the problem [with *Be Here Now*]. To write "The Masterplan", "Half the World Away", "Acquiesce", "(It's Good) To Be Free", "Headshrinker" . . . to write those for B-sides and be as stubborn an idiot as I was and say, "No, those are the songs I've written [for B-sides]," is ridiculous. Missed opportunity.'

The opportunity missed, he added, was bigger than anything that might impact only his career, though. A little more care in his selection of B-sides could have had far wider repercussions. 'There wouldn't be any religious wars any more, because I'd be a god on earth. The world would be a better place. History balanced on a mirror, with a little razor blade there . . . "Acquiesce", though, one of our better songs.' **TK**

'Headshrinker'

B-SIDE OF 'SOME MIGHT SAY'

One of the defining features of early Oasis songs was a pace that future guitarist Gem Archer would describe as 'just too slow'. Most songs on *Definitely Maybe* felt like this, as did 'Some Might Say'. Only on a couple of occasions did Oasis speed up into speed-addled punk rock territory: on 'Bring It on Down', on 'Fade Away' and on 'Headshrinker', the punkiest song they ever made.

'We used to have a lot of fast songs like that years and years ago in '92 or '93. We were more like a punk band then really,' Noel said of it. 'It's a really, really old one: written before we had a manager or anything like that. Really fast, really loud. Probably the best drumming track that the ex-drummer ever done. It's written about a girl that Liam was going out with at the time that was a pain in the ass. She followed the band everywhere. She's a bit of a weirdo as well. I don't know what a headshrinker actually is. Just thought it was a psychiatrist or something I suppose. It sounds like The Faces on speed, doesn't it?'

It does. Specifically, 'Headshrinker' lifts its intro and central riff directly from the Faces' 'Stay with Me'. Its chorus – *'Lost in the fog/Up a tree like a dog/And I'm out of here'* – has Liam almost just shouting, the Lennon dialled down and the Lydon pushed right up. He sounds incredibly comfortable doing so. There's probably an alternate timeline where 'Bring It on Down' is the debut Oasis single, and 'Headshrinker' is chosen over 'Some Might Say'. HM

'Roll with It'

SINGLE

RELEASED 14 AUGUST 1995

The managing director of Parlophone, Tony Wadsworth, and Marcus Russell were old music business friends and colleagues. Throughout early 1995, the pair discussed the planned release dates for Oasis's second album and Blur's fourth with respectful care. Blur's label, Food, was owned by Parlophone and Wadsworth was keen to ensure that the recent commercial gains acquired by their career-reviving *Parklife* LP were not squandered by a needless trade war with Oasis, who'd parked their tank on Blur's patch and were now firing hit records and aggressively combative quotes in their direction.

Wadsworth and Russell, however, were gentlemen who could see the bigger picture. Blur scheduled their album for September and Oasis chose October. Both camps agreed to alert the other if anything changed, checking in regularly on progress. The month's gap between the two albums was seen as optimum.

Andy Ross, who ran Food, told John Harris for his excellent *The Last Party* book about Britpop and New Labour, 'You aim for a number-one single, and number-one singles then develop momentum.' If each band gained similar chart traction around their singles being released two or three weeks ahead of their respective albums, they'd likely both have number one albums a few weeks apart. 'We thought, "We'll be doing that, followed by a similar pattern by Oasis. Everyone will be happy, cheers." That's what we assumed.'

Border skirmishes between the groups had quietened promisingly too. As is the case with any young, confident new act upon arrival on the first rung of the music business ladder, from the start Oasis looked towards who their potential rival might be and had punched enthusiastically upwards at similarly sixties-influenced Blur in print. There had also been some barbs delivered in person, too, usually by Liam Gallagher, such as when he first encountered Blur guitarist Graham Coxon in the Good Mixer pub in Camden. In May '94 Liam had also refused to share a photo with singer Damon Albarn for the cover of *NME* at that year's *NME* Awards, telling Albarn that the reason for this was that his 'band are shit.' Surprisingly, Coxon then leaned in and planted a kiss on a blind-sided Liam. Click! *NME* had its shot after all.

The 1995 BRIT Awards suggested that both groups' success had calmed things and helped engender a thaw. Oasis won Best Newcomer. When Blur went up to accept their fourth award, for Best Band, Albarn held his trophy aloft and told the room, 'I think this should be shared with Oasis.' Coxon, looking a little surprised, agreed. 'Yeah, much love and respect to them,' he said mournfully into the microphone.

As Blur played their 'Girls and Boys' that night, Noel rose to dance, followed by the rest of the Oasis table. Later, Noel told reporters, 'What Blur did was a great gesture, and I want to go on record as saying it's us and them now against the world.'

Peace in our time. Well, maybe. Coxon noted that some fault lines remained open between parties. 'Liam was trying to intimidate us all night,' he said of the ceremony. 'Every time we came back from the stage [with another award], he'd glare at me and say, "You fucking look me in the eye and tell me you deserve that award." Then he'd make to hit [me].'

Nevertheless, their respective album release dates remained set in stone throughout the spring, with the lead singles for each group pencilled in to be unleashed, as was typical, three weeks before their albums. Blur's single was to be 'Country House,' they'd decided. It had been successfully debuted at their recent big outdoor London Mile End show, and all concerned felt confident afterwards that this sing-along Madness-meets-The Kinks bierkeller knees-up would be number one when it was released on 21 August.

But then storm clouds appeared on the horizon. Word reached Food that Oasis planned to release their new single, 'Roll with It,' six weeks ahead of their own album, rather than three, and just one week ahead of 'Country House.' Panic. Albarn, Ross and management met to discuss the news in a central London pub. They came swiftly to the conclusion that they had to move their release to the same date as Oasis.

'The thing is,' said Ross, 'a number-one record tends to have a better-than-evens chance of being one the week after, just because it's on *Top of the Pops*, and all the kids hear it.' If Oasis came out first, they'd nobble both Blur's single and consequently their album's chance of the top spot.

In the back of Albarn's head, perhaps, was also an encounter with Liam earlier that year. To celebrate Oasis's number one with 'Some Might Say,' Creation threw a party in the Mars Bar, a chaotic but exclusive drinking hole in Covent Garden. News of the party reached Albarn and bassist Alex James, as news of parties always did in this era. In the spirit of their recent détente, and also encouraged no doubt by Noel's declaration at the BRITs of both groups taking on the world together, the pair popped into the Mars Bar to congratulate their friendly rivals. As soon as Albarn had negotiated the rickety metal staircase into the party, however, Liam stepped nose-to-nose with him. 'Fuckin' number one!' he sneered.

Albarn was taken aback, having arrived, he claimed, with nothing other than good intentions. *OK*, thought Albarn, *let's see then.*

And so, the date for Blur's 'Country House' was pulled back a week in line with 'Roll with It'. It was on.

History now tells us that Oasis went into this seemingly high-stakes battle that they'd provoked curiously under-armed. 'Roll with It' was one of the first songs recorded during their second album sessions at Rockfield Studios in Monmouthshire (see page 107). There are without question stronger singles contained on . . . *Morning Glory*, not least the next singles that came out after the album, the pan-generational anthems 'Wonderwall' and 'Don't Look Back in Anger', both of which amplified Oasis commercially into a global force.

'Roll with It', by contrast, sounded even at the time like a bridging song between the two albums, a by-numbers Oasis rock-boogie tune that lyrically explored the same themes of personal empowerment found on 'Supersonic' or 'Rock 'n' Roll Star', i.e. say what you say, don't let anyone get in your way. Take your time and don't ever stand aside. Just roll with it. Valuable advice, and arguably more profound and relatable than Blur's satire about a rich man living sadly in pastoral luxury, rhyming 'Balzac' with 'Prozac'. For a single that was to be heavily inspected and debated, though, it was also unfortunately easy to lampoon, as Damon Albarn demonstrated when interviewed by Chris Evans on the Radio 1 *Breakfast Show*. Evans played him 'Roll with It'. Albarn responded by singing some of Status Quo's shaggy blue-denimed cover of John Fogerty's 'Rockin' All Over the World' back down the line to him. The similarities were undeniable and, given Status Quo's brand as cheery but bland old MOR rockers, somewhat unflattering. Later, Oasis would double-down on this comparison, making T-shirts that read 'Quoasis'.

It did appear as if the only effort Oasis put into winning this chart battle was scheduling the date for the single in the first place – and even that, Creation employees insisted, was a mistake. At that time, despite being funded by Sony, Creation still operated with an outsider indie mentality and had fewer than twenty employees. Therefore, they just put singles out as soon as they were ready to be released: so was the case with 'Roll with It,' they said. Moreover, in the mid-nineties, any chart-eligible single could be released on up to three formats. Blur's marketing team took full advantage, releasing two CD singles each with entirely different B-sides as well as a cassette version. Oasis, on the other hand, put the same A-side and B-side out on two vinyl and a CD format for 'Roll with It.' There was no additional material available for Oasis completists between formats. Blur's CD also retailed for a pound cheaper. It all handicapped Oasis.

For the media, the scheduling conflict was manna. By 1995, it was abundantly clear that the Oasis juggernaut was already providing a rejuvenating effect on bottom lines far beyond their label, a power source so strong that many British music-related businesses could plug into them without dimming the source whatsoever. Nowhere was this clearer than in the offices of the weekly music press. Typically, around this golden early Britpop time long before the advent of broadband, *NME* sold around 100k copies per week, with *Melody Maker* on average selling 25k fewer. An Oasis front cover guaranteed at least a 10 per cent uplift for either organ, largely because nobody provided copy remotely as entertaining – a fact that has remained true throughout their career.

In the *NME* office, the paper's pugilistic editor Steve Sutherland spied editorial opportunity. It finally gave him the chance to commission the mock-up boxing poster he'd long hankered for. In that week's editorial meeting he bullishly told the room that the cover would read 'BRITISH HEAVYWEIGHT CHAMPIONSHIP ... BLUR vs OASIS . . . AUGUST 14: THE BIG CHART SHOWDOWN.' A headshot of Damon Albarn split against another of Liam Gallagher. Other than a splash for a festival review in the top corner and a single line of band names along the foot of the cover, nothing else was sold on it. There was no need. The main story had it all.

The *NME* cover helped alert the rest of the nation's printed media to the battle, as well as broadcasters, and soon enough the national media pitch hit fevered. All awaited Sunday's chart rundown excitedly, knowing that the results would also provide another week's oxygen for further splashes across front pages and airwaves . . .

Before that early Sunday evening Radio 1 chart rundown, the offices of Food and Creation had the final totals relayed to them just after lunch. 'Country House' was number one with 274,000 sales against 'Roll with It' at 216,000. *NME* had held printing their front cover and news section to accommodate this information, a luxury normally only afforded to their Glastonbury coverage or the death of an icon. The simultaneous release of these two singles was viewed as being on a par. This *NME* cover read 'TOP DOGS! Number One! BLUR beat OASIS by a nose!'

Music, of course, is not a competition. The disappointment, however, was no doubt keenly felt in Camp Oasis, while Blur's celebrations were hearty and long, feted on news broadcasts and the tabloids. The sweet smell of success did not last, though. Blur had only secured the first battle. The war was comprehensively won by Oasis when . . . *Morning Glory* sold a record-breaking 345,000 copies in its first week, twice as many as *The Great Escape* had managed a month earlier, before spending an incredible ten consecutive weeks at number one in the UK.

If true success can be measured by legend and immortality, too, then 'Roll with It' is also the victor: it remained one of the most enthusiastically received live anthems throughout Oasis's touring career, every word sung and every limb thrown throughout the mosh pit whenever performed.

'And,' as Noel noted wryly, in 1998, 'Blur don't even play "Country House" live any more.' TK

'It's Better People'

B-SIDE OF 'ROLL WITH IT'

There wasn't huge attention paid to the B-sides of 'Roll with It' in the media hysteria surrounding the chart race between Blur and Oasis for number one in August 1995. For critics, it was a clear battle between A-sides, and all eyes were focused on that prize. A shame, as Oasis's support acts for 'Roll with It' were two Noel Gallagher gems. 'Rockin' Chair' – as described next by Hamish – was one of Oasis's best songs to date. And 'It's Better People' also took Oasis into a new dimension, Noel playing a fast-paced, rhythmic acoustic guitar and voicing a positive message of love and unity (*'It's better people love one another/Cos living your life can be tough'*), sounding like some beatnik Britpop version of Richie Havens opening Woodstock. TK

'Rockin' Chair'

B-SIDE OF 'ROLL WITH IT'

It is true that – as writers of both have at one time or another noted – 'Country House' was not Blur's finest hour, and 'Roll with It' was not Oasis's finest hour. But had that chart battle been between the two singles' B-sides, there would have been a clear, indisputable winner.

On the flipside of 'Country House', alongside some live versions of Blur's biggest songs played live at Mile End Stadium in London, was a song titled 'One Born Every Minute'. To be polite, it is not memorable. To be impolite, its two minutes and eighteen seconds are the dictionary definition of 'will this do?': destined to be forgotten by even the most dedicated of Blur fans within seconds.

On the flipside of 'Roll with It', meanwhile, is one of the greatest ever Oasis songs.

You can tell that 'Rockin' Chair' dates back to Noel's pre-Oasis days because, like so many of his songs from that period, it's about feeling stuck in the place where you were born, yearning to escape.

'I always wanted to move to London, it seemed to be the place to be,' Noel said while discussing it. 'Every time I came down there, I hated going back 'cos it was "grim up north". After the acid house thing the club scene died, and every time I came to London there'd be 500 different clubs to go to in one night. Everyone was buying us drinks 'cos the head of our record label was off his head at that point, and it was, *I'm gonna move down there and get a flat next to him – seems like the good life to me!*'

By the time they came to record it, Oasis were in the eye of the storm, becoming more and more famous by the hour, worries such as these a thing of the past. Songs like this – like 'Half the World Away', or 'Going Nowhere' – were thus hidden away on B-sides: like the guests at the best house party of all time, sat upstairs on their own in one of the bedrooms.

'Rockin' Chair' exhibits the influence of Johnny Marr's playing: lots of unshowy, cleverer-than-they-sound acoustic guitar parts entwining beautifully in its instrumental middle section. Powered along by Alan White, no electric guitars feature. Liam Gallagher had not sung over backing like this up until this point but, stripped of the noise that ordinarily backed him, 'Rockin' Chair' showed the depth of his voice, coming along at a time when he was at his absolute peak as a singer.

Oasis tried to play it live in this format just once: at a night-before-the-day-of release instore set at the Virgin Megastore that used to sit at the bottom of Oxford Street. It was aborted, just a verse or so in. They attempted an amped-up version live a couple of times in 1995, but after that it was quietly retired. There were plans to revive it for the tour that followed 'Don't Believe the Truth', but it didn't happen. Both Gallagher brothers, though, would eventually revisit it as solo artists.

Someone else who revisited it was Rod Stewart. In 1998, clocking the influence he and The Faces had had on some of the biggest bands of the era – not least Oasis – he recorded an album of covers of their songs. Serving as an opener to both the album and the shows that followed in support of it was 'Cigarettes & Alcohol'. He did 'Rockin' Chair', too, but it didn't make the cut, his version not emerging until the release of the 2009 rarities album *The Rod Stewart Sessions: 1971–1998*. A shame, but proof of how far and wide even Oasis's B-sides were spreading. **HM**

(What's the Story) Morning Glory?

(ORIGINAL UK RELEASE: 2 OCTOBER 1995)

1.	'Hello'	3:21
2.	'Roll with It'	3:16
3.	'Wonderwall'	4:18
4.	'Don't Look Back in Anger'	4:48
5.	'Hey Now!'	5:41
6.	(Untitled)	0:41
7.	'Some Might Say'	5:29
8.	'Cast No Shadow'	4:51
9.	'She's Electric'	3:40
10.	'Morning Glory'	5:03
11.	'(Untitled)'	0:39
12.	'Champagne Supernova'	7:27

Songs: Noel Gallagher (2–12)

Track 1: Noel Gallagher/Gary Glitter/Mike Leander

Produced by Noel Gallagher, Owen Morris

Bass guitar: Paul McGuigan

Drums, percussion: Alan White (except Track 7: Tony McCarroll)

Lead guitar, vocals, Mellotron, piano, E-Bow: Noel Gallagher

Rhythm guitar, Mellotron, piano: Paul Arthurs

Vocals: Liam Gallagher

Lead guitar, backing vocals on Track 12: Paul Weller

'Hello'

Depending on which Noel Gallagher is relating the story, it took Oasis just twelve or sixteen days to record their second album. Either timeframe would be an unbelievably quick turnaround for an entire LP.

'I tell other bands that it took us twelve days to record the album and they don't believe me,' Noel said, looking back in 2020. 'They say it takes them twelve days to get the drum sound set up.'

Oasis approached *(What's the Story) Morning Glory?* with an added obstacle in their path.

'We went to Rockfield with half the songs unfinished,' continued Noel twenty-five years after the fact, 'which is quite the thing. It's the sort of thing you'd only do when you're young because you wouldn't second-guess it. It's staggering.'

The plan, such as it was, was to go in the spring of 1995 to Rockfield, Kingsley Ward's storied residential studio in the Welsh countryside of the Wye Valley near Monmouth, built with his fellow farmer and brother Charles. It's where Queen famously recorded 'Bohemian Rhapsody' among many other big records nailed there, and a five-minute drive from their affiliated Monnow Valley studio, scene of Oasis's aborted debut album sessions. There, they'd record their second album in the same way as *Definitely Maybe*, i.e. getting each track down more or less live.

There was one significant change from the *Definitely Maybe* sessions, other than the drummer and studio: Mark Coyle would not be involved this time. Owen Morris, who'd so successfully mixed the first album, produced the whole caboodle, as his work on *Definitely Maybe* had been so important in finally realizing the record.

'Noel and Owen were in charge of the recording sessions,' Coyle told the *Supersonic* documentary makers. 'There is no discussion because what's the point? Noel knows what he's doing, there is not time for sentimentality. I was broken-hearted, absolutely broken-hearted.'

There was also a huge environmental shift from *Definitely Maybe*. 'It was May,' recalled Morris. 'Brilliant time to be recording. Sun shining. Rockfield, the posh studio, as well-equipped as anywhere in the world. Kingsley is a farmer, and he built a studio on his farm because he liked music. The accommodation was magnificent, food was good. Just a great recording place.'

For inner-city boys like Oasis, there were many earthy pleasures to be found in these pastoral surroundings – such as the bountiful supply of magic mushrooms that grew in abundance nearby. Liam Gallagher told me of a trip he took with Morris during these sessions, which almost resulted in disaster as the sun rose over Rockfield . . .

'I wanted to climb over the fence into the next field because I could see white mist there,' he said. Despite Morris urging Liam to come back, Liam climbed the fence. 'I could just see this white line in the distance, rolling towards us like beautiful mist. I'm going, "Yeah, let's walk into the white line." He's going, "No fucking way, man!" I'm walking towards it, walking towards the white line, the white line . . . suddenly, the white line is coming towards us much quicker and forming into a V-shape. It's fucking hundreds of sheep and they're all running towards us! They're charging! Back over the fence and into the kitchen. Noel's up, having his granola. "Where have you been?" "Chased by a load of sheep, mate."'

Despite these distractions, work progressed swiftly.

'On the very first day, we did two takes of "Roll with It",' Noel said. They released the first take, which is unusual for a high-stakes single, especially as it was also new drummer Alan White's recording debut for the band. 'On the master tape you could hear Alan saying, "Right, boys, first take, we'll get it first take,"' said Noel. 'At the mastering, I decided we can't have a cockney talking at the beginning of a single and wiped it off. I should have kept it because it's poignant.

A moment in time.' Initially, the speed of the recordings was breathtaking. 'We were doing a song a day, finished, completely done,' recalls Morris. 'That first week we recorded "Roll with It" on the first day, "Hello" on the second, "Wonderwall" on the third, "Don't Look Back in Anger" on the fourth day . . . He's like God, isn't he? Ninety per cent of "Champagne Supernova" on the Friday. Extraordinary.'

Then, however, even God had to abandon the idea of recording the songs live together as a band.

'Trying to do a load of songs live that nobody has ever heard before is a waste of time because nobody knows how it goes,' admitted Noel. 'It's really hard being in a musical collective when you're the only one who knows how a song goes. I'm shit at explaining anything musically to anyone. My musical vocabulary goes "faster", "louder", "more", "less", "don't do that".'

Morris suggested that they record it 'how Marc Bolan used to do it'. This involved Noel sitting with his acoustic guitar and a click track, gradually building the song up instrument by instrument.

When Noel was done with his initial tracks, he'd call each member in to record their part to the backing he'd laid down. 'It was a different way of working, but we had a producer who knew us and knew what he was doing,' said Bonehead. 'Alan would come in and do his drums, and we'd have this incredible drum track with this incredibly tight bass track Guigs had put in. Then you'd have Owen being Mr Enthusiastic, cheering you on, "Come on!"'

'Owen came up with that way of recording for the record and it suited me,' said Noel. 'It's something I've done from that day forward.'

One of the songs that was entirely finished before they got there, however, was 'Hello', which had been in Noel's armoury ever since demoing it at Mark Coyle's house in Chorlton long before recording *Definitely Maybe*.

'If you listen to the record, it's split into two halves,' says Noel of . . . *Morning Glory*. 'Half of the songs have a second verse, they were all written before I got [to Rockfield], and the rest have the first verse repeated twice or maybe three times. Owen would say, "Have you got another verse?" and I'd say, "Oh, we'll do it later." Then when it'd come to it it'd be, "Does it need a second verse? Don't think so . . ."'

'Hello' definitely had a first verse, a second verse, and the guitar dynamism of two of Noel's fundamental influences in Johnny Marr and Paul Weller: one could easily imagine it opening albums by either The Jam or The Smiths.

It's also the closest song to anything on *Definitely Maybe*, but perhaps Noel knew when demoing it at Coyle's that it would provide a perfect opening to a follow-up album, even if the chorus voiced a familiar pre-fame anxiety about time running out from Noel in *'we live in the shadows . . . had the chance but threw it away . . .'* It was the playful outro that perhaps most influenced Noel in thinking it should be held for the band's second coming, however.

Noel Gallagher was just about to turn six when Gary Glitter's 'Hello, Hello, I'm Back Again' was released in April 1973. And, like most British kids at that time, he would have been transfixed by his weekly dose of *Top of the Pops* on Thursday evenings, the most influential music platform at the time, regularly hitting viewing figures of 15 million back then. Between 1972 and '75, Gary Glitter – an extravagantly quiffed showman in platform boots and twinkly catsuits with plunging necklines – was a fixture on the show. He had eleven top-ten hits in that three-year period, including three number ones. For context, David Bowie had seven top-ten singles in that same timeframe, and no number ones. Gary Glitter was huge – one of the biggest British male pop stars of the era.

As well as a popular and preposterous pop singer, Glitter also had very catchy songs, none more so than 'Hello, Hello, I'm Back Again', which was adapted by football fans for decades to suggest that their team was on the way up.

Noel Gallagher's an unapologetic magpie, unafraid to telegraph the lifts in his earliest songwriting, as demonstrated already on the likes of 'Shakermaker' and 'Cigarettes & Alcohol', and he spied a perfect outro for 'Hello' by incorporating Glitter's *'hello, hello (said it's good to be back, it's good to be back)'* for the ending of Oasis's first song on their second album, the lines repeated three times to reinforce the message: Oasis have returned. It started, as many good ideas do, as a joke, though. Noel began singing it to the rest of the band when unveiling the song and 'everyone just fell about laughing. As the track progressed, we found we couldn't get rid of it, so we stuck it in.'

At the time, in 1995, most recognized the cheek and good humour in the lift. No doubt it was worth the writing credit and royalties due to Paul Gadd, aka Gary Glitter, along with his song-writing partner Mike Leander – it's the only song not entirely credited to Noel Gallagher on the whole album – because it was a great way to reintroduce the band.

It wasn't until 1997 that this lift truly soured, after Glitter was arrested when a technician found child pornography on his laptop that he'd taken in for repair. After that, the charges spiralled, and in 1999 he was sentenced to four months in prison for the offence; later, he was convicted of serious child sex offences in 2006 and again in 2015. None of this was known in 1995, though, and Glitter no longer receives any royalties on his songs, ensuring guilt-free purchase of *(What's the Story) Morning Glory?* is possible.

After they'd completed recording 'Hello,' Morris asked what was next.

'I've got this song finished,' replied Noel, and played him 'Wonderwall' for the first time. They recorded it the next day . . . **TK**

'Roll with It'

SINGLE RELEASED 14 AUGUST 1995 (SEE PAGE 98)

'Wonderwall'

Right now, somewhere on Planet Earth, just as someone will be snapping a KitKat or kicking a football, somebody, somewhere, with an acoustic guitar strapped around their neck with a capo on the second fret, will be placing their little and ring fingers onto the bottom two strings, three frets along, where they will stay for the next four-and-a-bit minutes.

Their middle and index fingers, meanwhile, will be on the third and second strings respectively, two frets along. With just three simple movements of these two fingers, they will play a chord sequence that is about as easy as it gets: Em7, to G, to Dsus4, to A7sus4, if you want to get technical. And then come the lyrics that everyone they are playing in front of will know every last word of.

The first person to perform this song in public was, of course, Noel Gallagher. He did so backstage at Glastonbury Festival in 1995, on 24 June, soon after Oasis had played their headline show on the Friday night. During that show, he had unveiled another new, yet-to-be-released song with the full backing of the band, called 'Don't Look Back in Anger'. Then, in solo, acoustic form, for the benefit of the people tuned in to Channel 4's coverage of the festival, he played a song that had had the working title of 'Wishing Stone' but was now called 'Wonderwall' in honour of the George Harrison soundtrack to the psychedelic 1968 film of the same name.

Oasis had finished recording it a month previously at Rockfield. But its writer was unaware, surely, of what this song would become. Like most of their songs during this period, 'Wonderwall' was written quickly. But when time came to record it during the sessions for *(What's the Story) Morning Glory?*, Noel Gallagher wanted to try something different with its production. He had, like a lot of music fans, been taken by the startling originality of Portishead's *Dummy* – a debut album that had been released just a week before *Definitely Maybe*. *Dummy*, like *Definitely Maybe*, would shape popular music for the rest of the decade and spawn legions of imitators. And it's unlikely 'Wonderwall' would sound the way it does without it.

Noel took full advantage of the newly installed Alan White's talents, getting him to play a shuffling, off-kilter drum beat far more complex than anything featured on an Oasis song up until then. Over the top, he played a dub-tinged bassline – beyond Guigsy's capabilities – that would lead Liam to dismiss what he heard as 'reggae music'. A moody cello part was added, a four-note piano motif at the end, some very subtle picked acoustic guitar. Liam's vocal – he quickly came round to the song once he had sung it – stays at the same register throughout (the highest he goes is on the '*I don't believe that anybody*' line that comes at the end of its three verses). There is no big, soaring, 'Don't Look Back in Anger'-style chorus. You might, had you heard it before the world did, have called it understated.

But within what seemed like hours of ... *Morning Glory*'s release, 'Wonderwall' had achieved a ubiquity that made it an unavoidable part of British life. You could not walk down the street without hearing it blasting out of a shop or being played on repeat on a pub jukebox. Pretty soon it had made its way onto the football terraces – '*And all the runs Kinkladze makes are winding*', sang Maine Road's Kippax stand of their newly installed Georgian midfielder – and, as soon as Oasis played it live, every single person in attendance sang every single word of it, just as they would forevermore.

To date, on Spotify, 'Wonderwall' has a billion more streams than the next most played Oasis song. It has been certified septuple platinum in the UK alone. But even numbers such as these don't get across the enormity of what 'Wonderwall' is, and what it had already become by the end of the year it was released. Very, very few songs achieve this kind of everlasting cultural ubiquity: 'Hey Jude', 'Bohemian Rhapsody' and ... not many others.

Astonishingly, 'Wonderwall' did not reach number one in the UK when it was released. Or ever. It was kept off by Robson & Jerome's 'I Believe': a version of the Frankie Laine standard by two actors who were starring in an enormously popular television show called *Soldier, Soldier*. A then-up-and-coming music executive had seen their performance of 'Unchained Melody' in one episode and persuaded them there might be money to be made in some more covers. That executive's name was Simon Cowell.

What 'Wonderwall' did do, however, was stick around high up in the charts for a long, long time. This was unusual. In the nineties, bands like Oasis were in the albums business, and singles were mainly put out to try to convince people to buy an album. Only hardcore fans would buy post-album singles for the B-sides. For 'Wonderwall' to be remaining so high in the charts for so long meant that it was being bought, repeatedly, by people who were far from music obsessives.

The cover versions came quickly. By the end of 1995, an easy-listening group called the Mike Flowers Pops, fronted by thirty-five-year-old Michael Roberts, had their version played on BBC Radio 1's *Breakfast Show*. The host, Chris Evans, claimed that it was the long-lost original, and that it was the Oasis version that was a cover. The ruse was taken seriously by many.

'We were in America,' Noel remembered. 'I get a phone call off the wife. And it's another one at 7 a.m., and I'm like, "What do you want at this time?" She's going, "You know that song you wrote for me?" "Yeah . . ." "Well it's not even one of your songs, is it?" I was going, "What are you fucking going on about?" She says, "Listen to this" – and she's taped it off the radio! She's going, "That's the original." I said, "Play that again!" Then she sent the tape over and eventually we found out what it was. But for a minute I was going, "Did I? Maybe I did!" She was well pissed off for about an hour and a half. "No, honestly, I did write it about you . . . !"'

Many more versions, by artists well known and not at all well known, followed for years. The 2004 version recorded by Ryan Adams – a much darker, ethereal version – would become one of his most famous songs. Noel approved of it: to the extent that, around that time, he started playing a version at Oasis shows that far more closely resembled Adams's than his own, which he was sick of. Soon after . . . *Morning Glory* came out, in fact, he had strolled into a guitar shop in Manchester 'and there was a sign banning people from playing "Wonderwall". When I walked in, they all groaned, "Fucking hell, man, do you realize how many times we've heard 'Wonderwall' over the last six months?"'

Oasis themselves experimented with lots of different versions of their most famous song. Initially, it was played solo by Noel – just as it had been that first time at Glastonbury – as part of his mid-show acoustic set. By the time they started playing their own open-air concerts, it was played acoustically – much faster than on record – and sung by Liam. On the Be Here Now and Standing on the Shoulder . . . tours, it was played with electric, distorted guitars: the only way it would not be drowned out entirely by the mass sing-along. Only on their final tour did they play a version that resembled the original.

As with many bands who have a song that takes on a life of its own, Oasis expressed mixed feelings about 'Wonderwall'. I was at one show at Brighton Centre where Noel had to abort his solo acoustic version because he couldn't hear himself over the crowd. By the end of Oasis, Liam had, to say the least, had enough of it. 'I can't fucking stand that fucking song!' he said. 'Every time I have to sing it, I want to gag.'

He came around to it, with time realizing what exalted company he was in, having sung a song that so many people all over the world know every word of.

'There's certain places where I have to play it,' he told me as he was getting ready to tour as a solo artist for the first time. 'Otherwise, it'd be, "Who the fuck is this cunt!?"' **HM**

'Don't Look Back in Anger'

Some special songs have multiple lives, existing on new planes for future generations far beyond their creator's original blueprint. 'Heroes' by David Bowie, for example.

Conceived by Bowie with art-rock maestro Brian Eno and born as a two-chord experimental piece in West Berlin in 1977, 'Heroes' tells the tale of lovers from either side of Berlin's Wall, dreaming of unlikely freedom together. Over time, though, 'Heroes' enjoyed many other lives beyond the political avant-garde: it was used in the opening ceremony of the 2012 Summer Olympic Games, for example, and to soundtrack mainstream TV or films, such as *Ninja Assassin* or *The Parole Officer*. When Bowie died in 2016, the German Foreign Office credited 'Heroes' with actually bringing down the Berlin Wall. And, of course, it's been covered many times, including by Oasis, on the flip side of 'D'You Know What I Mean?'

Another celestial song like 'Heroes' that's enjoyed multiple lives beyond its creation is 'Don't Look Back in Anger'.

Noel Gallagher once claimed that he knocked it up in a Parisian strip club between Oasis playing and the strippers taking the stage, but he may have misremembered the occasion. (Oasis played the Erotika strip bar in Paris in June '94, long before a second album was a twinkle in Noel and Liam's eyes.)

More likely, he wrote the stately chord structure in his hotel room after playing the Bataclan in Paris with The Verve on 20 April 1995. Two days later, Oasis were due to play their first arena gig, in Sheffield, where Noel continued to work on it.

'At the soundcheck, I was strumming away on the acoustic guitar,' remembered Noel, 'and our kid said, "What's that you're fucking singing?"'

Noel told Liam he wasn't singing anything in particular, just making up words to go with the melody, as usual with a new tune. Liam thought differently.

'Are you singing "*so Sally can wait . . .*"?' he asked.

The words stopped Noel in his tracks.

'If you're not, you should be,' added Liam.

That's brilliant, Noel thought. He hadn't been singing it, but now he was. *So Sally can wait*. I'll have that. Years later, Liam claimed that Noel had actually been singing *'Jim'll fix it for you*,' the theme tune to the Saturday BBC kids' TV show of the same name from disgraced host Jimmy Savile. But that's probably not true.

Back in the dressing room, Noel wrote all the words down very quickly, with the title appearing, he said, from nowhere, just as the melody had. This has happened to him a few times.

'The great songs that I've written,' Noel reflected in 2019, 'they always just fall out of the sky. All the ones that will be forever remembered . . . they're just there.'

By now, as the sets had grown in length, Liam required a mid-performance break for his voice on account of the full-throttle manner of his delivery.

'And how he would rest his voice was to go to the side of the stage and drink and start smoking,' said Noel. 'Which as anybody knows anything about resting your voice, the best thing to do is to drink and smoke and shout and behave like a fucking dick.'

So Noel had begun to perform a two-song acoustic section in the middle of Oasis's set. 'I decided to play this new song I'd written on Tuesday, that nobody had heard, that nobody in the band had heard, in front of 12,000 people. I don't know what possessed me to do that really.'

Noel stepped out in front of the huge, packed Sheffield Arena, their biggest headline gig to date, and played 'Don't Look Back in Anger' live for the very first time, even though he'd only written about a third of it and announced it to the crowd as not even yet having a title. 'Just me, on an acoustic guitar. Sat on a stool. Like an idiot.' And singing a song about an imaginary girl's name his younger brother had misheard.

'I don't actually know a Sally,' Noel admitted when pressed, though sometimes this fact was not taken in good faith. A decade later, after an open-air Ian Brown concert in Thetford Forest, Norfolk, a saucer-eyed young woman grabbed Noel to explain her theory that 'Sally' was in fact the 'Sally Cinnamon' from an early Stone Roses single, a theory that included an elaborate backstory of lost love letters on a bus and more. Noel, though impressed and somewhat regretful it was untrue, had to let her down as gently as possible.

And yet, from the moment that Liam had misheard Noel's nonsense words, 'Don't Look Back in Anger' lived independently of its author, finding its own way in the world.

This continued in the spring of '95, when the band came to record the song in Rockfield. At this stage, Noel imagined his brother might sing 'Don't Look Back in Anger'.

'I was originally going to sing "Wonderwall", recalled Noel. 'Liam said, "I wanna sing it!"'

Noel, however, knew that there were two definite songs-for-life on his second album selection, and he was going to be singing at least one of them. They were both within his range and he fancied some immortality too.

'I was, like, "I'm singing one of them, so you take your fucking pick." He chose "Wonderwall".'

The final composition highlighted Noel at his most magpie-like. A chunk of John Lennon's 'Imagine' for the piano intro. Some of Bowie's 'All the Young Dudes' for the chorus melody. Certain lines, such as *'start a revolution from my bed, because you said the brains I had went to my head',* were lifted entirely from John Lennon's Dakota tapes, the recorded memoirs stolen after Lennon's murder. He'd been listening to a tape of the memoir that had been given to him in the US on tour, becoming transfixed by Lennon saying, 'I love that thing they said about George Bernard Shaw, that his brains had gone to his head.' Thank you very much, said Noel.

Even the title was a play on Bowie's 'Look Back in Anger' (itself a nod to John Osborne's kitchen-sink drama of the same name). Noel, however, was refreshingly unrepentant; after all, how important is originality in the history of immortal pop songs? 'The opening riff's "Imagine", he agreed. 'Fifty per cent of it's put there to wind people up. The other half is saying, "Look, this is how songs like 'Don't Look Back in Anger' came about: they're inspired by songs like 'Imagine'."'

Noel, perhaps remembering how his great influence Paul Weller had also sent him scurrying to The Beatles and Motown nods in his biggest hits with The Jam, understands the breadth of his audience. 'There will be some thirteen-year-old kid out there who'll read an interview and think, *"Imagine?" I've never heard that song.*'

When Andy Bell joined Oasis in 1999, replacing Guigsy on bass, he memorably suggested – in an amusing echo of Billy Connolly's description of the ancient theme from Radio 4's *The Archers* – that 'Cigarettes & Alcohol' would make a better British national anthem than 'God Save the Queen'. In reality, though, 'Don't Look Back in Anger' had long grown into the UK's alternative national anthem. It was the central focus of every Oasis concert.

'"Don't Look Back in Anger" is the one where everybody will sing at an Oasis gig, particularly the first chorus,' noted Noel. 'It must do Liam's head in.'

But the many lives of 'Don't Look Back in Anger' did not end with its status as the new national anthem, nor with hitting number one when released as a single in February 1996. It also became a staple of small-screen sports montages of heroic failure for decades to come, as well as regularly floating through TV dramas – most convincingly in March '96 in the moving final scenes of *Our Friends in the North*, the BBC hit social drama series that helped establish the likes of Daniel Craig and Mark Strong. Few, however, would have hoped to predict the song's next incarnation.

On 22 May 2017, a suicide bomber at an Ariana Grande concert in Manchester Arena murdered twenty-two and injured many more. The next day, students at Chetham's music school, a residential facility that was inside the city centre police cordon, performed 'Don't Look Back in Anger' when their regular afternoon concert was cancelled.

There followed a nationwide minute's silence at 11 a.m. on 24 May. Hundreds gathered in Manchester's St Ann's Square, where floral tributes to the victims had been growing and where, also, television was recording the memorial live for the nation. The silence was impeccable, heavy, punctuated only by the sound of police helicopters and a ripple of applause when someone shouted, 'Rock on, Manchester!'

Clutching a bouquet in the middle of the crowd stood Lydia Bernsmeier-Rullow. As the silence grew to its climax, the thity-two-year-old started to sing 'Don't Look Back in Anger' a cappella for a few moments before she was joined by others in the crowd, the song slowly filling the square and, via digital reflection, the world.

'I love Manchester and Oasis is part of my childhood,' she told *The Guardian* afterwards. '"Don't Look Back in Anger" – that's what this is all about: we can't be looking backwards to what happened, we have to look forwards to the future.'

Watching live at home, Noel Gallagher swallowed his tears. 'It really brought it home to me,' he told the BBC's Dermot O'Leary, 'that in times like that, religious leaders, community leaders, they're all coming out with the same old bullshit. "We will stand together, stand firm . . ." It took a song to bring people together.'

But this particular song's healing work was still not done. On 27 May, five days after the bombing, local lads The Courteeners played 'Don't Look Back in Anger' at Emirates Old Trafford cricket ground, with singer Liam Fray joined throughout by the 50,000-strong crowd. A week after, on 4 June, the city came together for the One Love Manchester memorial concert, also at Old Trafford cricket stadium and beamed live across the world. Many global superstars performed, including Liam Gallagher. But the highlight of the three-hour show was, of course, provided by 'Don't Look Back in Anger', when Coldplay's Chris Martin and Jonny Buckland stood either side of Ariana Grande, announcing, 'Ariana, you've been singing a lot for us, so I think we in Britain want to sing for you. This is called "Don't Look Back in Anger", and this is from us to you.'

'For a not very extraordinary song, it's an extraordinary thing,' noted Noel. **TK**

'Hey Now!'

. . . *Morning Glory* was Oasis's very own *Thriller* – an album that at some point stops being an album and becomes a household appliance. Even months after the release of *(What's the Story) Morning Glory?*, were you to pick one of its songs at random and ask someone in the street to sing it, chances are they would be able to do it . . . unless you picked 'Hey Now!'.

Who knows why 'Hey Now!' failed to connect in the same way as every other song, including the instrumental snippets, on the second Oasis album? Maybe because it follows the one-two of 'Wonderwall' and 'Don't Look Back in Anger'; maybe because it was never played live (though Oasis soundchecked it a couple of times in the US); or maybe because you can only have so many songs on one album connect in that way. It's a mystery.

It's certainly nothing to do with quality: 'Hey Now!' is a strong piece of songwriting, beautifully sung and with all kinds of entwining guitar parts and orchestral grandiosity. Lyrically, it combines the profound – *'I took a walk with my fame down memory lane/I never did find my way back'* – with the ridiculous – *'It said you might never know that I want you to know what's written inside of your head'* – like so many of the best Noel Gallagher lyrics.

Noel's own ambivalent relationship to 'Hey Now!' is best described by an aside he made when discussing it after listening to the reissued version of its parent album, twenty-five years on. 'There's a fucking synthesizer on it that I heard today,' he said in 2020. 'I don't know who snuck that in. We didn't even have a synthesizer! I was listening to it on the train thinking, *Who's playing that?!*'

More than any song on . . . *Morning Glory* other than maybe its title track, it speaks to the moment that Oasis were in in 1995: their dreams now a reality, strapped in for what comes. HM

'The Swamp Song' (aka 'Untitled')

A week before his final show at Sheffield Arena on 22 April 1995, Tony McCarroll had made his final TV performance with Oasis on Channel 4's *The White Room*, playing on 'Acquiesce' and '(It's Good) To Be Free'. He was not required for their third song. 'Talk Tonight' featured only Noel and – for the first but far from last time ever – Paul Weller, who was also appearing to promote his single 'The

Changingman', which was, like 'Some Might Say', being released on 23 April 1995.

'The Changingman' would chart at number seven, meaning that the same day Noel Gallagher scored his first number-one single, his teenage idol and now friend got his first ever top-ten hit as a solo artist. (Side note #1: only Oasis could go on a primetime TV show the week before releasing a single that they were desperate to get to number one . . . and play three B-sides.)

There was much for both to celebrate, in other words. In the canteen afterwards, the two camps mingled. With the atmosphere between Tony McCarroll and Noel at its nadir, the Oasis leader mentioned to Weller that he was going to be getting rid of Oasis's drummer. Weller pointed over at his own long-term drummer Steve White and said, 'You know who's good? His brother.'

Seven years younger than Steve, Alan White had looked up to his older sibling from a very early age. His brother had encouraged him to start drumming, had sent him off to the same teacher he had learned from, provided him with his first kit (though he made Alan pay him for it) and hooked him up with Acid Jazz group Galliano. Later he would end up playing with a singer from Sweden called Idha, who was signed to Creation and married to Andy Bell. (Side note #2: this means that, having auditioned for Heavy Stereo when he was fifteen, Alan White had crossed paths with Andy Bell and Gem Archer long before they all played together in Oasis.)

Noel Gallagher was in Maison Rouge studios working on Oasis material in early 1995 when he heard Idha playing in another room and wondered who the drummer was. He made enquiries and was told it was the brother of Steve White. When it came time for Tony to go in April that year, he put a call in to the White household. Mother White passed on a message to Alan. He called back, and Noel instantly asked him if he could join Oasis. Didn't he need to audition, he asked? Time being of the essence – McCarroll played his final show on 22 April 1995; there was the second *Top of the Pops* appearance to mime on the 27th – Noel said that would not be necessary.

'As long as you're not eighteen stone and have got a nice jacket and a nice pair of Levi's,' Alan White was told, 'then you're in.' He met Noel at Cafe Delancey in Camden shortly afterwards and had a short rehearsal with the rest of the band, during which they played The Beatles' 'It's All Too Much' plus a few Oasis songs, and that was that: Alan White was in Oasis. Off to the BBC studios he went with the rest of the band to perform their first ever number one.

(Side Note #3: Steve White would, just as his brother had with Galliano, deputize for Alan – who had a thumb injury – on the Oasis Tour of Brotherly Love across the US with the Black Crowes. Highlights included going to see *The Mummy Returns* with Liam in Kentucky.)

Very, very soon after came Alan's first live shows with Oasis, the second of which, following a discreet warm-up in Bath, was – no biggie – headlining the Pyramid Stage at Glastonbury. Here they would debut 'Hello', 'Morning Glory', 'Roll with It' and 'Don't Look Back in Anger'.

Again: no biggie.

If Alan White was nervous, though, it didn't show. In fact, his drumming on the opener – another new glam-stomp instrumental called 'The Jam', that sounded quite a lot like Doctor and the Medics' 1986 number-one single 'Spirit in the Sky' – was so perfect that it was taped and used on the recorded version. Noel recorded the guitar parts over the top. Then, when he was at Orinoco Studios in south London mixing *(What's the Story) Morning Glory?* with Owen Morris, Paul Weller arrived to do his thing on 'Champagne Supernova'. Noel noticed he had a harmonica in his pocket. He asked what key it was in, and it turned out to be in the same key as 'The Jam'. Noel asked Weller if he would mind playing some harmonica on it, which he did brilliantly, as well as some extra guitar.

Though Weller would later say it would have been funny to have an Oasis song entitled 'The Jam (featuring Paul Weller)', Noel thought it was cheesy. So, when it first appeared, in the form of two brief snippets on . . . *Morning Glory*, it was listed on the sleeve, both times, as ' '.

By the time it was included on the 'Wonderwall' single, it had been retitled 'The Swamp Song'.

Noel remained very fond of it: so much so that when it came time to put out *The Masterplan*, he vetoed an online fan vote as to what tracks should feature, in which the only-ever Oasis instrumental up until that point had not scored highly, and on it went: chosen over fellow 'Wonderwall' B-side 'Round Are Way'. Its inclusion was justifiable given that 'The Swamp Song' had, before 'Fuckin' in the Bushes' came along in 2000, served as the opener to some of the biggest Oasis shows. Hearing it, Noel knew, would remind the thousands upon thousands who listened to it of those phenomenally exciting few minutes before Liam Gallagher walked onstage halfway through it and the party began in earnest.

(Side note #4: when Oasis tribute band No Way Sis, somewhat unbelievably, released their own single – an Oasis-ified version of 'I'd Like to Teach the World to Sing' – it featured, even more unbelievably, two of their own songs as B-sides. The second was an instrumental entitled 'The Quicksand Song'. Clever, eh?) **HM**

'Some Might Say'

SINGLE RELEASED 24 APRIL 1995 (SEE PAGE 85)

'Cast No Shadow'

It was not a huge surprise when Richard Ashcroft was announced as the main support act for the 2025 Oasis reunion shows. He had, after all, been a long-term associate, supporter and kindred spirit of the band, stretching back to his time as singer in Verve (the 'The' would come later, to differentiate them from an American record label).

At one particularly memorable show featuring both bands in December 1993 at Newcastle Riverside – the same venue at which, less than a year later, Noel Gallagher would be assaulted onstage – Verve's headline set was cut short by a power cut. Twenty minutes later, with the crowd growing frustrated, Ashcroft and Noel came onstage to bellow 'She'll Be Coming Round the Mountain', accompanied by Bonehead . . . on spoons.

The last song to be recorded for *(What's the Story) Morning Glory?* was 'dedicated to the genius of Richard Ashcroft'. When Oasis played 'Cast No Shadow' at Knebworth, Noel prefaced it with a dedication to him, urging him to 'get your shit together'.

'He always seemed to me to not be very happy about what was going on around him, almost trying too hard,' Noel said. 'That's why it goes, "*He was bound with the weight of all the words he tried to say.*" I always felt he was born at the wrong time, and in the wrong place, and he was always trying to say the right things, but they came out wrong.'

At the time, Ashcroft was not in the best place. Without warning, and just as they released the masterful 'History' as a single – 'All Farewells Should Be Sudden' read the sign above the band on the sleeve – The Verve had split up. This was in September 1995, two weeks before the release of . . . *Morning Glory*. Bar one solo appearance supporting Oasis in New York, Ashcroft was nowhere to be seen in 1996. He was busy trying to get a band together.

Eventually, The Verve re-formed. By 1997, they had released an absurdly strong trio of singles in 'Bittersweet Symphony', 'The Drugs Don't Work' and 'Lucky Man' – all credited solely to Ashcroft – and a third album, *Urban Hymns*, which remains one of the twenty biggest-selling albums in the UK. 'I remember hearing on the radio: "And number one . . . once again . . . *Urban Hymns* by The Verve"', Ashcroft recounted to me, 'and just thinking, *WHO IS FUCKING BUYING THIS ALBUM?*'

Oasis and The Verve were at this point on a similar journey musically: incorporating strings into the mix of what they did in a way that no British guitar band had done since Echo & the

Bunnymen's 1984 album *Ocean Rain*. By 1997, the Bunnymen were also re-forming: having their biggest ever hit with the Oasis-sounding 'Nothing Lasts Forever', a song featuring one Liam Gallagher on backing vocals. Before long, you could not turn on a radio in the UK without hearing a guitar band backed by an orchestra. Coldplay were taking notes. Many bands would go on to take notes from Coldplay. Something was in the air.

'Cast No Shadow' was a big part of why this happened. Like 'Wonderwall', it featured a more complex, off-kilter drum pattern than was typical of Oasis at that time. Musically, as a whole, it was a huge leap forward: Noel playing a dancing, melodic bassline – too tough for Guigsy to manage, as evidenced by the simpler version he played live – then adding layers of ethereal backing vocals that sat high up in the mix. In contrast to the 'just add strings' plastic grandiosity of the bands it inspired, the orchestration was sophisticated and subtle in its enhancement of the melody. Liam Gallagher's lead vocal, meanwhile, is just sublime. Once again, it took just one take. **HM**

'She's Electric'

'"*I'll be you and you be me*" is from *Stop, Look, Listen*,' explained Noel Gallagher around the launch of the remastered *(What's the Story) Morning Glory?* in 2014, referring to one of the lines from 'She's Electric'. 'We used to be at school and you'd have a class where'd they play TV. It was *Sesame Street*, but an English version. That stayed with me for years until I wrote "She's Electric."'

Noel Gallagher has written some of the most memorable songs of our lifetime, so it's not really on him to explain anything consistently about them. His work is done. But he can be an unreliable narrator for those looking for witnesses to a song's background, and here he is mistaken. *Stop, Look, Listen* was on ITV for schools, it's true, but on BBC at around the same time, between 1974 and 1992, was *You & Me*. It was a much more playfully psychedelic programme, designed 'for four- and five-year-olds, and the adults watching with them,' featuring puppets such as a dragon called Duncan, Alice the hamster and a nameless crow, as well as a folk-pop theme song that went *'you and me, me and you/Lots and lots for you to do/Lots and lots for you to see . . .'*

Not very far at all from *'I'll be you and you'll be me/There's lots and lots for us to see/There's lots and lots for us to do . . .'* as Noel had the chorus for 'She's Electric', his second album's one anomaly, go. 'I wrote it for *Definitely Maybe*, but it got bumped for "Digsy's Dinner",' he said in 2020. 'I think "Digsy's Dinner" sounded better live because it's a less complicated song.'

'She's Electric' performed a similar role on . . . *Morning Glory* as 'Digsy's Dinner' did on their debut, though, providing the levity on an otherwise intense second half. Based on a sped-up version of the chord sequence from 'Married with Children', 'She's Electric' is at odds with the swagger that otherwise defines Oasis's songs.

'Great words,' said Noel, of the kitchen-sink love triangle (or square, possibly?) at the song's core. 'I don't know how I came up with that shit. It's kind of like "The Importance of Being Idle" in its sixties-ness, and it's got a story too. And listen to Liam hit those high notes!'

Perhaps that's why it was not played live by Oasis in the nineties, revived instead by a solo Noel in the next millennium: he's a singer happier to reach regularly for that end of the scale. We may never have heard Liam's version of the song, however, had matters turned out differently.

'We were doing a song a day, finished, completely done,' recalled Owen Morris.

'We were rattling through it,' confirmed Noel. 'We were having a good time. I remember everyone being into it . . . and then there was the night where it went off.'

Owen Morris and Noel hated having people just hanging idly around the control room when they were working. Morris insisted that Liam and Bonehead should go to the pub in Monmouth if they weren't needed, as he found them particularly distracting.

‘When you have these nice recording studios, the villages, it has a pull,’ explained Liam to the *Supersonic* documentary makers. ‘I always had a pull towards the pub. You’ve got to be very strong-willed.’

It’s fair to say that, pub-wise, Liam Gallagher has not been historically very strong-willed, but especially so in the mid-1990s. That night, 12 May, was the night before Morris’s birthday and Oasis’s sleeve designer Brian Cannon had come down to Rockfield to celebrate with his pals. He, Liam, Alan White and Bonehead rode into Monmouth for a few drinks in the town boozer, while Noel put down his vocal for ‘Don’t Look Back in Anger’ in peace.

Everyone in the Royal Oak knew Liam Gallagher, naturally, and pretty soon he was mobbed with well-wishers, including John Robb, a journalist and musician they knew from Manchester who was producing a punky band from Derby called Cable at Monnow Valley. A high old time around the pool table in the Royal Oak ensued, before dozens of those present joined Team Oasis for a nightcap back in Rockfield.

‘We invite them all back, drunk,’ remembered Bonehead. ‘Probably a bad move, because Noel was still in the studio with Owen.’

Back at the studio, Owen Morris and Noel furiously told anyone poking their nose in to go up to the farmhouse if they were having a party, which they did, getting stuck into the spirits and playing Subbuteo, listening to the Small Faces. Then, Liam said he’d play everyone some new stuff, including the just finished ‘Don’t Look Back in Anger’.

Cable’s guitarist, Darius Hinks, was more drunk than he can previously remember being. Nowadays, he’s a middle-aged author of fantasy fiction novels called things like *Ghoulslayer* and *Daemonhammer*, but then he was in a John Peel-approved grunge band recording his first album, full of beans.

‘There was lots of posh whisky,’ he told the BBC in 2020, a little sadly. ‘They were rightfully really proud of the song that we now know is “Don’t Look Back in Anger”. I was more into alternative music and when you’re young you get quite po-faced. So I got on my indie high horse.’

Initially, he started tickling Liam, winding him up. Then he told him the new song was crap. It sounds just like The Beatles, he said. Why have you ripped off 'Imagine'? Soon enough, Liam snapped, and a huge bundle ensued.

'It was kicking off, big time,' said Bonehead. 'I hit one of this band that had come down. They were gobbing off, so I punched him.'

'It ended with me getting punched as our producer picked me up with Oasis members chasing us,' said Hinks. 'Now I'm embarrassed I was such a bad guest.'

Oasis were only just getting started, though. Noel arrived on the scene and starting kicking anyone still there out, his mood dark. 'Somebody must have got on my tits,' he said. 'My thing is, when I'm working, I am working. I don't particularly want people there, fucking about. I am in the studio.'

Bonehead says, 'It just exploded into a big bunch of chaos like you've never seen.'

Details are hazy, decades after the fact, but some remain etched into memories. Liam upturning tables, smashing chairs and any nearby object, running up to the studio to attack Noel's guitars, thwarted by the bars on the window. Bonehead and Liam trading blows. Alan White and Bonehead seizing the studio's air rifles so that Liam couldn't use them. Guigsy punching a stranger attempting to enter his room. Noel being attacked by Liam and grabbing cricket fan Guigsy's small bat, smashing his brother with it until it snapped . . .

'It was bad,' said Liam. 'The whole place got smashed to bits. There were loads of little bits – electrical bits – going "*pfzz*". Whitey was locked in a room while I was going to town on the living room.'

Furious, Noel went to his room, but Liam started kicking that door, badly injuring his foot in the process. Luckily for Noel, he was on the ground floor. So he climbed from the window, collected Alan White and asked him to drive him to London.

As they made off across the gravel, Liam loomed out from the dark and launched a rubbish bin lid at the car. After a few minutes, White – who'd been a member of Oasis for less than a month – turned to Noel, gauged that he'd reduced from boiling to a simmer, and asked, 'Have I joined The Troggs?!' Noel almost smiled.

For the next two weeks, Noel Gallagher thought Oasis were over. He'd rather do it solo than like that in a band with Liam again, he told friends. Liam saw a doctor for his injuries and then skipped off to Portugal. Noel spent some time in London alone, then travelled to Jersey to see Meg Mathews, his girlfriend, who he'd started seeing at the end of '94 (see 'The Girl with the Dirty Shirt', page 185). While he grieved the band, he was also upset about hitting his brother so violently with the cricket bat.

Liam agreed. 'There was no need for the cricket bat around the head,' he said. 'I remember going home and thinking my foot was fucked, my arm was in plaster.'

Eventually, the studio rang Ignition asking when the band were coming back. Oasis's management replied that they thought they'd been banned. 'For that?! You should've seen the studio after Ozzy Osbourne and Black Sabbath!'

'We didn't care less,' Kingsley Ward told the BBC. 'They're lovely boys. They came back, paid the damage – about £800 – and went in the studio and did one of the greatest records afterwards.'

The reunion in Rockfield was pretty low-key. Liam apologized. Noel called Liam a dickhead, then gave him a Beatles belt buckle he'd found. That was pretty much it. 'Every time there was a scene in Oasis, when we got back together it was always like nothing had happened,' said Noel in *Supersonic*. 'I don't remember any airing of grievances. If there was any bad blood ever, it happened at that moment and then it was gone. I live day by day. I don't carry shit with me.'

Back together in the studio, Oasis picked up exactly where they left off, nailing six songs in that week, including 'Cast No Shadow'. First up, though, was 'She's Electric'. **TK**

'Morning Glory'

The attempts by the UK tabloid press to concoct a furore around Oasis and their drug use were, even by UK tabloid press standards in the 1990s, extremely disingenuous. 'We've been on the front page of a paper where it said, "Oasis in drug shock",' Noel Gallagher noted the week after those two nights at Maine Road in 1996. 'Shock to who? It would be a bigger shock if we all went to church: "Oasis in religious shock".'

He was right. It had been there for all to hear – or at least for all who were worldly enough to decode euphemisms like *'white line'* or *'mirror and the razor blade'* – from the get-go.

Even so, on the attempts to concoct a scandal went, culminating with the infamous BBC interview in January 1997 in which Noel said that, to most people, 'drugs are like getting up and having a cup of tea in the morning'. The tabloids had their line. No, not that sort of line. (See 'Angel Child', page 168, for more.) None of the innocent little lambs who worked at a tabloid newspaper knew what the reference to the white line in the chorus to 'Cigarettes & Alcohol' from three years previous had been. Or read the interview in which he had said he liked to sprinkle cocaine on his cornflakes.

Nor had they heard the title track of *(What's the Story) Morning Glory?*, which, in the above-mentioned opening line – *'All your dreams are made/When you're chained to the mirror and the razor blade,'* to quote it in full – contains the most explicit drugs reference that would ever feature in an Oasis song. And certainly, too, the most explicit drug reference contained within the five biggest-selling UK albums of all time.

On 'Be Here Now', Oasis would take the overblown sound that results from too many drugs too far. But 'Morning Glory' is just right: the exact split second just before the line that tips its inhaler over from towering, king-of-the-world self-confidence into a gurning mess. It begins, just like 'Be Here Now', with helicopters. It continues with layer upon layer of heavy guitar and titanic-sounding drums, just like 'Be Here Now'. It is a perfect blast of just too much: the intro is the most intense and thunderclap-like moment in the Oasis catalogue.

When asked, years later, which great Oasis songs were not written on drugs, Noel Gallagher was characteristically blunt. 'None,' he said. 'Before 1997, I hadn't written a song without the aid of the old Colombian marching gear. Don't forget, I was on drugs before I was even in a band. I was a roadie for three years with Inspiral Carpets. What do you think I was doing then? Drinking mineral water and eating Twiglets?'

'The whole of the first three albums were written on drugs,' he continued. 'I remember being off my nut and going into the back room and setting the goal of writing a song in ten minutes. That was "Supersonic". All those albums and all the B-sides were written on drugs. That's why they're so good. And that pisses me off. I think, *Maybe I should get back into taking drugs, and then it would be brilliant again.* But that thought lasts less than a second.'

Trying to replicate the visceral, effortless, spontaneous thrill of these songs would indeed be a fruitless – not to mention risky – exercise. But the one-two of 'Morning Glory' and then 'Champagne Supernova' that closes the second Oasis album is the absolute top of the mountain. As invincible as Oasis would ever seem. Where could they – or anyone – go from there? At the time there was no time to worry about such matters. No time to do anything but bask in the narcotic excitement of it all, willing this most enormous of choruses to arrive. The worrying about needing a little time to wake up, wake up was approaching fast . . . but had not yet arrived. **HM**

'Champagne Supernova'

There's a cliché that insists you should never meet your heroes. Noel Gallagher's long friendship with Paul Weller provides powerful anecdotal evidence that that is not necessarily true.

The first time Noel laid eyes upon Weller was in 1978, while watching The Jam on BBC Two's *The Old Grey Whistle Test.* Chatting on the *Desperately Seeking Paul Weller* podcast in 2024, Noel remembered the trio playing 'The Eton Rifles', Weller's post-punk anthem depicting class war on suburban streets. And yet, though The Jam – dressed that night uniformly in black suit jackets and white strides, performing in front of a Union Jack – did appear on *TOGWT* in '78, their three-song set didn't include 'The Eton Rifles'. Perhaps Noel meant to say that he was transfixed by a furious '"A" Bomb in Wardour Street' that evening in front of the box. Or quite possibly the mists of time have mixed the memories up with The Jam's incredible live version of 'The Eton Rifles' in May of '79 on BBC's *Something Else* (a two-band bill shared with Joy Division's final TV performance), when Weller's forceful delivery had somehow matured ten-fold in six short months.

Either way, Noel was a committed, life-long Jam fan from that moment, like hundreds of thousands of British kids in the late seventies and early eighties tweaking his dress code modishly in tribute and tuning into all of Weller's life-or-death pronouncements on everything from music to politics in the press. 'They're as important to me as The Beatles,' he's said.

Disembarking the No. 50 bus outside the Mauldeth pub in Burnage after school on 30 October 1982, bad news awaited fifteen-year-old Noel, though. A pal was at the stop with the shock announcement he'd just heard on Radio 1: The Jam were splitting at the end of the year. 'It was a big deal,' says Noel. 'It was on national TV news. There was real anger among Jam fans, Paul had to go on to explain himself, saying he didn't want to be doing it at twenty-five and mean nothing. I didn't get signed until I was twenty-seven!'

But while many Jam fans, still smarting at the biggest band in the country splitting at their peak, turned away sulkily from Weller's radical new soul-jazz-pop direction with the Style Council, Noel Gallagher remained on board. 'I absolutely loved the Style Council, they're still one of my favourite groups.'

Later, in 1992, when a post-Council Weller at his lowest commercial ebb toured the country solo, Noel Gallagher turned up to the Manchester Academy to watch him with his brother Liam. 'As soon as he played the riff to "Into Tomorrow" – 'gonna play something new for ya!' – me and Liam looked at each other, "Oh hello".' Then, in 1994, he finally met Weller. In the backstage bar of that year's Glastonbury, a broadcast acquaintance of Noel's told him that he'd just done an interview with Paul Weller, who'd declared that the group he was most looking forward to seeing that weekend was Oasis. Noel took another swig of Dutch courage and marched over to introduce himself.

'Where are you living?' wondered Weller after a few minutes of sympathetic chat. London, replied Noel. With a nod and the instruction to call him sometime, Paul Weller gave Noel Gallagher his phone number. A few days later back in town, a nervous Noel dialled. Weller answered in characteristically straightforward terms, 'Who's this?'

'It's Noel, from Oasis . . .'

'Oh nice one, fancy a drink?'

Since then, they have remained the firmest of friends, as well as musical allies. *Definitely Maybe* was sandwiched between two Weller LPs, '93's *Wild Wood* and '95's *Stanley Road* that helped him forge a large and loyally appreciative new audience – most of whom were also Oasis fans (and the older members had probably once been Jam fans too). Alongside other groups such as Ocean Colour Scene – who contained two members of Weller's band – they formed a loose alliance of successful British acts in the mid-nineties who wore their hair like the Small Faces, hung out socially together and were mockingly dubbed 'Noelrock' by the weekly music press. The name never really stuck, largely because by 1995 the music press already needed all things Oasis far more than Oasis needed *NME/Melody Maker* etc. The group's allies also felt the warmth of this commercial heat: OCS's first two albums, '96's *Moseley Shoals* and '97's *Marchin' Already,* sold huge numbers despite rotten reviews.

At the heart of this alliance lay the close comradeship between Noel Gallagher and Paul Weller. Noel was warned by a mutual friend when they met that 'Weller falls out with everyone eventually', but three decades later they remain the best of buddies. 'I think he was born virtually the same day as I was,' Noel told *NME* in 1995, early in their romance. 'He's a Gemini, too, we've both got a chipped front tooth, which he sees as a sign because McCartney's got one and he's a Gemini as well and we've all got blue eyes . . .'

For years, the balcony of Weller's house looked onto the kitchen of Noel's home. Weller would text him when he was having a smoke outside so they could look at each other while chatting on the phone. They still live within a moment's walk from the other in Maida Vale and so many of Noel's warmest anecdotes involve his neighbour, the man he once described as (TV sitcom grouch) 'Victor Meldrew with a suntan'. For example, the time they danced together to the Style Council's 'Shout to the Top' at one of Noel's house parties. Watching Weller from his bedroom window chanting his own name, topless, in Noel's garden in the early hours after a big night. Noel sending a photo of himself arm-in-arm with two of Weller's ideological musical enemies, Bono and Elton John, and Weller replying simply by text message with 'you've gone too far this time.' Or Weller's response when Noel played back his contribution to 'Champagne Supernova' to him for the first time . . .

Noel knew the song was good from the moment he unveiled an acoustic version of what he envisaged to be a psychedelic ballad to the rest of the band while on tour in November 1994. Oasis were parked outside a hotel in Germany at the time, waiting for their hotel rooms to be made available.

'Play us some new tunes, then,' requested Bonehead.

Alright then, thought Noel. *I will.*

'I played "Champagne Supernova" in its entirety on an acoustic guitar,' recalled Noel. 'At the end, silence. I looked up and Bonehead was crying. I said, "It's not that bad – it could be our 'Stairway to Heaven'!" He said, "You've not just written that, have you?" I'm looking at him thinking, *You soft lad*. Either that or it's shit.'

It wasn't that it was shit.

'We were like, "Fuck, do it again," remembers Bonehead. 'He did "Champagne Supernova" from start to finish, in the back lounge of the tour bus, at about eight in the evening . . . I fell apart. I was a blubbering wreck. It was just Noel's voice and an acoustic guitar, not a million miles from how it came out. It got me. It touched a nerve.'

'Champagne Supernova' is an uncanny mix of euphoria and sadness, a song of such supreme, stately elegance that it seems to be describing both the absolute pinnacle of an era as well as its imminent decline, its lyrics either nonsense masquerading as profundities, or vice versa. One line in particular has been repeatedly picked out for ridicule over the decades by sneering music writers: *'Slowly walking down the hall/Faster than a cannonball'*, as if this is a ludicrous, physical impossibility. However, as anyone who's crept in the front door carrying their shoes and whatever remains of their mind while chemically retuned in the early hours can attest, it describes the desperation not to draw attention to oneself in an otherwise silent home perfectly.

'It means different things when I'm in different moods,' Noel told Keith Cameron for *NME* around release in '95. 'When I'm in a bad mood, being caught beneath a landslide is like being suffocated.'

Meanwhile, the lilting refrain that Liam repeats with slightly different emphasis each time – *'where were you when we were getting high'* – was actually an old Noel Gallagher catchphrase. 'We used to say it to each other all the time,' he recalled, but sung to an international audience across the decades, it assumes heavier, more melancholic meaning. Those were the days, my friends, we thought they'd never end . . .

'There is a great sadness to that song,' Noel admitted in the *Supersonic* documentary, 'and yet it has generated the most joyous thing ever when you look out to the crowd and 60,000 people are singing it. I put that down to magic, I really do. And I wish I could tell you the ingredients to that magic potion. But when you see that, who cares what it means? It means something different to every one of them.'

‘I haven’t a clue what it’s about,’ decided Liam, when quizzed. ‘It just reminds me of getting pissed, in a big style. Fucking having loads of drugs, that’s what it means.’

Noel knew when he was recording it that ‘Champagne Supernova’ deserved some extra magic, so he invited his hero/pal Paul Weller down to play guitar on it. Weller obliged happily, adding a great swirling solo to the song’s climax. Then everyone celebrated with a drink.

‘We all got absolutely steaming pissed,’ said Noel, sadly. ‘Mixed it drunk. It still breaks my heart when I hear it.’ Paul Weller was not happy with the final mix either, as he let Noel know.

‘Why didn’t you turn my solo up?’ he asked.

‘He starts having a go at me,’ recalled Noel. ‘“You fucking turned it down on purpose, you cunt!” And I’m like, “Why would I do that, mate, you’re a miles better guitarist than I am.”’

Time judges the mix more fondly. You really wouldn’t think the guitar has been massaged away. It sounds glorious, as it did at Knebworth in 1996, when another of Noel’s prime influences, John Squire of the Stone Roses, strapped the guitar on for a rare live appearance, playing Weller’s parts (and then some) on ‘Champagne Supernova.’ To have had both Paul Weller and John Squire add their imprints to the same Noel Gallagher song is significant, as they both provide key DNA strands of Oasis.

Noel first saw the Stone Roses at Manchester International 2 in 1987, when the band were emerging from a gothic period, singer Ian Brown performing in ‘a harlequin shirt, with a walking stick and slicked back hair, like Dracula.’ Noel was into the sound, but not yet entirely on board.

That changed a year later in ’88, when Noel returned to the International 2 to watch the Stone Roses again, this time with his sixteen-year-old brother Liam also in the sold-out crowd for his first ever gig. The metamorphosis from goths into the quartet who strode on stage that night in loose-fitting streetwear was stark, Brown having swapped his cane for a large silver bell, which he sounded to announce the start of the show – the singer’s only interaction with the audience: a take-it-or-leave-us attitude noted approvingly by Liam. But it was the music that rang loudest for the Gallaghers.

'The songs were so simple,' marvelled Noel, describing the aspirational desire of the set's opening 'I Wanna Be Adored.' 'I thought, *Well, if they can do it, I can definitely do it.* Liam was also entirely enraptured, for the first time imagining that he – an unskilled manual labourer – could possibly belong on a stage. 'Most groups looked like fannies,' he told me. 'The Roses were cool as. I thought, *Yeah, I'll have a bit of that.*'

Noel once said that the Stone Roses were entirely responsible for the existence of Oasis. 'Without the Stone Roses, Liam wouldn't have bothered to join Bonehead's band and I wouldn't have subsequently joined Liam's band.' The logic of this statement is undeniable, though the fact is the Gallaghers had simply fallen under the Roses' same freeing spell that entranced Britain's musical youth between 1988 and '91.

Few groups' reputations can have been founded on a solitary album quite as profoundly as the Stone Roses and their eponymous 1989 debut. Revelling in the free-spirited attitude of acid house and filled with sixties-styled songs of freedom elevated into life-affirming terrace-chants, the Stone Roses' debut contained the blueprint for Oasis. Together with like-minded Mancunian associates Happy Mondays, they influenced a renaissance in bands cast in their image, including Inspiral Carpets, by whom Noel was once disciplined for wearing a Stone Roses T-shirt while working side of stage by his insecure employers.

The Roses also helped briefly redefine ambition for British alternative bands, most arrestingly in gathering 30,000 of their baggy-clothed tribe at Spike Island, near Widnes, in May 1990. The crowds making the best of a windy sound that day included several future members of Oasis. Noel was there with his pals, as was Guigsy. Local press captured images of a van parked at the top of the site redecorated in the style of John Squire's paint-splattered sleeve design for *The Stone Roses*, surrounded by its lairy-looking occupants. On the side of the van a sign read, 'Paul Arthurs, Plasterer,' i.e. Bonehead.

The scale and youthful religious fervour of the event was noted enthusiastically by Noel. 'The Stone Roses kicked the door open for us,' he said, 'then we came in and nailed it to the wall.' What Noel took beyond everything from the Stone Roses, though, was admiration for John Squire's playing. 'He's always been the guitarist I most admire,' he once declared. At Knebworth in August 1996 both these things came beautifully together for Noel.

In April 1996, after two albums – the long-delayed second of which, '94's *Second Coming*, initiated a precipitous fall in listener affection – John Squire announced he was leaving the Roses. Barring a few contract-fulfilling shows without Squire, that was it for the band before a lucrative live reunion between 2012 and '17. By 1996, Oasis's star had already totally eclipsed the Roses. Yet the gasps throughout the vast numbers in attendance at Knebworth that year when John Squire strolled on stage to add extravagant colour to 'Champagne Supernova' were significant. Noel had entered by declaring the event to be 'history,' and he was correct, but this meeting of musical minds appeared to be a fleeting, pinch-me, once-in-a-lifetime moment. It wasn't. In June 2022, who did Liam Gallagher invite onstage for the 'Champagne Supernova' encore at Knebworth for his two sold-out solo dates at the country estate? 'I had the hang of it by then, I wasn't nervous really,' Squire told me later about his second appearance at the venue in twenty-six years, despite having not been on a stage in five. 'Well, not until Liam introduced me as "the coolest man on the planet", which I am definitely not.'

Reminded of Squire's prowess, Liam subsequently agreed to sing on a new collection of Squire songs for the *Liam Gallagher John Squire* album that came out in March 2024, his last recordings before Oasis announced their own reunion later that summer. All of which is to say, some heroes are definitely worth meeting. You never know where it may lead. **TK**

'Bonehead's Bank Holiday'

(WHAT'S THE STORY) MORNING GLORY? BONUS TRACK

'You know how The Beatles used to get Ringo to sing the odd tune here or there?' Noel Gallagher smiled in 1995. 'Well, he's our Ringo, you see. Completely untalented. The luckiest man in rock. So we thought we'd write him a song, you know? "Bonehead's Bank Holiday" is about going to Spain and nicking cars and meeting girls whose mothers are nuns.'

If any member of Oasis deserves their own tribute song, it's original rhythm guitarist Paul Arthurs. In many ways he is the soul of the band: a balding Bez with barre chords only. Like Ringo, though, as the years have gone by, his musical importance has started to be more and more recognized. His brutalist, minimalist approach to rhythm guitar – one chord shape only, moved up and down the fretboard – was and is an absolutely critical part of the Oasis wall of noise and the early sound of the band.

When Liam Gallagher went solo, Bonehead made a guest guitar appearance at his very first show at Manchester Ritz in 2017, stepping up to play on the finale of 'Be Here Now'. Gradually, over time, he snuck into Liam's band almost by stealth: appearing on more and more songs. And, if you closed your eyes, you could tell. Like a secret sauce, his playing made the Oasis songs sound as titanic as they should. A guitar player with a simple but truly distinctive sound.

The same, though, could not be said for his singing. Which he knew more than anyone. When Noel Gallagher woke up one morning at Rockfield Studio and told him that his vocal talents were needed, he was nonplussed. He was aware of the existence of 'Bonehead's Bank Holiday' – the demo had been recorded at the Club Quattro soundcheck in Japan at the end of 1994 – but assumed that Noel would be singing it. And also . . . really? That song? The one about polluted beaches, girls called Avaline (geddit?) and a mum with a face like a nun in a pain? 'She's Electric' was already in the mix. Did it need any more comedy?

It did, for the same reason that 'Sad Song' ended up on the vinyl version of *Definitely Maybe*: without it, the grooves on the record would have been too close together and the sound thus too quiet. Bonus tracks should probably sound a bit more like 'Bonehead's Bank Holiday' anyway and, Noel thought, if you're going to record it, there's only one man who can sing it.

Daunted by the prospect of adding his pipes to album sessions that by then already had Liam performing 'Champagne Supernova' and Noel doing 'Don't Look Back in Anger' in the can, Bonehead did what lots of British people do when they're nervous and went to the pub, taking Liam with him.

Several hours and sixteen pints of cider each later, he entered the vocal booth with an equally drunk Liam by his side offering moral support. For two hours they tried to sing it but managed nothing but gabbled nonsense and the 'la la la la' chorus. Noel had to step in and do the lead vocal, but Bonehead's drunken rambling remains on the recording, adding a sense of bonhomie to his theme song without which it would not be the same. A different kind of secret sauce, born of a day out on the sauce. **HM**

'Wonderwall'

SINGLE RELEASED 30 OCTOBER 1995 (SEE PAGE 111)

'Round Are Way'

B-SIDE OF 'WONDERWALL'

When it came time to compile an album of Oasis B-sides, pretty much everything from all the *Definitely Maybe* and *(What's the Story) Morning Glory?* singles was included. The only exceptions were the couple of songs that had only been demos ('I Will Believe', 'Alive') and some of the Noel solo acoustic songs, in the spirit of keeping *The Masterplan* upbeat.

And then for some reason 'Round Are Way' – the brass- and harmonica-laden stomp that had appeared on 'Wonderwall' – was also omitted.

This was certainly not due to its quality. It had been played live, when most of the other B-sides from that era had not, at Earls Court, Maine Road, Knebworth – all of the biggest, most culturally significant Oasis shows. They'd chosen it, too, to be part of the five-song set played on the 1995 New Year's Eve edition of *The White Room*. Like so much of *The Masterplan*, it would have made a great single. In fact, more so than most of *The Masterplan*. It's one of the poppiest, most out-and-out fun songs they ever recorded.

Introduced with a Blues Brothers-style brass section, it stomps along like a second helping of 'Digsy's Dinner', but with a much bigger, more soaring chorus. The drums were fed through the same phasing the Small Faces used on 'Itchycoo Park': a playful classic to which it bore more than a passing resemblance. It's one of the few times Noel put Ray Davies-esque characters just going about their day: Ernie banging the sound as the day begins; meeting at the office before the staff clock in; paperboys lying to teachers; next-goal-wins games of football in the park. It is also surely the first time anyone ever put the word 'minging' in a song (and some years before *Big Brother* contestant Jade Goody made 'Am I minging?' a national catchphrase).

And it was the song that introduced harmonica player Mark Feltham, a storied harmonica virtuoso who had come to fame with blues band Nine Below Zero and then gone on to appear with all manner of artists, from The The to Robbie Williams, Rory Gallagher to Talk Talk.

Though he wasn't present at the sessions – his parts were added at the end during mixing – the band were enamoured enough by what he did to invite him back for live shows shortly afterwards, from the end of 1995 right up until the *MTV Unplugged* show on 23 August 1996 – where Liam bailed at the last second and left Noel to sing – that followed Knebworth. Given free rein to do what he liked onstage, he threw everything at 'The Masterplan', 'Whatever' and others, giving them an entirely new feel.

It may not have made *The Masterplan*, but 'Round Are Way' found a second life nonetheless: appearing in a 2020 Christmas TV advert for Co-op supermarket, busked by two very young brothers from the north of England, about six years apart in age, one of whom sings and plays guitar and the other of whom just sings. Who do you think the Co-op were hoping their audience might assume these two might be? **HM**

'The Masterplan'

B-SIDE OF 'WONDERWALL'

It sounds as if it was first strummed in a hotel room, late at night, a long, long way from home, when the inner demons are quietly knocking, producing rare self-doubt that needs to be contextualized lyrically and destroyed melodically . . .

Which is exactly where and how it was conceived: on tour in Japan, in the full flush of the mania that accompanied *Definitely Maybe* echoing around the globe, most manically in the Far East.

As soon as Noel Gallagher had finished 'The Masterplan' he knew it was special. A lovely melody, initially an acoustic rhapsody in blue before it was transported to Maison Rouge studio in Fulham to have the sweeping orchestra, warmly swelling brass and sparkling guitar breaks applied to the canvas. It's Noel's version of The Beatles' 'Across the Universe' – a grand state of human existence address that doubled at the time of composition as a motivational creative speech, directed at himself. The opening line, *'Take the time to make some sense of what you want to say'*, is literally Noel's instruction to the songwriter to take a moment to weigh his thoughts. 'But it is a good line,' he considered years later, pointing out that the following line – *'cast your words upon the waves'* – 'means the airwaves.' It is satisfyingly meta.

The twenty-seven-year-old sitting in that hotel room writing 'The Masterplan' had no real reason to fear death, even though twenty-seven is a dangerous age for rock stars at the peak of their powers (as Jimi Hendrix, Kurt Cobain, Jim Morrison, Brian Jones etc. can attest from the beyond). But he may have felt at an existential crossroads, nonetheless.

The band that released *Definitely Maybe* was powered by a clear mission: to first become the biggest band in Britain, then the world; to reject the prevailing indie band mentality whereby number seven in the album chart was the height of success. For Oasis, number seven would've have meant failure. They arrived through the door they'd kicked in proclaiming they were mad for success, for everything on offer, for 'it'. And these proclamations had all come to pass, they were on a trajectory far beyond what anyone outside of Oasis had forecast for them a year earlier.

What, wondered Noel, however, was the masterplan? What do you do in the next bit, as you grow a little tired, slower, older? The conclusion he came to through his chosen therapy – i.e. singing along to this melancholic melody – was just go with it. Dance if you wanna dance, sing if you wanna sing. Do what you want. That's the meaning of life. We're all part of a masterplan, and that masterplan is that there is no masterplan. Enjoy it while you can.

Back home in his basement Camden flat, he polished and shined the piece, then he headed to Maison Rouge, playing it on acoustic to the band and Owen Morris to a chorus of awed silence. This, he told them, was one he was going to sing himself.

The recording was similarly Noel-centric, with the song's composer playing all guitar and bass parts, Bonehead adding a little piano and Alan White supplying percussion.

The critical response to 'The Masterplan' was an approving blanket of praise when it finally made its understated, almost apologetic way into the world on the B-side of 'Wonderwall''s CD single.

The first time Liam Gallagher heard 'The Masterplan' – as detailed in Paolo Hewitt's essential *Getting High* – was at Maison Rouge. The mood was turbulent. Liam arrived at the studio while Noel enjoyed a break after mixing the 'Wonderwall' B-sides, sharing a Chinese takeaway with wife Meg Mathews and friends in the reception of the studio, which is right around the corner from Chelsea's Stamford Bridge stadium.

Having just heard the finished mix for 'Round Are Way,' Liam confronted his brother without greeting immediately upon arrival in the reception. 'What the fuck do you think you're doing?' he asked of Noel instead.

After some back-and-forth, it turned out Liam thought his vocals were not mixed 'right.' Noel understandably disagreed, as he'd just finished work on the song. Neither was convinced by the other's position and the disagreement continued venomously down the corridor and into the studio control room, where Owen Morris continued to make final mixing tweaks on the songs. He also attempted rather forlornly to mediate between the Gallaghers, but he had one ace up his sleeve. Calling for quiet, he played the mix for 'The Masterplan' through the desk.

As the magisterial song flooded the room, the mood was overwhelmed. Liam had absolutely no notes to give his brother for this mix. 'This is as good as any Beatles song,' he gushed to Noel, awe-struck. 'You don't know how good you are, man. And it's a fucking B-side!'

In time, though, the fact that Noel assigned 'The Masterplan' a place as a B-side on the UK CD single of 'Wonderwall' came to niggle Liam. It didn't even make its way to the USA until Noel sang a live version for *MTV Unplugged* at the Royal Festival Hall, in August 1996. Liam felt aggrieved they'd underplayed their hand sneaking it out on the undercard.

As Noel noted later, 'Our kid was just walking around going, "Why did you write that now, you knobhead. You couldn't have waited a year so it could go on the next album? You dick!"' Time, however, relegates commercial decisions to their appropriate standing. 'I can see how mental it was to put it out as a B-side, but we were all off our tits in the 1990s.'

Now we can see the true value of 'The Masterplan' as one of Noel Gallagher's very best compositions and performances. 'I got the sound right in the studio,' he reflects proudly. 'I got the words right. When I read the lyrics back, I thought, *Fucking hell, this is it! I've come to age as a lyricist!* Then I wrote "Bonehead's Bank Holiday" or something ridiculous.'

Noel knew the true worth of 'The Masterplan', though. 'I think it's the best song I've ever written, everyone's favourite B-side.' For a song that extols the virtue of the journey rather than the map, this is the perfect destination. TK

1996

On 3 January, the first ever flip phone goes on sale. Danny Boyle's adaptation of Irvine Welsh's Trainspotting *is released in cinemas. A nineteen-year-old Briton becomes the first human being to die of mad cow disease. Jay-Z releases his debut album* Reasonable Doubt *in June, with the Spice Girls' first single 'Wannabe' coming soon after. England host the UEFA European Football Championship but are knocked out by eventual winners Germany. Football is not, as the popular song released that summer by the Lightning Seeds with Frank Skinner and David Baddiel has it, coming home. Take That announce they are splitting up, with the UK government setting up an emergency phone line to counsel fans. Nelson Mandela steps down as president of South Africa. George R. R. Martin publishes* A Game of Thrones *in August, a month that will also see Osama bin Laden declare war on the United States. Tupac Shakur is shot dead in September. Rupert Murdoch launches Fox News in October. Bill Clinton is re-elected in November and Kofi Annan becomes secretary general of the United Nations in December.*

'Look at you now/You're all in my hands tonight': Noel surveys Maine Road, April 1996, shot by Jill Furmanovsky. 'When I look at this picture, I don't hear the crowds roar or find myself standing back on the stage,' he said. 'All I remember is the nightmare of trying to walk to the front without tripping over the cables and making a cunt of myself!'

'Don't Look Back in Anger'

SINGLE RELEASED 19 FEBRUARY 1996 (SEE PAGE 115)

'Step Out'

B-SIDE OF 'DON'T LOOK BACK IN ANGER'

Of course, Noel Gallagher knew everyone would recognize the chorus of 'Step Out' as being exactly like Stevie Wonder's 'Uptight'. *Of course* he did. He knew, too, that the guitar riff is exactly the same as 'Rosalie' by Thin Lizzy. Both were borrowed with the same knowing, wink-wink intentions as Gary Glitter's 'It's Good to Be Back' was lifted for 'Hello'.

'I laugh to myself when I'm writing these songs,' Noel said in '95. '"Wait 'til the lads hear this!" I always promised myself that I'd change that "Hello" bit, but it just wouldn't go away. In the end, I just said, "Fuck it, it must be the song because I can't get rid of it."'

A very similar thing happened when Oasis came to record 'Step Out' during that second post-ruck session at Rockfield. 'We thought, *Well, alright, it's got the "Rosalie" guitar riff, probably get away with that.* But then the chorus . . . well, oops! I thought I'd change the melody in the studio, come up with something else . . .'

As with 'Hello', though, it just wouldn't go away. 'We weren't snobs,' Noel said in 2020, describing his instincts for borrowing from whomever. 'It's like when people would say, "'Cigarettes & Alcohol' sounds like T. Rex" No! No shit. Does it? No way, I'd never noticed that . . . "Aren't those two chords the same as 'Imagine'? You can't do that!" I can, and I will, and I have. And you'll buy it, so fuck off.'

They'd have to buy 'Step Out' as a B-side, though. Originally, it was the opener for side two of *(What's the Story) Morning Glory?*, even appearing on (now very valuable) promo copies of the album, before Stevie Wonder's intervention.

'We went to get clearance,' Noel said, 'we were going, "We'll credit you, man, don't fucking worry about that," and the cheeky bastard wanted six points on the album!'

A point is equal to 1 per cent of the royalties earned on an album. Typically, the producer will earn around four points on an album. Six points on an album for using a similar chorus for one song is, therefore, ludicrous.

'We said, "Do you know how much money you're gonna get? Nothing, because it's not going on the album. So you can fuck right off!"'

The interaction may have soured Noel's opinion of the song somewhat. 'It's not that good anyway. The thing about "Step Out" is, it is "Rosalie" mixed with "Uptight", but it's also "Step Out" by Oasis. The inspiration for the two parts of the tune come from Thin Lizzy and Stevie Wonder, but the tune wouldn't exist without me.'

The biggest mystery surrounding 'Step Out' isn't who provided which bits as influences for it, though. It's why Noel chose to sing a song so within Liam's register.

Online, passed around by fans in recent years, is one and a half minutes of Liam singing 'Step Out' in a recording booth, headphones on, so we can't hear his backing track, just his isolated vocal. It sounds even in these conditions immense, as good as any of his most passionate vocal recordings from the . . . *Morning Glory* sessions. At the time of writing, a Liam-fronted 'Step Out' has not made its way officially into the world. Hopefully, by the time of reading, that's changed. **TK**

'Underneath the Sky'

B-SIDE OF 'DON'T LOOK BACK IN ANGER'

Another great example of how easy Oasis were making it seem in 1995 and 1996, this not-often-mentioned song has the kind of effortlessly classy-yet-catchy melody their contemporaries would have killed for.

'Underneath the Sky' is also a good example of how instinctively Oasis were working in the studio at this point, the freedom of it being 'just a B-side' giving Noel Gallagher room to try things out. If you listen to the acoustic version with him singing – Noel did this a couple of times for radio, the only time it's ever got close to a live airing – it works fantastically. Then Oasis bring it into the studio, throw on the distinctive guitar part that is fed through a rotary speaker (partially inspired by Blondie's 'Call Me') plus layer upon layer of backing vocals and, within the space of a morning (they had 'Cum On Feel the Noize' to get done that day also), it becomes something else entirely.

The song was written the night before Oasis went in to record it. 'I can remember sitting with a tape recorder with Owen in a little flat that was rented in Camden,' Noel remembered. 'We needed one more track. It's a little like "Dead End Street" by The Kinks in the middle. It's not identical but I always liked that bit. So I think I got that bit first and wrote the verses around that.' Lots of the lyrics were pulled from a little book he had picked up in an airport, with travellers sharing their wisdom: hence 'all he needs is his life in a suitcase' and 'wish me away to an unknown place.'

The one-finger piano solo, meanwhile, took both Noel and Bonehead to play. They were pissed, obviously. **HM**

'Cum On Feel the Noize'

B-SIDE OF 'DON'T LOOK BACK IN ANGER'

Slade guitarist Dave Hill's autobiography, *So Here It Is*, tells the inspiring story of a working-class kid from a council house in Wolverhampton who goes on to achieve fame and fortune playing guitar with one of the most popular and flamboyant bands of the 1970s. He's endured an onstage stroke, crippling depression, all three original members of Slade leaving the band and has lived to tell the tale. In some ways, however, the biggest revelation comes in the book's afterword, written by a certain Noel Gallagher.

'The Stone Roses? Yeah, they played their part,' writes Noel. 'The Beatles? Well, they were undeniable . . . but Slade? I felt their songs could've been written at the end of my street, in a house just like mine. No Slade = No Oasis. It's as devastating and as simple as that.'

Given this huge accolade, it's no surprise, perhaps, that Oasis should pay Slade the ultimate compliment of covering their barnstorming 1973 hit, 'Cum On Feel the Noize,' a song about the sheer power of their live audiences, about 'feeling the sound of the crowd pounding in the chest,' as frontman Noddy Holder explained. Noel has also described 'the love and the vibe and the passion, the rage and joy coming from the crowd . . . that's what Oasis was.' There's a lot in common there.

'It just sounds like an Oasis song,' Noel said of 'Cum On Feel the Noize' in a 1999 BBC documentary about Slade. *'Come on, feel the noise/Girls grab your boys/We'll go wild, wild, wild . . .'*

Nevertheless, it's a complete fluke that Noel decided to record the song. He was preparing for a guest radio DJ spot with Oasis's plugger Dylan White in late '94, rifling through the station's CDs, when White spied Slade in there. 'You've got to play some Slade!' White implored.

'If it wasn't for him, we wouldn't have done the Slade cover,' admitted Noel. Playing it on air, though, connected him back to the group he'd loved as a kid, the original good-time lads' band. Slade started off as skinheads in the mid-sixties but found mainstream success with a richly melodic, stomping wall of glam sound that delivered six number-one singles.

'They were a proper geezers' band, but they dressed like the Diddy Men,' said Noel. Something fundamental connected him with Slade. 'I'm not a student, I've not been to college, I've never been to art school, I'm not very good with words. But Slade speak to me, through the energy and the guitars more than anything. It's brilliant, it's just pure emotion.'

The first time most people saw Oasis play 'Cum On Feel the Noize' was on *Later . . . with Jools Holland*, on BBC Two in November 1995. Forced to pick a number without Liam singing as he'd cried off with a sore throat, Noel fronted a solid if unspectacular take on Slade at the last minute. Afterwards, sitting with Holland at his piano for the routinely slightly awkward main interview, Holland thanked him for doing Slade ('very badly,' replied Noel, convincingly) and then played him the original, as mimed on *Top of the Pops* twelve years earlier. It wasn't really a fair comparison: anyone can mime to a record. 'What did you like about Slade?' asked Holland.

'I'll have to be boring and say the music,' replied Noel, with the mildest contempt.

The following February, Oasis were given an opportunity to mime their own version of 'Cum On Feel the Noize' on *Top of the Pops*, when on Thursday the 22nd the BBC decided in an unprecedented move to allow Oasis to deliver both an A-side and a B-side performance. So, after Noel fronted 'Don't Look Back in Anger' with Liam pretending to play the piano on his left, Liam sprang to the front of the stage and Oasis launched into their recorded version of 'Cum On Feel the Noize,' which had all the emotional punch and boozy power of the original. There was one hiccup that eagle-eyed viewers may have spotted, though.

'If you watch the footage of *Top of the Pops*,' points out Noel, 'Liam being Liam, he is so blatantly miming out of time.'

This is particularly true as he mouths the line, *'So you think my singing's out of time, well, it makes me money . . .'* 'It cracks me up every time,' says Noel.

But the moment that Oasis truly made 'Cum On Feel the Noize' their own – for five minutes or so, at least – was on 4 May 1996, when they played their landmark homecoming show at Maine Road, then the stadium of their beloved Manchester City.

It seems almost quaint, cosy nowadays, seeing Oasis perform in front of 40,000 fans, but then, before Knebworth, Wembley and all the rest, this was a step into a new dimension for the band. This was where they became a stadium band, and they did so with extraordinary aplomb. Without any stage set or pyrotechnics, nothing showy really beyond Noel's Union Jack guitar, Oasis held the entire stadium in sing-along raptures with just their two albums' worth of material. And for a final encore, they reached into their covers bag and plucked out 'Cum On Feel the Noize', received as if an Oasis original.

'It's uncanny for me that I write a song and people say, "Oh, it sounds like Oasis!", reflected co-writer and Slade bassist Jim Lea, ruefully. 'It's a bit putting the cart before the horse.'

At Maine Road, the other writer of 'Cum On Feel the Noize' stood on the VIP balcony beaming, though. 'It was great seeing forty thousand singing along to a song that was more than twenty years old,' said Noddy Holder afterwards, defining the best possible outcome for a cover version. TK

'I'm being chased by the God Squad!'

On the frontline with Oasis #3

Be there then, June 1997

Liam Gallagher was first in, squeezing through the heavy metal doors. Wearing a blue Kangol parka and accompanied by three hulking security guards, he pointed across the photo studio. 'Have we met before?' he shouted at me.

Noel was right behind him in a matching green Kangol parka and his own heavies in tow. He denied they'd synchronized their coats. 'Do you think I'd be wearing the same clobber as that cunt on purpose? he asked, rhetorically.

We were no longer in Lily la Tigresse's 'world famous topless bar', Toto. After months of negotiations and some nail-biting deliberations, bluffs and passive-aggressive grandstanding, we were finally all together in snapper Kevin Westenberg's fancy Fulham photo studio for our exclusive Oasis *NME* cover shoot and interview to run around their insanely anticipated new single, 'D'You Know What I Mean?'

Our personal and professional circumstances had all changed somewhat since we were last together as a trio, in Paris in 1994. Oasis were by some considerable distance the biggest band in the world now. I'd had a promotion at work too.

As *NME*'s features editor, I'd spent several weeks, perhaps months (certainly felt like it), on the phone negotiating the piece with their laconic, low-vibes in-house PR, Johnny Hopkins, who was very much making the most of his new role as kingmaker and press puppeteer – a powerplay he may not have anticipated when joining Creation in 1993 as a junior PR, handling the Felt reissues, the Bandulu album and some new Mancunian group named Oasis.

He now made lots of commissioning editors who wished that a ray of Oasis's glory might reflect momentarily upon their publications dangle, but I suspect he enjoyed the dangling more with me, bearing in mind the hassle I'd caused him a few years before.

The Jukebox Fury I'd surreptitiously organized with Noel for the 1994 *NME* Christmas issue had gone spectacularly well in the basement conference room of the Kensington Hilton. Noel and Justine had got on like a small house fire, tongues loosened by several bottles of Jack Daniels. Jarvis Cocker, who Noel was meeting for the first time, charmed everyone with a magical display of deadpan Jarvisness before throwing up quietly in the wastepaper basket in the corner of the room. We discussed records by Blur, Primal Scream, REM and Whigfield's 'Saturday Night'. Noel called Tom Jones 'a Welsh cunt' and railed hard against junglist UK Apache's 'Original Nuttah': 'Jungle schmungle – bet the closest he's been to a jungle is Chester Zoo'. Guigsy, in one of his very few public speaking engagements, repeatedly embarrassed Noel, saying things like 'you buzzed off Slash's guitar playing' to him, like an elderly nan airing ancient laundry in front of her grandson's cool new mates. Guigsy's role in Oasis was mainly as a staunch companion to all in the band; a man of few words normally, a lover of cricket and reggae who acted, as fellow bass player Derek Smalls from Spinal Tap said, as calming 'lukewarm water' between the fire and ice of singer and guitarist. This time, though, he'd said too much. 'I'm never bringing you to one of these again,' Noel informed him, as Noel and Justine head off into the night together.

Back at the office, it was decided to pull the feature forward a week and stick a photo of Noel and Justine laughing together on the cover. Its appearance on newsstands on the second to last cover of the year was the first that Ignition, Creation, *Melody Maker* or any interested parties such as Johnny Hopkins knew of the event, and all our phones at *NME* rang with the not angry, just disappointed tones of Hopkins letting staff know how we'd ruined his *Melody Maker* exclusive Christmas cover (which still ran, of course).

Since then, Oasis had sold several million copies of their second album, delivered two Knebworths and were as good as printing their own supply of £50 notes. New, more business-minded players subsequently arrived to help Creation with their endeavours in this respect and manners had become incredibly heavy, particularly for us goofballs on music magazines. For example, in order to hear the music I was to interview the Gallaghers about, I had to sign a contract saying I wouldn't discuss any of the said music with anyone whatsoever, including romantic partners or colleagues, ahead of publication. Which would be quite a feat as I had to hand the piece in first to be edited. Still, I signed the contract and listened to the magnificent 'D'You Know What I Mean?', while wondering nevertheless if perhaps a little conversation about it might have cut that long opening minute of airplane noise down a touch.

Shortly before he finished recording *(What's the Story) Morning Glory?*, I'd interviewed Noel about how it was going at Rockfield, and he delivered some typically magnificent quotes about Paul Weller being 'Victor Meldrew with a suntan', only considering an MBE 'so I could flog it', and meeting Morrissey walking down his street in Camden and accidentally inviting him to his birthday party. Fearful he'd have to cancel the do to avoid his mates and Moz mingling, Morrissey had saved Noel by slipping a note through the door saying, 'Sorry, I can't make it, but give us a ring if you want to go shoplifting.'

The quote from the piece that got most traction, though, and probably haunted Noel in the following year of interviews, was him declaring that 'I see it as three albums and that's it', suggesting that after a third album the band would either end or some other radical change would occur. As the third album dawned upon us, however, that possibility seemed as remote as Coca-Cola declaring that it would fold after the launch of Coke Zero. Oasis was a business juggernaut, a brand now as unstoppable as Star Wars, about whose forthcoming *Phantom Menace* there was a similar level of anticipation as *Be Here Now* (and possibly even more long-term disappointment).

We had three hours before the pair left on a Paris promo trip, so after a debate about whether Tina Turner was any good or not

– Liam said yes, Noel forcefully not – we all cracked open that most nineties of alcopop, Hooch, and each Gallagher separately took a seat opposite me to describe where they were at on the last day of June 1997.

Liam was up first, unveiling his unhealthy sexual obsession with Helen Daniels, the fictional sixty-something character on the Australian soap opera *Neighbours*, his love of the word 'cunt' (which he fired off in a multi-purpose demonstration), and how he was not afraid of the aliens he hoped to encounter on his first foray into space: 'I'm probably as smart as them,' he decided. 'Probably thick as fuck, the big goggly-eyed big heads, man, they haven't a fucking clue. I wouldn't want to get lost in space, though. Fancy just nipping in and nipping out. I'd do their heads in, them aliens. They'd be like, "Farking hell! Farking hell! Let's get back to Planet Knob!" I'd take them out and get them slaughtered, they would turn green then.'

After Liam had left for the pub with his minders, Noel sat down to weave ninety minutes of anecdotal magic, some of which is recounted elsewhere in this book. There was one line from our interview that cut through with the wider world and faced back at me on the tube to work from the front of everyone's tabloids on the morning of 7 July – and it wasn't the bit about how much he liked the Chemical Brothers.

'NOEL: OASIS ARE BIGGER THAN GOD!'

This seemed to be the consensus across *The Sun*, *Mirror* and all the rest. It was a bit of a stretch. I'd gone in with the studs-up challenge of 'do Oasis mean more to the youth of today than God?', and, knowing the reaction it would get, Noel agreed with the statement, saying football meant more to him than religion. 'Has God played Knebworth recently?' he asked. Naively, I was thinking of the headline we could manufacture from his statement for *NME*, rather than the distance it would travel beyond our 100k readers. It travelled further.

At some point that morning, my colleague Paul Moody arrived

in the *NME* office saying he'd just bumped into Noel in Marylebone High Street, but after a quick handshake Noel had made a getaway. 'Can't stop, Paul,' he said, laughing, 'I'm being chased by the God Squad!'

My phone rang. It was a reporter for *BBC News at Six* called Paul Newman (no, not that one) wondering if he could come in with a crew and interview me about Oasis being bigger than God. *Thanks, but no thanks* – some ancient law dimly ringing in the back of my mind about journalists not becoming the story.

'Come on, Ted!' implored Newman. 'This is your big moment. You've created this story. Have your say: you're in the eye of today's hurricane.'

For twenty-four hours, I had the briefest glimpse of what it was to be in the eye of the Oasis hurricane. I could step away, so I did. '*I'm being chased by the God Squad.*' For Noel and Liam Gallagher, there was no stepping away, and, besides, they exhibited absolutely no intention to dial down their contribution to the noise surrounding them. Rather, they leaned into it with relish. Just a couple of lads from Burnage with music and the media on strings, playing conkers. The noise, meanwhile, was only going to get louder, day by day by day . . . TK

1997

The year begins and ends with the Spice Girls at number one in the UK Singles Chart. Tiger Woods becomes the youngest ever golf world champion at twenty-one. In Manchester, the Haçienda finally closes, soon to be turned into flats. Paul McCartney becomes Sir Paul McCartney. Channel 5 begins broadcasting in the UK. The world is shocked by the Heaven's Gate mass suicides; thirty-nine bodies are found in San Diego, their aim having been to reach an extra-terrestrial spacecraft. Manchester United win the Premier League for the fourth time in five seasons. On 1 May, Tony Blair is elected prime minister. On 2 May, New York realtor Donald Trump announces that he is to divorce his second wife (shortly afterwards he will begin dating Slovenian model Melania Knavs). Harry Potter and the Philosopher's Stone *by J. K. Rowling is published in June. August begins with the broadcast of the first* South Park *episode and continues with Oasis's* Be Here Now *becoming the fastest-selling album of all time in the UK and the founding of a DVD rental service called Netflix in the US. On the last day of the month, Princess Diana is killed in a car crash at the age of thirty-six, an event that will cast a long shadow over the rest of the year.*

Waiting for luggage at Schiphol Airport, Amsterdam, November 1997, taken by Jill Furmanovsky. 'I was just focusing on Noel and Liam, when suddenly in the background of my shot I saw a pair of legs sail past,' she recalled. 'It was Bonehead lying on his back with his legs in the air, being a piece of luggage on the now-moving conveyor belt. For part two of his comedy act, he leapt onto Noel's lap and kissed him.'

'D'You Know What I Mean?'

SINGLE

RELEASED 7 JULY 1997

Officially, Noel Gallagher composed 'D'You Know What I Mean?' at Mick Jagger's villa in Mustique in May 1996, during writing sessions for the rest of Oasis's third album.

In truth, though, he'd had the song's chords for a good year already. At soundchecks during *(What's the Story) Morning Glory?*'s long trek around the globe, he'd play them on an acoustic guitar, and though the melody was significantly different throughout this gestation, Noel felt certain from the start that it would be the lead single for the new album when that time came. He knew he had a big anthem to open the third campaign with, one that would blossom into a seven-minute psychedelic Crazy Horse-like rabble-rouser.

For that reason, it's one of the last songs they recorded at Air Studios in London, coming after they'd captured all the B-sides for this and other later singles. 'We tend to do that,' Noel told me. 'That's why it's got a sound that's a bit more advanced than the rest of the album.'

One big shift from the rest of *Be Here Now* is the rhythm, which is informed by a chunky sample of 'Amen Brother' by The Winstons, the drum loop that forms the basis of many golden-era hip-hop records and which Noel lifted from NWA's 'Straight Outta Compton,' with Alan White adding his own pattern over the top.

'It runs right through the song,' explained Noel. Years before Oasis, when Noel made bedroom dance tracks with Mark Coyle (also responsible for adding the backwards guitar flashes to 'D'You Know What I Mean?'), the pair would use the same 'Amen Brother' loop on hour-long mixes. Listening to an early version of 'D'You Know What I Mean?,' Noel thought he'd found the perfect place to repeat the trick. 'Just the pace and sound of it suits that song.'

'Anyway, like a knobhead, I did this interview with *Rolling Stone* and said, "There's an NWA sample on the new single." My manager goes, "Doh! Why did you say that? You daft cunt, we've got to pay them now!"'

The song's biggest controversy, however, was a landmine that Noel laid in the song's lyrics, and which he knowingly stepped upon in an *NME* cover story with us upon its release.

The song, explained Noel, was a call to arms for Oasis's legion of fans. For all his people, right here, right now. What he was asking of them was unclear, even to him, but he felt certain that they understood. Hence, 'D'You Know What I Mean?'

'It's all about cultural images,' Noel expanded. 'I know what it's about, the band know what it's about, even though you couldn't easily define it. It's not a song about religion, it's not a song about shagging birds, it's not a song about taking drugs: it's a song about all them things.'

Despite claiming the song was not specifically about religion, however, it does seem to be squaring up to God when Liam sings, *'I met my maker and I made him cry.'* This Noel acknowledged. 'On judgement day, if there ever is one, I will have some things to say to that fucking cunt.'

The media storm that accompanied Noel's comments to us at *NME* comparing Oasis favourably to God did not adversely affect sales. The following Sunday, 'D'You Know What I Mean?' charted at number one, selling an eye-watering 370,000 copies in its first week.

All that was left to speculate about was whether there were any messages that might be hidden within the layered wash of reversed sounds and Morse code that surrounds the central melody. 'We did this American interview and the fella thought [the backwards voice in the song] goes, "The walrus is Bonehead." I said, "You are definitely smoking too much pot if you even think that I think Bonehead is a walrus!"' In fact, the talking is courtesy of a visiting Mark Coyle, who was in the studio sampling snatches of conversation and then running it backwards. 'Just random bits to fill out seven and a half minutes.'

A decade later, in 2008, Noel would ruefully look back on the writing and recording of this and the other songs that make up *Be Here Now*. 'I regret going to the Caribbean island of Mustique with Mick Jagger, Jerry Hall, Johnny Depp and Kate Moss and trying to write *Be Here Now*,' he said. 'I was doing it for the wrong reasons. And that's how you get a situation where at the beginning of "D'You Know What I Mean?" there's no music for the first minute.'

'It's the sound of an airplane landing, which we recorded on the airstrip outside the house I was renting,' he continued. 'And, of course, we thought it was the most amaaazing thing we'd ever recorded. We took the tapes back to Sony in London, and you've got all the suits sitting round the boardroom stereo thinking, *These fucking jokers are riding on the biggest expectations of any band this decade, and they have recorded a plane landing*.'

As for the Morse code that kicks the song off alongside the swoosh of that plane landing: 'It was inspired by "Strawberry Fair" by Tony Newley,' Noel improbably explained to BBC Radio, referencing Anthony Newley's 1960 novelty hit that does not noticeably feature Morse code. 'We got hold of a code book and tried to tap out "bugger all" to follow the line *'Don't look back 'cos you know what you might see'*. But if anyone can tell me what we really said, please let me know.'

At the time of writing, it is one Oasis mystery that remains unsolved. TK

'Stay Young'

B-SIDE OF 'D'YOU KNOW WHAT I MEAN?'

Imagine you're the biggest band in the world and you haven't released any new music for over a year. Your last album is still selling in astronomical quantities, and you cannot leave your house without journalists or fans pestering you about what is happening next. Finally: you are ready. You sequence the songs you've recorded into an album and choose one that will act as a statement of intent, an indicator of what you want to say, as the first single. There are a few songs left over, one of which is a poppy, throwaway, almost bubblegum song. It's great, but it doesn't speak to where you're at. So you hide it away on a B-side.

And then the biggest radio station in the country decides that they like the poppy, throwaway, almost bubblegum song just as much as the big, dark statement-of-intent song and start playing it on heavy rotation, effectively upgrading your B-side to an A-side.

In 1997, the influence of BBC Radio 1 in the UK was such that it was pretty much impossible to have a hit single without it. Making it onto the A-list meant that a song would be guaranteed at least twenty-five plays to a listenership of about 15 million people: a quarter of the country. Most artists would tailor their singles to give them the best chance of being selected for this list. A short intro over which the DJ could talk. Vocals coming in quickly. Big, catchy chorus. Three and a half minutes long.

Oasis, of course, did not have to adhere to these rules at this stage. The public's appetite for their new material was such that they could supply an eight-minute song whose vocals did not arrive until over a minute in and the radio stations would have to play it. What they didn't bank on was that the radio stations would clock that, tucked away on its B-side, was a song that could not have been any more radio-friendly. So, in the spring of 1997, the bright, light, happy vibes of 'Stay Young' blasted out of car stereos as often as 'D'You Know What I Mean?'.

Within a week of its release, Noel Gallagher was making no secret of his feelings about the song. 'As soon as we'd finished it,' he said to Ted, 'I just kept seeing the word "Britpop" everywhere. It's a bit too jolly, y'know. Nice sentiments, though: "*Stay young and invincible . . .*"'

By 1997, Britpop was indeed as dirty a word as you could imagine. Blur had just released their self-titled fifth album: a record that dispensed with all the bouncy whimsy that had made them stars and replaced it with discordant, alternative America-influenced guitars and a dark lead single about heroin. Pulp had retreated to the studio to make their paranoid, druggy, end-of-the party album *This Is Hardcore.* Supergrass were refusing to play 'Alright' and putting out an album called *In It for the Money.*

At the other end of the spectrum, former boyband member Robbie Williams had just released his debut single: an ersatz Oasis song called 'Old Before I Die'. Television heartthrobs – see Sean Maguire's 'Today's the Day' or Ant & Dec's 'Shout' – were doing similar. Even the likes of Bryan Adams and Bon Jovi were producing music that was unashamedly, overtly Brit-guitar-influenced – with the specific purpose of getting back on the radio. Britpop, a smart/subversive reaction to the grandstanding misery of grunge, had now been fully co-opted by the mainstream. Nobody with any credibility whatsoever wanted to be associated with it.

'Stay Young' was written before this period and became one of the first songs to be recorded during the *Be Here Now* sessions at Abbey Road, immediately after Knebworth (and a chaotic US tour that Noel walked off) at the end of 1996. 'When you start doing an album,' said Noel, 'you usually start with the ones you like least, just to get into it really.' By the time it came to sequencing the record, 'Magic Pie' was favoured over 'Stay Young', and it was discarded from the tracklist.

'I don't like it,' Noel would reiterate. 'I don't like the guitar solo on it. I don't like the sound of it either.'

When it came time to tour *Be Here Now,* though – with the help of a set that saw the band emerging from a big red phone box in the middle of the stage – he had relented somewhat. 'Stay Young' took pride of place as the second song of the evening at every show, its value as something that would get people immediately bouncing up and down recognized. 'This is a song that could start a party at a funeral,' an early *NME* review remarked.

Once *Be Here Now* was put to bed, though, it was never to be heard from again. When compiling *The Masterplan*'s tracklist of B-sides, Noel conveniently omitted it. But then the phone rang. It was Liam. 'I never get a phone call from Liam unless it's a problem,' he said. '"ALRIGHT, MATE! Why's fucking 'Stay Young' not on that album?" "Um, I was gonna put it on." "Right, that's alright then . . ." So he wanted it on, 'cos he likes it. But I don't. I suppose people like it because it says, "*Hey, stay young and invincible*". And "*Come what may my faith's unshakeable*". I like that line. But it's a bit happy, it's a bit of a jolly pop song. And I don't really like the way it sounds, either. But if other people like it, and if Liam likes it, then it must go on. And on it went.'

Stripped of the context of the era, though, with guitars once more a rarity on commercial radio, 'Stay Young' sounds fantastic: as straight-ahead pop as Oasis ever got and one of the biggest radio hits they ever had, despite the best efforts of its composer. **HM**

'Angel Child'

B-SIDE OF 'D'YOU KNOW WHAT I MEAN?'

It's hard to quantify the manic appetite in the UK for anything Oasis-related in the summer of 1997. The only real comparison since then has been the manic appetite for anything Oasis-related in the summer of 2024, when the Oasis reunion was announced, or the summer of 2025, when that reunion actually took place . . .

By June 1997, ten months after Knebworth, Britain – and in particular the British media – had completely lost its mind over Oasis. The pitch was fevered. There was no Gallagher-focused story, the kind of item that a year earlier would've been confined to the news pages of *NME* or *Melody Maker*, that didn't instead make splashes across all the tabloid press, and often the main TV and radio news broadcasts. Let's look at a small selection of Gallagher-focused items that somehow made UK red-top front covers and items on BBC and ITV news broadcasts between the autumn of 1996 and early summer of 1997:

- Liam Gallagher returns home fifteen minutes before the band are due to fly from Heathrow to tour the States, prompting the immortal line from heavyweight ITN news reporter Ian Glover-James camped among dozens outside Liam's St John's Wood house, starved of information to relate beyond a glimpse of a newly shaved singer: 'Liam Gallagher is still here. His beard is gone.'
- Noel leaves the same US tour early after a row with Liam, provoked, he said many years later, by having to witness a disagreement 'over a leather jacket' between Liam and Bonehead – probably just the final straw on a tense tour. Cue covers of *The Sun* and the *Mirror*, TV crews at Heathrow to meet his return
- Liam is arrested and cautioned for possession of a small amount of cocaine.
- Liam's 'cycle rage' incident with a cyclist who gives him a wanker sign through the window of his car at the lights in London, and who Liam leaps out to confront, becomes a soap opera on London news channels.
- Noel tells BBC Radio 5 Live at the *NME* Awards in February 1997 that, for many people, 'taking drugs is like having a cup of tea in the morning,' going on to say that most people in the room are on drugs, as are many MPs in the House of Commons. By the morning, this line – 'Drugs Are Just Like a Cup of Tea' – is splashed on the covers of both the *Mirror* and *The Sun*, and the Conservative government home secretary, Michael Howard, appears across

> news bulletins suggesting that, in light of these disgraceful comments, Oasis should fire Noel Gallagher . . .

When I interviewed Noel for *NME* in early July 1997, his first sit-down with a publication since all these stories, I asked what 'Angel Child', the B-side to new single 'D'You Know What I Mean?', was about. It's a stark acoustic number, strummed and sung by Noel alone, recorded in Mustique. One line in particular leapt out: *'I gave all my money to people and things/And the price I'm still paying for the shit that it brings/Doesn't bring me hope for the songs that you sing . . .'*

Who was that aimed at? I wondered. Noel had quite a lot more to say about that than I expected, considering that generally he didn't really care for analysing his lyrics.

'I suppose it's about the way that whenever I open my mouth, I get a letter off some cunt telling me how much money it's gonna cost me,' he said.

Noel gave an example of how, after he'd foolishly said (and immediately regretted) that he hoped Damon Albarn and Alex James died of AIDS in an interview with the *Observer* magazine, an AIDS charity got in touch. 'The Terrence Higgins Trust wanted all the profits from the Earls Court gigs. Which profits? There are no profits because the money goes into putting the thing on. The song's about that sort of situation.'

There was more, though. 'And, I suppose, it's about that thing when I said about taking drugs being like a cup of tea.'

In November 1995, an Essex teenager called Leah Betts celebrated her eighteenth birthday by taking a tab of ecstasy, but, after drinking approximately seven litres of water in the next ninety minutes, fell ill and, through a combination of these factors, died after entering a coma. Her understandably grief-stricken parents aggressively campaigned against drug use in the media for years afterwards. They were particularly unhappy with Noel's comments.

'I had Leah Betts' parents on the phone, giving me a hard time.

Fucking hell, I don't know your daughter, I don't know your circumstances. You don't know me, so why don't you fuck off and leave me alone?'

Those 'drugs are like a cup of tea' comments had acted as a kind of cultural Rorschach test: many young music nuts – and certainly most Oasis fans – saw it as the tongue-in-cheek wind-up it was delivered as; others took high-horse umbrage.

'The best thing about the whole scenario,' said Noel, 'was I've got a cover of the *Daily Mirror* that says "98 per cent back Noel on drugs". Which is a great headline, one for the grandkids. What I was saying – and they only used a soundbite – was, "Look, you know I do drugs, I know you do drugs, there's probably someone in this room doing drugs right now. What's the big deal? For some it's like a cup of blah blah blah . . ." I guess I may have gone a bit far saying that all the Members of Parliament were heroin addicts, but the rest was just stating a fact.'

Straight after the *NME* Awards, Noel took his gong for Best Band up to Birmingham to meet up with Ocean Colour Scene, who were working on an EP for Ronnie Lane, the Small Faces and Faces bassist who died shortly after, in June '97. Merry at 5 a.m. with his friends in the studio, Noel was flicking through the Ceefax news pages on TV looking for the football scores.

'This page flashes up,' he recalled. '"Noel Accuses Cabinet of Drug Addiction". Wind that one back!'

Soon after, Marcus Russell called Noel, advising him to come back to London: there was a storm brewing. He'd have to check into a hotel, though, as there were too many cameras and TV crews outside his house.

The next evening in his hotel room, Noel was watching the *London Tonight* news programme.

'Michael Howard's on talking about me. I'm sitting there chopping one out and Michael Howard is going, "He should be kicked out of the country." I'm going [acts chopping a line of cocaine], "He can't say that!" But he came out with a classic. He said, "I hope he gets kicked out of the band!" I thought, *Yeah, imagine that.* Imagine

Bonehead coming up to me and going, "Listen, man, we've had enough of your mouth, you've got to go. Me and Guigsy, man, we've had it up to here!"'

When he'd composed himself, Noel looked quizzically to the ceiling. 'What was the question?'

'Something about "Angel Child",' I replied.

'Right, well, that's what "Angel Child" is about. What's next?' **TK**

'Heroes'

B-SIDE OF 'D'YOU KNOW WHAT I MEAN?'

At some point in 2006, an A4 notepad that Noel Gallagher made full use of in 1994 – and which had mysteriously disappeared – was auctioned at Bonham's in London. In it were lots of lyrics for songs yet to come (among them 'Champagne Supernova' and 'She's Electric') and one page, titled 'Rebbelius Jukebox', contained his thoughts on some of his favourite songs. (This was for music magazine *Melody Maker*'s regular feature, Rebellious Jukebox, where a musician would choose their favourite songs by other artists, which Noel did in September 1994.)

'My first memory of Bowie,' he had scribbled underneath one entry titled 'Diamond Dogs/Heroes', 'is of seeing all these sixth-formers wearing makeup and stupid hats and lipstick round school. I was curious. "Oh, we're into Bowie!" I thought to myself: *Anyone who stays at school one second longer than they have to and wears their sister's eyeliner seems to be into this guy David Bowie*.'

Quite a few years later – he was just five when 'Ziggy Stardust' came out – a fourteen-year-old Noel was sat around at somebody's flat watching television when a programme called *Five Minute Profile* came on. The subject was David Bowie, 'and there was this video of him, looking clearly coked out of his fucking mind, singing this song with the light behind him. It totally fucking blew me away.'

The song was 'Heroes'. The next day, Noel was off to his local record store to buy a 'best of' and immerse himself in one of his most underdiscussed influences. For a start, there is 'All the Young Dudes', of which he would later say: 'I've had two songs out of that now: 'Don't Look Back in Anger' and 'Stand by Me'. And he's still not sued me yet.' (Oasis would also often incorporate the chorus of 'All the Young Dudes' – as well as The Beatles' 'Octopus's Garden' – into live versions of 'Whatever'.)

And in 1997, on the B-side of maybe the most hugely anticipated Oasis single ever, there was a more complete tribute: a full-band version of the song that had been Noel Gallagher's introduction to Bowie, sung by him rather than Liam. Ditching the initial baritone verses of the original, he goes straight into the higher, climactic verse, backed by the barrage of guitars that were characteristic of Oasis at that point in time. In the notebook detailed above, he had written that 'Heroes' connected with him because 'it actually said something: "*We could be heroes/Just for one day*"'. You can see why he liked it: this is pretty much exactly the same sentiment offered up in 'Live Forever'.

There is a brilliant photo of Noel meeting David Bowie, which was taken backstage at the latter's Wembley Arena show in November 1995 (his set opener that night was 'Look Back in Anger', not to be confused with . . . oh you know), a couple of weeks after Oasis's shows at Earls Court. In the image, Bowie is laughing at something that Noel has said to him. Noel has no idea what it was. But making David Bowie laugh has got to be up there with his achievements.

Years later, he would email Bowie, who wrote back immediately – he was an early enthusiast of the internet and doing the he's-always-just-on-his-emails! thing a decade or so before anyone else – and told him to 'keep writing'. Soon after, he was gone. **HM**

Be Here Now

(ORIGINAL UK RELEASE: 21 AUGUST 1997)

1.	'D'You Know What I Mean?'	7:42
2.	'My Big Mouth'	5:02
3.	'Magic Pie'	7:19
4.	'Stand by Me'	5:56
5.	'I Hope, I Think, I Know'	4:22
6.	'The Girl in the Dirty Shirt'	5:49
7.	'Fade In-Out'	6:52
8.	'Don't Go Away'	4:48
9.	'Be Here Now'	5:13
10.	'All Around the World'	9:20
11.	'It's Gettin' Better (Man!!)'	7:00
12.	'All Around the World (Reprise)'	2:08

All songs: Noel Gallagher

Production by Noel Gallagher, Owen Morris

Bass guitar: Paul McGuigan

Drums, percussion: Alan White

Guitar: Paul Arthurs

Guitar, backing vocals: Noel Gallagher

Vocals: Liam Gallagher

Slide guitar (Track 7): Johnny Depp

Harmonica (Track 10): Mark Feltham

'D'You Know What I Mean?'

SINGLE RELEASED 7 JULY 1997 (SEE PAGE 163)

'My Big Mouth'

The first time Oasis played 'My Big Mouth' live was in August 1996, at the cosy warm-up gig of Balloch Castle, Loch Lomond, to 80,000 fans over two nights. They needed to break it in in a no-pressure situation, because its next appearance would be at Knebworth, in front of 125,000 fans for two nights running.

The tune-up worked a treat. At Knebworth, 'My Big Mouth' confidently lived up to Noel's billing before he struck its first note 'as rocking'. He'd long used Neil Young's work with Crazy Horse as a mood board, on 'Slide Away', 'Morning Glory', but at Knebworth 'My Big Mouth' seemed the most convincing approximation of the windy, free-wheeling, declarative rock song that teeters on the line between confession and confrontation that Young had patented. Though new, 'My Big Mouth' introduced itself that night as if already one of Oasis's cornerstone heavy anthems, like 'Supersonic' or 'Acquiesce'. '*A sound so very loud*', in fact, as Liam sang in the second line.

By the time they got in the studio to record their third album, however, it was decided that the sound wasn't quite loud enough. So, as with all of the recordings on *Be Here Now*, the remedy was just to ladle as much instrumentation imaginable on top of the basic track, and to stretch the song out for as long as possible. For 'My Big Mouth', that meant a couple of dozen extra guitar tracks smothered on top, the intro and outro elongated beyond logic, and everything turned up into the red. You can still tell this is a classic Oasis song, with a great Liam vocal fighting to be heard over the cacophony, but it's been brutalized by trebley noise. A sound perhaps a little too loud.

'Why does it sound like that?' asked Noel rhetorically, when speaking with Keith Cameron for the remastered reissue in 2016. 'Cocaine, baby. It's a hell of a drug. I can only tell you that on the night it was mixed it sounded fucking amazing.'

This was the defining characteristic of the chaotic recording of *Be Here Now*. Firstly, they shouldn't even have been in the studio recording.

'We should've let *(What's the Story) Morning Glory?* land properly after Knebworth. It was still in the top five everywhere, selling loads,' said Noel. 'We were a mess. We needed to go off for a bit, get pet monkeys or whatever. Hang out with arms dealers. Spend some money. You know how northerners solve everything with a cup of tea? "Oh, your dog's got cancer? Would you like a cup of tea?" With us it was, "You're in a mess? Would you like to go in the studio?" Yeah.'

Another issue was the sheer popularity of the band, then the biggest in the world. Nobody working for, with or around Oasis had anything to compare it with, never mind the band themselves. It was peak Beatles intensity. 'I do festivals all over the world and there are big bands,' Noel told Gibson TV in 2022. 'Oasis then were a hundred times bigger than all of them put together, particularly in England.'

Wherever Oasis went, so did dozens of newspaper reporters and paparazzi. 'You're the biggest band in the world making this much-anticipated record,' said Noel, describing the press pack who awaited their every move. 'It was the birth of celebrity culture and what became known as Britpop crossing over into the tabloids. The circus never ended. No way to make a record.'

But make the record they did. First, they went to the closest studio to their north London homes, Abbey Road Studios, from which they were quickly asked to leave. Too noisy, too disruptive, too fond of the quaint in-house studio bar.

'They're making classical records next door. You opened the door to our studio, and it was like Animal House,' remembers Noel. 'Smoke billowing out, screaming. We were playing it back extremely loud, and I mean extremely, painfully loud. I think they got a little pissed off with us.'

Next the band and their press outriders went to Ridge Farm, in the Surrey countryside. Here, they experienced different hurdles. 'You were always looking out the window paranoid: "That sheep's got a camera! He's working for the tabloids."'

Light relief was supplied by Liam's wariness of the paranormal.

'If ever we were anywhere remotely spooky, we'd tell Liam the house was haunted,' said Noel. 'We convinced him his bedroom was haunted. When he'd go for his breakfast, someone would go in his room and turn all his pictures back to front or move his bedside lamp across the other side of the room. "You been in my room?" No. "My lamp's in the toilet!" No way.'

In the end, after a visit from the police who were intrigued by the number of media nearby ('Closest I've ever come to shitting myself, watching that police car pull up,' recalled Noel), Oasis left for Beatles producer George Martin's Air Studios in Hampstead. 'I don't know why we went back to London. Probably just because of . . . chaos.'

Back in the capital, work continued with the same modus operandi, Noel remembered. 'In Air, we had this huge desk, the size of Bradford, and then we had a tape machine that couldn't handle the number of tracks. We had to get another tape machine, which is the only time I've ever seen that in the history of music.'

Neither Noel nor Owen Morris, the two men helming the process, look back fondly at the recordings. 'Massive amounts of drugs. Big fights. Bad vibes. Shit recordings,' was Morris's frank appraisal. But the real damage was done in the mix, which Morris describes as 'an utter disgrace'.

Noel agrees. 'Absolutely shocking. Owen mixed *Definitely Maybe* on his own. It's the best mix of those three albums. The second album we did together, I'm flying in on days off from tour: I don't think we're pissed or stoned.'

Be Here Now, though, involved everything you shouldn't do when mixing an album, he admits. He listed those to Keith Cameron: 'It was excruciatingly loud in the studio. There were two tape machines, one of which was not working at any given time. We were both high as kites. We didn't know what we wanted. Subconsciously we didn't believe it was a great album, it was just a case of "will this do?" Really, we shouldn't have mixed it. We should've given it to someone else, someone fresh. It is awful, I have to say. It's terrible.'

In 2023, Noel identified the problem clearly. 'The lesson I learned from it is when you shouldn't be making a record, don't make a record. We went into the studio with a load of songs that weren't good enough for the first two records.'

One song that was good enough for the first two albums was 'My Big Mouth,' though – as proven at Knebworth. Unlike much of the rest of the album, it was also a song with something on its mind, a fact that helped provide its drive. Speaking with Phil Sutcliffe for *Q* in 1997, Noel partly identified what that was.

'*"I ain't never spoke to God/I ain't never been to heaven,"* that's about fans who think you're on the phone to John Lennon and you have all the answers,' he said. 'I understand where it comes from, people meeting their heroes, they talk to you without thinking because they only have a minute.'

There were also a sizeable number of music journalists who imagined the song might be partly aimed in their direction. There certainly wasn't an *NME* writer who didn't hear the magazine's name in the second verse, especially given the paper's occasionally techy relationship with Oasis in the previous year or so . . . *'Around this town, you've ceased to be/That's what you get for sleeping with the enemy.'*

One certainly couldn't blame Noel for returning a little dig, for big mouth striking back. He'd been doing interviews relentlessly for three years. It must have been wearing.

'I'm going into these interviews thinking, *This is it, I'm a fucking rock star*,' he told the *Supersonic* documentary makers. 'And I'm sat opposite a journalist and within thirty seconds I'm thinking, *You're a knobhead*, asking me the same questions a guy asked me two months ago. I get bored quickly and think, *Alright, I'm going to jazz this up and threaten to kill Prince Philip or something*.'

Perhaps the same impulse, to have some fun doing something that was fast becoming gruelling, drove the over-egging of *Be Here Now*. 'I don't like it as a record. But I loved it at the time,' said Noel in 2023. He was left with an overblown piece of work, but it also opened up some of his happiest memories of his band. 'As much as I don't like that period musically, that was the best time Oasis ever had on the road. We had such a laugh. That was when the chaos went up ten notches. It was brilliant.' Given these reminiscences in 2023, about those halcyon days on the road with your family and friends, was 2024's announcement of a reunion tour really a surprise? **TK**

'Magic Pie'

'Being interviewed by *The Sunday Times* today,' wrote Noel Gallagher in his (extremely funny) Oasis tour diary, *Tales from the Middle of Nowhere*, in February 2009. 'Wonder how long it'll take the geezer to mention Tony Blair? 30 mins, I reckon.'

To the more serious, grown-up sections of the British media, Noel Gallagher's most significant act of the nineties was not writing its soundtrack, nor playing its biggest concert, but turning up to a party at No. 10 Downing Street on 30 July 1997. Given that a) Blair was elected Labour leader within a month of *Definitely Maybe* being released, and b) Blair won a historic, landslide election within a month of the feverishly anticipated *Be Here Now* being released, it's not unjustifiable that their respective, meteoric rises are often so inextricably linked. But since that party, pretty much every broadsheet profile of the Oasis leader had included, or at least made mention of, the famous image of him from that day: in one hand a flute of champagne, in the other the hand of the then-just-elected first Labour prime minister since 1979. ('The photograph looks a bit shit, doesn't it?' Noel would later shrug.)

Largely because of its involvement in the USA's 2003 invasion of Iraq, history has not been especially kind to New Labour. At the time, 6–10 million people took to the streets of Britain to protest their country's involvement in it. The infamous 'dodgy dossier' – a report that deliberately exaggerated the nuclear capabilities of Saddam Hussein's regime – became public knowledge very soon afterwards. Many artists had already publicly distanced themselves from Blair, claiming that they knew all along that he was not to be trusted. By 2016, Blair himself was expressing 'more sorrow, regret and apology than you can ever know or believe' about his actions.

Understandably, this would come to overshadow just how exciting and different he and his revamped Labour Party seemed to young people in 1997. Noel Gallagher himself had known nothing but Tory rule since he was twelve years old. A large proportion of Oasis's giant fanbase, meanwhile, could barely even remember Margaret Thatcher being in office, let alone James Callaghan: the last Labour resident of No. 10, ousted in 1979.

And then, suddenly, here was the youngest UK prime minister since 1812: a decidedly unfusty character (43) who played header tennis with footballer Kevin Keegan on TV, presented David Bowie with a lifetime achievement statue at the BRIT Awards and played electric guitar (a decidedly uncool, un-Oasis-y red Fender Stratocaster, but still). Cynical and superficial? Perhaps. But this was a leader who was successfully engaging with young people in a way that would alter the manner in which politics could be conducted forever.

On some of *Definitely Maybe*'s songs – in the lyrics of 'Up in the Sky', 'Bring It on Down' and 'Cigarettes & Alcohol' – there was a sense of raging against an established order that never seemed to offer much to young, working-class people. But nothing overtly political. 'We're overtly political once every five years, when we all go out and vote Labour,' its writer said at the time. 'Then we go back to being in a band again.'

By 1997, of course, Oasis were much, much more than just a band. They were a cultural force of the kind that has not been witnessed since the Sex Pistols. But though Noel may famously have eulogized Tony Blair at the BRIT Awards that year ('Go and shake Tony Blair's hand, he's the man'), on record they continued to never stray directly into politics. And the closest they, and Noel Gallagher, came to an in-song endorsement of New Labour was stealing the line 'There are but a thousand days, preparing for a thousand years' from Blair's party conference speech in 1996 for one of the verses of 'Magic Pie'.

The song's opening line – '*An extraordinary guy can never have an ordinary day*' – is about the ludicrous level of fame that by then was reality for Noel, whose face adorned the front page of at least one British tabloid newspaper every day. '*They are sleeping while they dream and then they wanna be adored*' from the second verse could very well be about the unrealized potential of the Stone Roses, who had slumped to their end in August 1996, just two weeks after their estranged guitarist, John Squire, had passed the torch to Oasis via a guest guitar appearance at Knebworth.

The steal from Blair's speech comes in the third and final verse. At the time – with Google a year away from even being registered as a company – there was no easy way for people to notice such links. Noel Gallagher mentioned it in interviews, but it passed without much comment. Maybe because by that point in the song, anyway, the volume and the quantity of guitars are at such levels that it is barely decipherable.

Following on from a short Mellotron interlude – 'All I did was run my elbows across the keys and this mad jazz came out and everyone laughed', its writer remembered – the sole *Be Here Now* song on which Noel Gallagher would take lead vocals initially offers respite from the onslaught of guitars that characterizes the album's opening two tracks. But not for long. After a low-key, electric piano-backed opening verse with the vocals sung quietly through a lo-fi, radio-style microphone, it explodes without warning into yet more titanic, deafening layers of guitar, and guitar solos, which stay that way for its duration.

So, decades on, the only overt link to Oasis's brief alignment with New Labour in their songs feels well weighted, in that most people will barely even notice that it is there. And for those that do want to remember it, to look back in anger, there will always be that photograph. 'I tell you what New Labour have achieved,' Noel told me in 2006, when I asked him to reflect on those heady days. 'They've destroyed politics in this country. Because I don't know anyone who, next time around, is gonna fucking vote. It means nothing.' HM

'Stand by Me'

There is a vague consensus among some heavy-duty music critics that Britpop died with the release of *Be Here Now*. It was such a colossal weight around the neck of popular music, it's said, that with its release, that jaunty, positive mid-nineties mood darkened. In Britpop's place came paranoid androids and drugs that did not work, that just made you worse . . .

There is a counter-narrative, though, that the day Britpop truly perished and music in the UK entered a new, more introspective and gloomier period from which it would not emerge for several years actually arrived a month after *Be Here Now*, on 31 August 1997. For that was the day that Diana, Princess of Wales, died in a car crash in Paris, after a high-speed chase away from paparazzi.

The national shock felt at the sudden, violent death of this glamorously omnipresent and popular thirty-six-year-old mother should not be underestimated. To live in the immediate aftermath was to enter a cloying, week-long period of national nervous breakdown and mourning. Floral tributes to Diana spread across London, numbering approximately 60 million blooms, with a carpet of flowers flowing for hundreds of metres out from her Kensington Palace home. One bouquet left there in tribute had a card that read 'Live Forever, Noel & Meg Gallagher'.

It's surprising, perhaps, to hear that a confessed staunch republican such as Noel would leave flowers for a member of the royal family. No doubt the then Mr and Mrs Gallagher were swept up in the national mood, but Noel also recognized the circumstances.

'I'm no fan of the royal family or anyone connected with the monarchy in any way, shape or form,' he told a press conference on tour soon after. 'But having been in that type of position myself, been in the back of cars being chased through the streets by paparazzi, I stopped to think about it for maybe half an hour. And I thought, *Well, that could've been me in that car.* I was quite upset about that.'

As far as Noel could estimate, Diana was the most valuable tabloid hide – but he and his brother were also in contention. 'Me and Liam are number two, closely followed by a footballer by the name of Paul Gascoigne. The Spice Girls are up there with us as well.'

At Diana's funeral in Westminster Abbey on 6 September, broadcast live across every TV channel in the UK to a national audience of 35 million and an international audience in the billions, Elton John played a reworked version of his mawkish ballad 'Candle in the Wind' in tribute.

A week later, on 13 September, 'Candle in the Wind' was released as a single, selling 658,000 copies on day one and more than 1.5 million in its first week in the UK. A week after that, on 22 September, Oasis released 'Stand by Me', their second single from *Be Here Now* and the song that had long been earmarked as the album's big hit, the love song that label and management imagined would give the group another 'Wonderwall' moment.

'Candle in the Wind' spent five consecutive weeks at number one in the UK (and fourteen weeks at the top of the US charts), ambushing all of Oasis's well-laid marketing plans, as well as the cultural mood of the nation. 'Stand by Me' was certified gold within a month, selling a huge 600,000 copies – but it had to play second fiddle to 'Candle in the Wind'. It did not rise above number two. Its performance was in some ways a mirror of *Be Here Now* generally, in being an underwhelming, disappointing, enormous success.

As arguably the best song on *Be Here Now*, 'Stand by Me' deserved its stolen 'Wonderwall' moment, but, as with most of the third album, it soon disappeared from the Oasis live set. It's nevertheless one of Noel's most memorable and catchy melodies, 'a bit like "Live Forever" with a touch of "All the Young Dudes"', as he said at the time of release.

While most of the song extols the virtue of solidarity, both romantically and spiritually, in the broadest of terms, the first verse had its roots closer to home. 'It starts, *"Made a meal and threw it up on Sunday"*,' Noel explained. 'When I first moved to London my mam kept on ringing up and asking if I was eating properly. So I tried to cook a Sunday roast and puked up for two days with food poisoning.'

Liam Gallagher was the first to revive 'Stand by Me' after Oasis split, playing it most memorably at his own Knebworth performances in 2022. Noel waited a little longer, but at the Royal Festival Hall for a Paul Weller-curated show in honour of Sir Peter Blake in December 2022, he'd reinvented 'Stand by Me' as a kind of soul-folk song, slow and bluesy with a lovely accompanying electric piano. Its new life continued when he returned to 'Stand by Me' with his High Flying Birds in the spring of 2024. The song had further softened with age, filled with a new longing that had been obscured by the layers of electric guitars on the original. It deserves its new life. TK

'I Hope, I Think, I Know'

Inauspiciously, Noel was as good as disowning 'I Hope, I Think, I Know' before it was even released.

He told *Q* magazine in a track-by-track preview of *Be Here Now* that the only reason it was on the album was for balance, 'as it's quite fast', which didn't read as a ringing endorsement. Noel went on to say that 'I quite liked the demo, but it's too pop for me now.'

Like 'Fade Away', 'I Hope, I Think, I Know' has a touch of Buzzcocks' pop-punk about it, something its writer acknowledged. But he still understandably wasn't having it, nonetheless. It sounded dashed off in '97 and time has not reframed that view. 'I think it's going to be like "Hey Now!" on *Morning Glory*,' he told Q, whetting appetites, 'the one that nobody mentions.' TK

'The Girl in the Dirty Shirt'

Noel Gallagher is always happy to paint himself as a romantic. 'You don't write a song like "Wonderwall" if you're not,' he's said on numerous occasions. This is true: he's authored several unabashed love songs in Oasis, the most explicit being 'She Is Love'. The most directly autobiographical, however, is 'The Girl in the Dirty Shirt', a song released in honour of his new wife Meg Mathews in 1997 that was conceived in the first flush of their romance, during the final month of 1994.

They'd known each other for a little while, as Noel was going out with Meg's flatmate Rebecca de Ruvo, a Swedish MTV presenter. As that relationship started to fizzle out in the early winter of '94, Noel and Meg began hanging out more, partly because Noel needed somewhere to stay when he got back from Europe. His new place wasn't working out and de Ruvo was away, so it was decided he could stay in her room. When Oasis's seemingly endless UK tour kicked off again in December '94, their paths crossed again. Meg was staying with her family in Liverpool and Oasis's last date before Christmas was a hometown show at Manchester Academy, so the pair travelled together to Oasis's next riotous show, at Glasgow Barrowlands on 27 December. Heading back on the coach afterwards, the pair became a couple somewhere between Scotland and London . . .

Two days later, Oasis played their second last gig of the year at Brighton's Exhibition Centre, supported by Ride – featuring Andy Bell on guitar – and The La's, who were making a rare live appearance that super-fans Noel and Liam made sure they watched. In fact, that turned out to be Ride's final UK gig for two decades, as they split the following year – and The La's wouldn't play very regularly either.

Before Oasis took to the stage, Noel grabbed a shower. Returning to his room, he found Meg ironing her shirt, which was dirty, as she hadn't brought any clean clothes. 'What the fuck are you doing ironing a dirty shirt?' he laughed.

'I was so embarrassed,' Meg told Paolo Hewitt in *Getting High*. 'You know what it's like when you don't really know someone.'

Later that night, Noel dedicated a song to 'the girl in the dirty shirt, she knows who she is,' repeating the phrase twice. Afterwards, Noel listened back to Mark Coyle's recording of the gig. *Hmm,* he thought, *'the girl in the dirty shirt' has a good ring to it.* And so he wrote a tribute to his new partner on the back of it, a sweet love shanty that inevitably goes on for a bit too long but features a goofy electric piano break towards its end and adds some unvarnished personality to *Be Here Now*. TK

'Fade In-Out'

The A-list hangers-on had arrived quite soon into the lifespan of Oasis. Even as early as August 1994, prior to the release of *Definitely Maybe*, there was one familiar extra face onboard their tour bus in the shape of Evan Dando – pin-up of the grunge era, bohemian dreamer and the singer and songwriter behind The Lemonheads. At some point that Noel could not remember, Dando and Noel had written a song together, 'Purple Parallelogram,' which he intended to release as a single. Noel heard it, thought it wasn't much cop and didn't want it released with his name underneath.

When Oasis played Slane Castle in the summer of 1995 as support to REM, Johnny Depp was present (at this time pre-*Pirates of the Caribbean*, four years on from *Edward Scissorhands*). Depp was spending a lot of time in the UK because he was dating Kate Moss, and as such had a more visceral sense of what was going on with Oasis than he would have had if he'd just been reading about them in the *Los Angeles Times*. 'What's great about them is they're just completely themselves,' he said. 'They're just honest and themselves, and not particularly concerned about what people think about them. I'd say there's something admirable about that.'

By September, he was (with Moss, who contributes tambourine) adding his not-inconsiderable guitar-playing skills to the version of 'Fade Away' – with Noel on lead vocals, backed by Liam – that featured on the *Help* charity album for War Child. Recorded in one day and released within a week, this version was credited to 'Oasis & Friends.' By December of that year, Depp had convinced Oasis, without friends, to make a surprise appearance at his Hollywood Club, the Viper Room, that ended up being their final show of 1995.

The following May, Noel Gallagher was on holiday in Mustique with Meg Mathews, staying at Mick Jagger's house, where he was also demoing songs for what would become *Be Here Now* (these were serious enough demos to warrant Owen Morris coming out to help). As it so happened, Johnny Depp and Kate Moss were also there at the same time.

'He was staying up the road,' Noel said. 'And we got to the bit in "Fade In-Out" where the slide guitar solo is, and I was playing just a regular guitar solo. And it was rubbish. It was doing me head in. So he came up for a drink. He was sat there and I said, "Can you play slide guitar?" He said, "Yeah," so I gave it to him and he played it. We recorded the one bit that he'd done separately, brought it back to England and played it over the top of the final tune.'

The final tune is quite unlike anything Oasis have done before or since. Instructed by its writer to 'pretend you're a Black man from Memphis,' Liam Gallagher duly obliged with a vocal that is throat-shredding even by his standards ('He couldn't sing for a week after,' remembered Noel). In contrast to the barrage of multi-layered guitar noise that characterizes all the songs previous to it on *Be Here Now*, the first two minutes of 'Fade In-Out' are raw, downbeat blues. Then, out of nowhere – or *'coming in out of nowhere'* as the song has it – there's the sound of Liam and Noel Gallagher primal screaming in unison, before the band crash in. (By the time Oasis came to play 'Fade In-Out' every night on tour, it was a more straight-up electric version, and a highlight of the set.)

'It's going to be weird how that's perceived, having a Hollywood star on the album,' Noel said, immediately prior to the release of *Be Here Now*. It speaks volumes of where Oasis were at and what stars they had become themselves that this fact was barely mentioned. HM

'Don't Go Away'

They say imitation is the greatest form of flattery, and that is certainly one way of looking at it.

Listening to 'Don't Go Away' as part of a radio track-by-track unveiling of *Be Here Now*, Tony Griffiths had a different reaction. 'I punched a hole in the ceiling,' he told the *Behind the Curtain* podcast.

The Real People guitarist and singer had an acknowledged influence on Noel Gallagher's early songwriting, having worked with Oasis at the Real People's Liverpool base before *Definitely Maybe*, adding backing vocals to 'Supersonic', helping to shape 'Columbia' and earning a co-write on 'Rocking Chair'. Hearing the chorus of 'Don't Go Away' for the first time, he couldn't believe his ears, though. It was identical both lyrically and melodically, he believed, to the bridge in the Real People's 'Feel the Pain'.

At the time, this similarity was not apparent to anyone beyond Griffiths' immediate circle, as 'Feel the Pain' was unreleased, a track on the Real People's second album, *Marshmellow Lane*, recorded in 1992 but shelved by their label Columbia. It was self-released in 2012 and the evidence is there for all to hear, word for word.

'Shit happens,' reflected Griffiths in 2024, philosophically. 'What can you do? It breaks your heart, especially that one.'

Shit happens. Had Noel lifted it consciously for the chorus of 'Don't Go Away'? He's never said as much, and he's not normally shy of namechecking influences. There's every chance that he hadn't consciously done so, of course, that as he jammed out the verses to the song, that chorus just presented itself to him from some forgotten vault. Creativity and memory can work mysteriously together.

Besides, the sentiments conveyed by both bands' songs were aimed in different directions. 'Feel the Pain' is a song with a story as old as mankind, about someone breaking up romantically with you. The angst at the core of 'Don't Go Away' is also timeless, but it's existential, essentially about the death of a loved one and specifically about their mother Peggy, who had a health scare while Oasis were on tour. Noel was explicit about this at the time: 'It's a very sad song about not wanting to lose someone close to you.'

'We talked about it a lot, life and death really. Thinking about all our mams passing away,' he said in a 1997 *Q* interview. '"Don't Go Away", that's about my mam.'

Liam also felt the weight of the song. While recording his vocal and fearing he was about to cry, he had to leave the booth to compose himself. Witnesses describe that upon his return, he banged on the window and shouted to Noel in the control room about what a brilliant songwriter he was. He then delivered his vocal in one take, one of his personal favourites. 'I had to go away and sort myself out first,' he recalled.

Peggy's health scare turned out thankfully to be just that, but Bonehead's mother Delia had also suffered medically at the same time, and she sadly died from cancer before *Be Here Now*'s release. The album is consequently dedicated to 'the eternal memory of Delia Arthurs.' 'Bonehead's normally the flag-bearer,' said Owen Morris. 'But he was in a right mess. We were recording "All Around the World" at the time, and it became one for his mum.'

A year after its release, an analysis of 'Don't Go Away' was provided by a surprising listener. In 1998, the highbrow British Conservative philosopher, provocateur and writer Roger Scruton published a much-discussed (in the *Telegraph*, *Times* and *Spectator*, at least) book called *An Intelligent Person's Guide to Modern Culture* – a title that provides some hint of the book's mood – that included a section on Oasis. Scruton wrote dismissively of the band, comparing their output a little unfairly to Beethoven's: '"Be Here Now"! says Oasis. Fine, if you acknowledge the cost. To live properly in the present tense you must be conscious of the past and the future.'

The tension between the past and future, about how understanding both helps one to navigate the present, was something Noel had actually already addressed three songs earlier on *Be Here Now*, in 'I Hope, I Think, I Know'. Perhaps Scruton hadn't played that one, not heard Liam sing, *'The future is mine and it's no disgrace/'Cos in the end, the past means nothing'.*

Scruton, surprisingly, arrowed in on one particular line from 'Don't Go Away' instead: *'Damn my education, I can't find the words to say/About the things caught in my mind'.* Scruton saw this as a gotcha moment for Liam (or, in fact, Noel): 'Trapped in a culture that treats articulate utterance as a capitulation to the adult world, the singer can find no words to express what most deeply concerns him. Something is lacking in his world – but he cannot say what . . . knowing that nothing will be changed for him, that the void will always remain unfilled.'

If given a right-to-reply (not something Boris Johnson's great political hero Scruton was much prone to), Noel might have merely flipped over the single version of 'Don't Go Away' that was released in Japan and pointed to its B-side, a live version of 'Cigarettes & Alcohol'. Noel and Liam Gallagher had long declared their own winning philosophy about how to fill voids. TK

'Be Here Now'

Every night on the tour in support of their third album, the house lights would go down and Oasis's new, garish, elaborate stage set would be revealed: a working bar to the left of the stage, containing not one but two keyboard players; Alan White's drums at the back, housed in a white Rolls-Royce poking out of a swimming pool; a huge clock above that ticked backwards; and, behind Alan White's drums, a slanted red British phone box, out of which the band would emerge, as the toy-keyboard loop that powered 'Be Here Now' (the song) went around and around.

On opening night, there was a problem: no one had been given the very important job of pulling the phone box door open to reveal the band. As the music started up, lighting engineer Bear stepped forward. 'So it was then his job every night,' said Noel. 'And as the tour progresses, he starts getting a bit giddy with the crowd, and we could hear all this, "Whoooooaaa!" In the end he ends up dressed as a fucking ringmaster: we'd gone, "Why don't we get him a fucking top hat, and a thing," and it ends up he's like some mad clown onstage, who did a little routine as the door was opened.'

In 1997, Oasis were at a point – in being not just the biggest band in the world, but the biggest cultural event in the world – that few human beings get to experience. The Beatles' *Magical Mystery Tour*. *The Rolling Stones Rock and Roll Circus*: follies that grew out of their creators reaching a status where they could say, 'What about . . . [insert literally anything]' and ten people would immediately jump to attention and say, 'Yeah, we can make that happen.' If John Lennon could have a dream about being a waiter shovelling spaghetti onto a fat woman's plate and then end up, the very next day, dressed as a waiter shovelling spaghetti onto a fat woman's plate in a film, then why couldn't Oasis have a phone box to come out of that's opened by a clown?

Nobody was saying no. To anything. Least of all to drugs, which may have been a factor here.

Be Here Now was an album born out of this sort of bubble, and its title track reflects this. Copying the formula of the greatest Oasis songs, it offers up one brilliantly quotable line – '*Been kickin' up a storm/From the day that I was born*' in place of '*I need to be myself/I can't be no one else*' – then surrounds it with nonsense poetry ('*Be my magic carpet ride*') and a line featuring a Beatles title ('*Sing a song for me/One from "Let It Be"*'). Digsy makes a second cameo, like a superhero movie fan favourite popping up for one scene near the end. It builds to the same '*Come on, come on, come on . . . yeah, yeah, yeah!*' refrain as 'Columbia'. The toy-keyboard that made the loop belonged to one of Mick Jagger's children: stumbled across by Noel on a beach in Mustique. There's a kazoo. What about if we made the loudest, cocaine-iest album of all time and then put a kazoo on it?

'Yeah, we can make that happen.'

In comparison to a lot of the album, 'Be Here Now' the song is a lot of fun. No, the lyrics are not Noel Gallagher's finest hour. Especially given that at this stage, a year on from Knebworth, it felt like the world was waiting for prophet-level profundity from Oasis. Had this song appeared on a B-side in the whirlwind first eighteen months of their rise, no one would have even noticed the lyrics: especially when sung by a singer with Liam's conviction.

'Be Here Now' made a lot more sense as a pandemonium-inducing live show opener than it did tucked away at the back of the album of the same name, trailing the more overblown, often darker songs that preceded it.

And that was then as far as elaborate stage sets went. 'We had a go at it, with the telephone box on that tour, decided it didn't work and never did it again,' Noel told me years later. 'We know our limits.' **HM**

'All Around the World'

Back in the late summer of 1994, it was still possible to go and watch Oasis perform in the United Kingdom among an audience who had never seen nor even perhaps heard the band before. Such was the case when Oasis played the tent in the early evening of Sunday 31 July at the T in the Park festival, Strathclyde Park, a twenty-minute drive from Glasgow.

You could just wander into the big top, through the gaps in the stationary, curious crowd and position yourself right down the front as the first notes of 'Shakermaker' ushered in their brutally effective nine-song set. A week before the release of third single 'Live Forever', the experience was like watching a trailer for the first year of their career: they'd walked on to blank, hard stares and a few disparate cheers; they left the arena to ecstatic, roaring adulation.

Afterwards, in the bar of the Glasgow Hilton Hotel, Noel enjoyed a G&T while playing down the performance. 'That's nothing. Just you wait.' He explained that his band were not in competition with anybody on the festival bill that weekend, not even headliners Rage Against the Machine, Blur or local heroes Del Amitri. He had his sights on the Rolling Stones, U2 – i.e. the big dogs.

'We're not worried about some student twat in London singing about pantomime horses,' he said, describing Suede. 'We've got a song called "Cigarettes & Alcohol". Wait until the American truck drivers get hold of that. Driving along singing that out the window. Kids buzzing on E to "Live Forever". We're gonna be the biggest band in the world.'

There was more.

'I've got a song,' he continued, leaning in, whispering conspiratorially, 'that's so big I've got to hold it back. It needs orchestras and choirs and all sorts, so it isn't on the first album. I don't think it'll get on the second one, it might get on the third, but probably I'll just hold on for the fourth.'

This seemed very presumptuous talk for a songwriter yet to release any album whatsoever, but Noel's ambition and planning appeared without limit. 'I might just enter it for Eurovision,' he decided, swishing his ice around the glass, 'it's that big. It's like "Let It Be", but twelve minutes long with key changes and all sorts.'

And what was the name of this enormous, multi-purpose future megahit?

'"All Around the World". I've had it a while, but I'm biding my time for when I need to buy my own desert island.'

Indeed, Noel had had 'All Around the World' since the start. He'd written it long before the band were even signed, playing it with Oasis as far back as 1992, when he was still splitting his time between touring as a roadie with Inspiral Carpets and rehearsing with Oasis.

'Bonehead used to ask, "Why aren't we doing that ['All Around the World'] song?"' said Noel twenty years later. 'Number one, it's eleven minutes long. Number two, this is third-album gear. He'd go, "Third album?! We've not even got a manager!" But, you know, I believed, man.'

Gigs in those early days would have setlists that often included other long-life songs that wouldn't appear until well after the debut album, such as 'Hello' and 'Whatever', but 'All Around the World' was born first.

'It was a matter of being able to afford to record it,' said Noel, when it finally made its recorded appearance on *Be Here Now*. Circumstances had changed in the song's favour. 'Now we can get away with a 36-piece orchestra.'

Did 'All Around the World' warrant the five-year wait to be recorded and released? Well, when it became the third single released from *Be Here Now* in January 1998, it peaked at number one on the UK Singles Chart, securing a bunch of first and lasts for Oasis in the process: at nearly ten minutes, it was the longest song to ever be a number one, the longest, too, to earn a Gold certificate. It was also the last single by Oasis to feature the guitar and bass of Bonehead and Guigsy, as they left the following year.

It certainly was a big old bash, with an orchestra, brass section, Mark Feltham's (somewhat unnecessary) harmonica, backing vocals from Gallagher wives Meg Mathews and Pasty Kensit, the former pop singer and now actress, who Liam had met on a plane in '95, married in '97, had a son called Lennon with in '99 and divorced by the end of 2000 – as well as The Verve's Richard Ashcroft. Noel had been correct when he originally compared it to The Beatles' 'Let It Be'; there was a strong resemblance. But it also had the arm-in-arm feel of a charity single, something like 'We Are the World,' in the repetition of the chorus – which is ironic as, many years later, when Noel detailed amusingly exactly why he hates Christmas, that song was a named factor.

Like much of *Be Here Now*, it would've been a more enjoyable listening experience if it had been a significantly shorter song with less layered instrumentation. Noel agrees.

'Coyley and Phil, my old mates in Manchester, they've always said *Be Here Now* is the best album,' said Noel in 2016. 'It was just meant to be played once, on that day, high as a kite, preferably in the park, pissed, then never to be listened to again. Should have put it as a sticker on the front: "Do not listen after 48 hours!" Owen [Morris] and I were just high as kites mixing it.'

Decades later, when doing the commentary for a DVD collection of Oasis videos, Noel discussed the psychedelic, semi-animated nature of 'All Around the World' in brilliant, deadpan self-deprecation. 'This is obviously a parody,' he said as flying saucers orbited a winking Big Ben on the screen, 'it's a parody of . . . a parody of a music video. If anybody's at home listening to this, you'd be advised to go mow the lawn because this goes on for ages and ages. The three key changes, you know, I'm having the scope of it and the sentiment. It sounded great at the time, but it doesn't sound too clever now. *"Pigs won't fly/Never say die".* Fuck me. Why didn't someone stop me?!'

By the end of the song Noel sounded exhausted by it. Even if there were brief moments of it that he enjoyed, there was one thing he'd never forgive himself for about 'All Around the World': 'Robbie Williams based his entire career on this, that's what I hate about it.' TK

'It's Getting Better (Man!!)'

Of the two new songs debuted at Knebworth, 'My Big Mouth' seemed more like where Oasis might be going: an edgy, darker journey into the hollow side of fame. And the other? It was like 'Roll with It' but even more dumb-slash-fun, fully earning the two exclamation marks in its title. 'The big party tune,' as Noel described it, would, with the title track, bring a very excitable end to *Be Here Now*. The opening lines are '*Say something/Shout it from the rooftops of your head/Make it sort of mean something/Make me understand or I'll forget*.' As a document of the lyric-writing process around this era, it's a pretty good one. HM

'All Around the World (Reprise)'

And now, for the listening pleasure of those who did not regard nine minutes and twenty seconds of 'All Around the World' as enough, comes . . . another two minutes of 'All Around the World', with added piccolo trumpet. HM

'Stand by Me'

SINGLE RELEASED 22 SEPTEMBER 1997 (SEE PAGE 182)

'(I Got) The Fever'

B-SIDE OF 'STAND BY ME'

When I interviewed Liam a few months prior to his first solo show, he surprised me when he said that his new band were considering doing '(I Got) The Fever'. 'Nobody will fucking know it's Oasis, eh,' he grinned. Which was true, unlike 'Stay Young' from its predecessor single or 'Going Nowhere' (see below).

It was not to have much of an afterlife having been recorded. A shame: it's a heavy, straight-up rock 'n' roll song with a long, soaring chorus that actually features the word 'soar' and the equal to lots of songs from that era. You can see why Liam was contemplating showing it some love years later. **HM**

'My Sister Lover'

B-SIDE OF 'STAND BY ME'

Demoed by Oasis in 1993, the song 'Lock All the Doors' was never released but remembered fondly by both Gallaghers: Liam revived it for his *Definitely Maybe* anniversary tour in 2024, while prior to that, Noel Gallagher recorded it properly for the second High Flying Birds album, *Chasing Yesterday*, in 2015. Noel's version, though, had a new first verse, the original lyrics having been upcycled in 1996 into 'My Sister Lover'. Musically it's a very different song to 'Lock All the Doors', bouncing along on a 'Digsy's Dinner'-type rhythm, before a moodier bridge in which Liam sings that '*faith in the Lord is something I could never have . . .*' not a line that would have been written in 1993. **HM**

'Going Nowhere'

B-SIDE OF 'STAND BY ME'

'Half the World Away' had made it clear how much of an influence the guy whose portrait was propped up against the sofa in the bottom-left corner of the *Definitely Maybe* sleeve was on Noel Gallagher. While on tour with Oasis in 1995, having been up all night and into the next day at a Los Angeles hotel, Noel had spied one of his songwriting heroes – or was it just someone who looked like one of his songwriting heroes? – walking into the lobby.

There was only one thing for it. Having approached and made certain that it was Burt Bacharach – the 'BB' on the back of his bomber jacket helped with this – they started chatting. Bacharach knew who Noel was by this point. He said he was coming to London soon. Noel said he'd be there. When Bacharach explained that he was using guest vocalists, Noel asked who was singing 'This Guy's in Love with You'. 'Well,' Burt Bacharach replied, 'why don't you do it?'

'And full of lager and cigs and whatever else,' Noel remembered, 'I was like, "No fucking problem, mate! You just call me."'

When that call did actually come through to the Oasis's management office, Noel was less full of Dutch courage. *I can't,* he thought. But after a London hotel meeting with the man himself – during which, with Bacharach at the piano in his suite, the two of them sang the song together – he was in. He made his first ever appearance singing without a guitar ('Like going onstage in your underpants') on stage at the Royal Festival Hall in June 1996, on a night he describes as 'the most stressful of my life'.

Not long after, in a rare quiet moment during the loud and chaotic sessions for *Be Here Now,* Noel and Alan White recorded the basic track for a song Noel had had for over seven years. Another song that, like 'Half the World Away', was about being stuck in a small life and dreaming of living in a big one. *'I'm gonna be a millionaire, so can't you take me there,'* it went, *'I wanna be wild 'cos my life's so tame.'*

In 1997, Noel Gallagher's life was of course far from tame. And he no longer had to dream about being a millionaire. He could afford to give 'Going Nowhere' the full bells-and-whistles Burt Bacharach treatment. So on to the basic track of Alan White's drums and his singing and guitar went French horns and sweeping, cinematic strings. If 'Half the World Away' paid homage to the maestro via its chord sequence, then this soon-to-be B-side of 'Stand by Me' did so in its arrangement.

'Going Nowhere' also continued Noel Gallagher's in-song dalliance with motorcars. Like another of his inspirations, Marc Bolan, he couldn't drive but sure as hell liked cool cars. At the Creation Records Christmas party in 1995, he had been led out of the Halcyon Hotel in London to be shown a chocolate brown 1978 Rolls-Royce that Alan McGee had bought him, as he had promised to do when Oasis got to a certain level. Later he splashed £110k on a revamped 1967 Mark II Jaguar, which, he reckons, 'has got about 12 miles on the clock.'

'*I'm gonna get me a motorcar, maybe a Jaguar*,' he had sung on 'Going Nowhere,' way back in 1990, before he even knew that his younger brother was in a band, let alone joined it. Turned out he was serious about it. **HM**

1998

A former White House intern named Monica Lewinsky signs an affidavit that denies her alleged affair with President Bill Clinton. Dawson's Creek *premieres on US television. Spice Girl Victoria Adams gets engaged to footballer David Beckham. Elton John is knighted by Queen Elizabeth II. Antony Gormley's giant steel sculpture* The Angel of the North *is erected in Gateshead. James Cameron's* Titanic *becomes the first film ever to gross $1 billion. On 14 May, Frank Sinatra passes away at the age of eighty-two. Coldplay release their debut EP,* Safety. *France beat Brazil 3–0 in the FIFA World Cup final, with Zinedine Zidane scoring twice. In August, Clinton is forced to admit he misled America about his relationship with Lewinsky. The first ever episode of* Who Wants to Be a Millionaire? *debuts in the UK, with Chris Tarrant as the host. Britney Spears' debut single, '. . . Baby One More Time', becomes a global number one. In November, Oasis release* The Masterplan, Shakespeare in Love *debuts in New York and Tony Blair becomes the first UK prime minister to address the Parliament of the Republic of Ireland. The Spice Girls score a third successive Christmas number one, their first single without Geri Halliwell.*

Liam Gallagher takes his mother, Peggy, to the Lyceum Theatre, London, for the opening night of Steve Coogan's show *The Man Who Thinks He's It* in September 1998, photographed by Dave Bennett. The first season of *I'm Alan Partridge* was not even a year old.

'All Around the World'

SINGLE RELEASED 12 JANUARY 1998 (SEE PAGE 193)

'The Fame'

B-SIDE OF 'ALL AROUND THE WORLD'

If anyone has ever been in a position to write a song entitled 'The Fame', it is Noel Gallagher in 1996. 'The lyrics go, *"I'm a man of choice/In an old Rolls-Royce/Sat here howling at the moon/Is my happening too deafening for you?"*' he said. 'Me being a sarcastic twat . . . It's about people who say fame's changed us, and us saying, "Well, it wouldn't fuckin' change you, would it? If you lived the life we fuckin' live . . ."' Demoed in Mustique, it was musically too close to 'I Hope, I Think, I Know' to make the cut on *Be Here Now* – not to mention the risk of lyrics like the above featuring on the most anticipated album ever, and thus being reproduced endlessly minus the sarcasm – but found a home as the B-side to the last Oasis number-one single of the twentieth century. **HM**

'Flashbax'

B-SIDE OF 'ALL AROUND THE WORLD'

Hidden in some of the lesser-known *Be Here Now*-era songs are some of the funniest ruminations on superstardom you will find. '*Sitting on a throne will give a bad back to you*,' Noel sings on the chorus of a song that really doesn't sound like it was recorded at the same sessions as its A-side, with just an acoustic guitar and a simple lead electric guitar line. '*In my well-paid opinion, these things they really don't matter*' is also pretty great. **HM**

'Street Fighting Man'

B-SIDE OF 'ALL AROUND THE WORLD'

Throughout the summer of 1997, the illustrious music writer Nick Kent worked on a documentary of Oasis for a French production company.

Although not officially endorsed by Oasis, it had their co-operation. Consequently, all members of the band, as well as Marcus Russell, filed into a Parisian hotel room on 1 July 1997, for separate filmed interviews with Kent, who lives in the French capital. This was partly in recognition of Kent's reputation, forged in the *NME* of the 1970s, for going toe to toe with all the main players of the pre-punk and punk eras. It was also because Kent had lined up filmed interviews with the likes of George Harrison of The Beatles, as well as Mick Jagger and Keith Richards of the Rolling Stones for this Oasis documentary. These were talking heads of an appropriate status to be paying tribute to the Gallaghers. Neither Echobelly nor Shed Seven's input was required.

When the documentary was finished, Noel and Liam Gallagher settled down in a London hotel room to gaze upon Kent's work. Noel had an inkling beforehand about Harrison's lukewarm appraisal because he'd been asked about it by Kent on screen.

'The one who writes the songs, he's OK,' said Harrison. 'But they don't have much depth. The other bloke's just a pain. I don't think they need him. The one who writes the songs, he can sing them just as well.'

Noel defended his brother. 'George Harrison doesn't know Liam because he's never met him. Unless you get to know him, you shouldn't be making statements like that. But we all love you, George. We think you're top!'

This collegiate spirit was not echoed by the other two heavyweights polled by Kent.

'Oasis basically copy Beatles/Stones sixties-ish sort of thing,' wheezed Richards, for whom being interviewed by sartorial disciple

Kent must've appeared like speaking into a smudged mirror. 'I don't think they're anywhere near either of us. I don't listen to them. I just hear them on the radio – I mean, I wouldn't go out and buy that crap! I wish them luck. I have nothing against them. But it's all a blur to me.'

Speaking in flamboyantly accented French, Jagger doubled down on Richards' analysis. 'I've listened to the new Oasis album once or twice. Their thing is quite melodic – but it's not good for dancing, Oasis. I stick on the new Oasis and it's impossible to dance to. *Vraiment!*'

As soon as the film was over, two decisions were made by Oasis and Marcus Russell. One, they would block the film being shown in the UK. Two, they'd record a faithful cover of 'Street Fighting Man' by the Rolling Stones to wind the old goats up.

On 1 November, a new front was opened in this surprising cross-generational rock god war of words. In an interview in the *New Statesman*, Paul McCartney was asked to cast an eye over the current musical landscape. What were his thoughts on those famous fans of his, Oasis? Not much, it seemed.

'They're derivative and they think too much of themselves,' he opened with. 'They mean nothing to me. They're not my problem. Oasis's future is their problem. I sometimes hear their songs and think, "That's OK." But I hope they don't start to believe their own legend. I wish them luck. I don't want to see them as rivals.'

What had riled the mildest of all the middle-aged music legends, McCartney? According to Kent writing in *MOJO*, McCartney had previously sent Liam a copy of *Flaming Pie* and received no reply.

Whatever the truth of that, the publication of the *New Statesman* piece came at an unfortunate moment for the surviving members of The Beatles and the Stones, namely the day that Liam and Noel Gallagher had a full schedule of media duties.

First, the pair journeyed to a Primrose Hill pub near the Creation Records office to be interviewed by Max Bell for *GQ* magazine. Standing on a table, Liam decided to address the remaining members of The Beatles. 'All these old farts, slagging us off . . . we can remember all their shit tunes. "I've Got My Mind Set on You", "When We Was Fab". The quicker they fucking go, the better for everyone. Anyway, John and Ringo were The Beatles. "Isn't It a Pity"? It will be when I meet George Harrison. I'm gonna stand on his head and play golf. I had a dream where I drop-kicked him in the throat, George, and smashed McCartney from here to Jupiter and back. He didn't have his seatbelt on.'

Still aboard the table, Liam then turned his attention to Mick Jagger and Keith Richards. 'Keith, Mick and any other old bag who decides to get out of bed in the morning to slag us off. Dirty old nipple. Sweaty old mushroom. I wanna meet you in the middle of Primrose Hill. Thursday afternoon, twelve o'clock, on the green. I'll hit him with me knob.'

It was only the start of Liam's retribution, however. Later that afternoon, after several more hours in the pub, Liam and Noel made their way over to BBC Radio 1 for an interview with Steve Lamacq on *The Evening Session*. After Lamacq opened the broadcast by gently asking what the pair had been up to, if they'd been working on any new songs, Liam seized control.

'I'm gonna shoot my mouth off here,' he began. 'All these old farts, I'll offer them all out right here on the radio. If they want a fight, be at Primrose Hill, Saturday morning at twelve o'clock. I will beat the living fucking daylight shit out of them, that goes for George, Jagger, Richards and any other cunts that give me shit.'

The next evening, BBC *Newsnight*'s heavyweight anchor Jeremy Paxman delivered a solemn condemnation on TV in his intro to a piece about it. 'Embarrassment and inquests at Broadcasting House, the home of BBC Radio today,' he opened with, 'about how was it that the Gallagher brothers of Oasis were able to spend the best part of an hour sitting in a Radio 1 studio, effing and blinding, praising drugs and threatening violence at eight in the evening. Are these people we want vaunted on the front of magazines as the epitome of cool, new Britain?' But back at *The Evening Session*, Lamacq simply wondered if 'these comments from Keith and George hurt you?'

'No,' replied Noel. 'Because at the end of the day, I still really like their music.'

'We've done a cover of "Street Fighting Man" just to piss them off!' announced Liam.

'Do you have to clear something like that?' asked Lamacq.

'No,' revealed Noel. 'As long as you don't change the arrangement, apparently you don't need permission.'

So that's what Oasis did: they recorded a heavy but faithful version of Brian Jones's final Rolling Stones single, their pumping exhortation to the London kids of 1968 to kick over a few statues. Whether it wound up Jagger and Richards is unknown, but no serious harm was done by this storm in Nick Kent's teacup. Everyone ended up friends.

In 2018, the Rolling Stones posted a photo of themselves arm-in-arm with Liam Gallagher backstage at the London Stadium, thanking him for supporting them at their hometown show.

And in 2021, on Absolute Radio, Noel told a story of meeting Keith Richards on holiday a few years earlier. 'I know all the Stones' kids, they're all Oasis fans. I see Marlon Richards in this hotel in the Bahamas, "Oh, Dad's here, come up to the bar for a drink tonight." I've never met Keith Richards. So . . . I go up to the bar and there is Keith Richards, looking exactly as you would imagine. Marlon goes, "Dad . . ." He turns around' – Noel slips into top-notch Keef here – '"Oh, you're still around, are you?" His second line was, "One thing I always wanted to ask you: who's the bigger cunt, your singer or mine?" I said, "'Well, as your singer wrote some of the greatest lyrics of all time, I'm going to say mine."'

The meeting was a big moment for Noel. 'He was great, such a dude. He kind of reaffirms your faith in meeting your heroes because he's the man. But Mick, Mick's great too. Been to his house a couple of times for parties. He's Mick Jagger. All the stuff about him being a businessman or whatever, that's bollocks. He's one of the Rolling Stones. The end.'

So all's well that ends well, though there was still one barb in the Bahamas between Noel and Richards worth repeating.

'Your band was quite interesting there for a while,' said Keith to Noel, no doubt with a twinkle in his eye.

'I could actually say the same thing about yours,' replied Noel. TK

On the frontline with Oasis #4

An evening at the Aquarium, October 1998

By 1998, four years into the love affair, the relationship between the music press and Oasis had grown stale. Or, rather, we loved them still very much, more than ever possibly. But did they love us, really? Only when it suited them.

Marriage guidance counsellors sometimes talk of a 'push–pull' dynamic, where 'one partner will feel embraced by the other's affection, only for them to become emotionally distant soon after, leaving you bewildered and uncertain.' They pull you in, then they push you out.

Can you guess which party was doing the pushing and pulling at this point? Counsellors also attribute this kind of relationship chiefly to a desire for control. Oasis were entirely in control, the biggest band in the world and a finely tuned business machine: their envoys were always happy to assert authority over the media, dictating all terms of engagement. We took what we could get because, frankly, nobody else sold music papers any more. Oasis did, though, in huge quantities, guaranteeing uplifts in sales that nobody – not Radiohead, not the Beastie Boys, not The Verve, Björk, Foo Fighters nor even U2 – could come close to.

This appeal wasn't rooted in the fact that Oasis sold the most records, though. Those artists were all doing just fine, thank you very much (better than *NME*, that's for sure). The uplift was because Oasis were, and are, the undefeated world champion interviewees across music or any other celebrity, artistic or sporting field. There has never been a more reliably excellent interviewee or subject to profile than Noel and/or Liam Gallagher. Readers knew it.

Writers and editors knew it. Oasis knew it. They were funnier, more open, more anarchic, more confrontational, more cheeky, more photogenic, and often more perceptive than any other star willing to talk to journalists for the cover of magazines or newspapers, for TV, radio, or whatever. This remains the case.

It was becoming a bit boring and repetitive for Oasis by 1998, though. They had done every publication many times over but would invariably keep doing music mags because despite the fact music journalists are, by and large, annoying idiots, we were at least *their* annoying idiots. We liked music. An interview with a music magazine wasn't going to involve someone who knew a couple of the hit singles turning up in yellow trousers and a Barbour and only asking questions about their wives, cocaine and going to meet Tony Blair. Music magazines were still their preferred place of promotion, despite the poor reach, because music would make up at least half the conversation. But Noel and Liam had met all the music journalists they wanted to meet, thanks, especially *NME* journalists, as they disliked the editor and worried that he was next in line to interview them. So, for a few years after *(What's the Story) Morning Glory*?, all *NME* interviews with Oasis were conducted by either Keith Cameron or me, on account of the Oasis camp knowing we'd been around the story from the start, had always written positively about the band and Noel didn't object to our company. I think he may have actually liked and respected Keith, in fact. Now was not the time to befriend new *NME* journalists (that would be after we both left *NME*, when Noel then met Hamish).

Our next go on the Oasis claw machine was just ahead of the release of *The Masterplan*, in October '98, when it was agreed Keith would go and talk through each B-side with Noel. What about pictures, though? Liam was up for those as well. We could, of course, shoot them in a studio, but how many times have we shot Noel and Liam Gallagher in photo studios looking moody? (Did I mention the relationship was getting stale?)

A year earlier, the London Aquarium had opened to local media fanfare. Someone suggested this would be a good backdrop for

Adrian Green to shoot the Gallaghers for our cover, so enquiries were made. The London Aquarium said yes, as long as it was after they were closed. Oasis also said yes, as long as there were no punters around.

I had one more question for Johnny Hopkins.

'Johnny, would it be OK if I come down to the shoot to ask Liam and Noel to pick some records for our Songs in the Key of Life feature? We'll run it in our Christmas issue.'

Silence.

'What do you reckon?'

Silence. Then, 'For the Christmas issue?'

'Yes.'

We had history in this Christmas issue malarkey, of course. 'Not for the cover?'

'No. Should take fifteen minutes.'

More silence. 'I'll ask.'

Ten days later, I walked through Ocean Tunnel halfway around a deserted London Aquarium, towards the sound of flash guns popping, cameras clicking and loud cries of 'fuck' coming from the vicinity between Shipwreck and Coral Kingdom.

'Fucking hell,' said Noel as he saw me. 'What are you doing here?'

I told him the score. 'Are you still doing this for those cunts, then?' he asked.

We both laughed. Liam, dressed entirely in black, hopped down from his perch high against a blue window filled with passing fish. 'I know you,' he told me. 'Where have we met before?'

When they'd finished with the shoot, we strolled back towards Ray Lagoon for our chat, passing through Ocean Tunnel as sharks, rays and turtles glided above our heads.

'I tell you what, this is not making me want to learn to swim,' Noel said.

Liam agreed. 'Reckon it's cold?'

At Ray Lagoon, our Aquarium sherpa offered the chance to find out for ourselves. 'Would you like to give the rays a gentle stroke?' he asked.

Noel and Liam declined in unison. 'Fuck off!'

I put my hand in and gave a ray bit of a rub, looking up to see Noel, who very unusually was wearing white jeans and a kind of chocolate kaftan with white piping, giving me a look that was a mixture of revulsion and concern.

'Should we get on with this?' he said. 'I'm meeting people for food in a bit.'

'Sushi?' asked Liam.

We began the inquisition.

We started off with the first records they could remember (Noel: 'Ticket to Ride'; Liam: 'Peters & Lee, "It Was You Who Tripped Me Up, You Cunt"' – not on streaming services yet), then songs that reminded them of school (Noel: 'Going Underground' by The Jam; Liam: Pink Floyd's 'Another Brick in the Wall').

There had recently been tabloid stories about Liam and wife Patsy Kensit being separated – they divorced just over a year later – so I approached the next two set questions hesitantly.

What was the song you fell in love to?

Noel: 'Erm, not sure about that one . . .'

Liam, however, was very keen to answer this. He grabbed my tape recorder and shouted 'WHICH ONE? THERE WERE SO FUCKING MANY!' into it.

Noel shook his head. 'You'll regret that,' he said. 'Me, I wouldn't like to say. Maybe something like "The Bitterest Pill" by The Jam.'

Liam: 'He's taking the piss out of me now!'

He grabbed my recorder again and shouted into it. '"The Bitterest Morning-After Pill"!'

The next question sat up invitingly. What is your heartbreak song? I asked.

Noel laughed. '"Always Look on the Bright Side of Life",' he decided.

Liam: '"Perfect Day" by whatshisname, Lou Reed.' A beat. Then he asked Noel, 'What does he mean by a heartbreak song?'

Noel: 'A record that reminds you of feeling sad when a bird leaves you.'

Liam: 'It's a "Perfect Day". D'yer geddit? Fancy a pint?'

Noel: 'You're gonna pay for that when this comes out.'

Liam: 'Fucking won't, mate. It's a "Perfect Day", what can I say? That's me heartbreak record. Ask me the next one, you cunt.'

We talked through some more records that meant something to the brothers, tunes attached to seasons and memories, including Liam accidentally saying he liked Dodgy's 'Staying Out for the Summer' (Noel: 'Don't say that!' To me: 'He didn't mean it,') and then making to throw the tape recorder into the ray tank to erase it. I asked which records were guaranteed to clear their tour bus. Noel listed a load of eighties pop groups that he suggested Bonehead was into. Liam also had a contribution.

'I'm going to be a right hard bastard and say anything by fucking Robbie fat-arsed Williams.'

At which he wheeled away across the room shadow-boxing the air and shouting 'WHO FUCKING WANTS IT' in the direction of Ocean Tunnel, to the alarm of our official London Aquarium attaché.

'Tubby-arsed Williams,' Noel agreed, approvingly. 'Not that we've ever played anything by him on the bus.'

Liam: 'If they played anything by Robbie fucking Williams, I'd run off. I'd rather walk. I'd rather be in the trailer. I'd rather trail the trailer.'

This carried on for a while. Eventually, perhaps five minutes later, I asked for the final record on the list: what song would you like played at your funeral?

'"Going Underground," deadpanned Noel, quick as a flash.

'"Natural Mystic" by Bob Marley,' offered Liam, before suddenly grabbing my groin, planting a huge smacker on my cheek and hissing 'Laters!' to me and Noel. He immediately started off towards the exit with his blindsided security in hot pursuit.

Noel offered a hand. 'Nice one,' he said, looking around for his own people, whose voices could be heard in the distance of the Aquarium. 'Until the next time then, eh?'

He set off back towards Ocean Tunnel while I turned in search of a way out to the damp South Bank night, the carnival lights provided by an audience with the Gallaghers extinguished for another couple of years once more.

Smoking through the press conference to announce the departure of Bonehead and Guigsy at Water Rats, London, August 1999, shot by Gareth Davies. 'They've got to be taller than me, have nice taste in shoes and a decent haircut. And not Man United fans. If they can do that, they're sweet,' Liam says of the characteristics sought in replacement members.

2000

With computers not having ended the world on the stroke of midnight, a new millennium begins. With 'The Millennium Prayer' still at number one, Cliff Richard becomes the first artist to have a chart-topping single in six consecutive decades. The PlayStation 2 is released in Japan. Ken Livingstone becomes the first ever mayor of London, and a week later Tate Modern is opened to the public. Eminem releases The Marshall Mathers LP, *and soon after is taken to court by his mother, who is suing him for $10 million. In Scotland, Section 28 – which outlaws the promotion of homosexuality in the United Kingdom – is repealed. Co-hosted by Belgium and the Netherlands, Euro 2000 is won by France. Brad Pitt marries Jennifer Aniston. Two months on from a chaotic Oasis show at the end of July, Wembley Stadium closes after seventy-seven years to be completely rebuilt. The result of the US presidential election contested between Al Gore and George W. Bush is deemed inconclusive. Madonna marries Guy Ritchie. The Millennium Dome in London is shut down, to be transformed from exhibition centre into entertainment complex, renamed the O2 Arena. After a recount in Florida, George W. Bush is declared the 43rd president of the United States.*

Fans gearing up for the first night at Wembley Stadium, July 2000, shot by Patrick Ford. The twenty-first-century Oasis logo on their flag was designed by new member Gem Archer.

'Go Let It Out'

SINGLE

RELEASED 7 FEBRUARY 2000

The film adaptation of Nick Hornby's book *High Fidelity* was released in July 2000, inspired by the cartoonishly snobbish, top-five-list-compiling men (always men) who staffed independent record shops around that time. In one of its most famous scenes, John Cusack's character looks around his store, then whispers smugly to his colleague: 'I will now sell five copies of *The Three EPs* by the Beta Band.' He puts it on. Every head in the store starts gently nodding along to the slow, shuffling groove of lead track 'Dry the Rain.' 'What is this?' one customer pipes up, to the satisfaction of the store owner.

There are not many things that Radiohead and Oasis have in common. But one thing is that, like most in-the-know music fans, they were taken by the Beta Band as soon as *The Three EPs* came out in late 1998. The next year, Noel Gallagher went to see them play at King's College in London, describing the show as 'one of the best I've ever been to.' So, when it came time to record the fourth Oasis album, they were very much at the forefront of his thinking. By the time 'Go Let It Out' was released as the first Oasis single of the twenty-first century, the Beta Band were well on their way to imploding: describing their debut album as 'fucking awful' and taking far too long to make its follow-up. In the meantime, they could at least console themselves with the fact they had been forever immortalized in a Hollywood film and provided direct, blatant inspiration to the biggest band in the UK.

Over a drum loop sampled from Johnny Jenkins' 'I Walk on Gilded Splinters' – a Dr John song sampled by Beck, the Beastie Boys and many others, and covered by Paul Weller – Noel Gallagher strums an acoustic guitar in a manner that bears a striking resemblance to the Beta Band's 'Inner Meet Me.' At the climax of 'Go Let

It Out,' a siren-like one-note guitar solo and then the shriek of a whistle introduce a descending three-chord sequence that recalls the segment of 'Dry the Rain' used in *High Fidelity*, over which Liam, his voice more of a sandblasted treat than ever, sings the final refrain.

Its bouncy bassline, played by Noel, veers close to funky territory. And 'Go Let It Out' also heralds the arrival of an instrument that would go on to characterize the sound of Oasis in the new century: a sixties Mellotron (essentially music's first sampler) that their leader had bought a few years previously. It was one of only six ever made – Paul McCartney owns one, Noel Gallagher owns one, the other four are unaccounted for – and had been used extensively by The Beatles. When pressed, one button on it plays the Spanish guitar intro heard on the White Album at the start of 'The Continuing Story of Bungalow Bill.' Another the 'Strawberry Fields Forever' flutes – which would now underpin the chorus of the new Oasis single.

'Go Let It Out' would go on to be held in high regard by everyone involved in making it. It's one of just a handful of Oasis songs that has been revisited live by both Noel and Liam during their solo careers. On its release, it immediately became the fifth Oasis UK number one, pulling off the trick of sounding both very much like Oasis and yet somehow quite unlike anything else they had ever done before. 'It's the first time we ever got close to the modern-day Beatles, I think, which is what we were striving for for years,' Noel would later reflect. This was exactly what Mark 'Spike' Stent – fresh from making British band Mansun's experimental second album *Six* – was brought in to do on *Standing on the Shoulder of Giants.*

'Hopefully, the new producer will make it sound like it's been recorded in 1999 rather than 1969,' Noel said prior to the recording sessions for the album beginning. 'Again, it could go arse over tit and end up sounding like *Exile on Main Street*.'

By common consent, the fourth Oasis album would end up being a bit of both of these things. But as a taster for what was soon to come, 'Go Let It Out' was an exciting one. It sounded different because everything was different. You only have to look at its video, featuring Oasis playing live on a bandstand as a four-piece – Gem Archer had just joined; Andy Bell was yet to arrive – with Alan White on drums, Noel Gallagher on bass guitar, Gem on guitar and Liam Gallagher strumming an acoustic guitar while he sings. In every conceivable way, the twentieth-century iteration of Oasis had been, five weeks into a new millennium, very much put to bed. **HM**

'Let's All Make Believe'

B-SIDE OF 'GO LET IT OUT'

In 1997, Noel bought 'a big, fucking heavy house' on Steele's Road in plush Belsize Park, north-west London. He named it Supernova Heights and immediately opened the drinks tab in his name. 'The place turned into a night club,' he recalled. 'The bar was always open, the door was always open, there were more people coming and going than I ever knew.'

Supermodel Kate Moss moved in for a bit. 'So much happened there,' Noel's then-wife Meg Mathews said. 'I can still see one of The Charlatans breaking his leg falling down the limestone floating staircase . . .'

No song in the Noel Gallagher songbook says, 'the party is over, everyone out' quite as clearly as 'Let's All Make Believe'. 'Where Did It All Go Wrong?' is also about closing the bar in his Supernova Heights home, but there's the suggestion of romantic turmoil in that song too. 'Let's All Make Believe' is explicit about the need to clear your front room of hangers-on at 4 a.m. – and revoking all future passes too.

It probably didn't happen, but had Noel played the song at any of the gatherings in his home during the high old times there before he sold Supernova Heights in 1999, everyone would've got the message, not matter how clouded their minds. The first two lines lay it on as thickly as tarmac: *'Is anyone here prepared to say/Just what they mean or is it too late?'* And, if that didn't make the message clear, then the chorus is absolutely brutal: *'So let's all make believe that we're still friends and we like each other/Let's all make believe, in the end we're gonna need each other.'*

Of course, it could also most obviously be interpreted as a song about relations within his band, about the changing personnel, as this was released six months after Noel and Liam sat in front of a press conference at the Water Rats, scene of their first London gig five years earlier, to explain that Bonehead and Guigsy had both left Oasis. A few weeks before, Noel had confirmed the Bonehead rumour to *NME*, saying that he had told the band his intentions in March, that he wanted to spend more time with his two kids in Manchester. 'It's hardly Paul McCartney leaving The Beatles,' Noel added.

At the Water Rats on 25 August 1999, the two Gallaghers also revealed that Guigsy was taking permanent leave, having handed his notice in a couple of days earlier. 'They've been mates for fifteen years,' said Noel, 'so it's going to be weird. It's a bit of a bummer, but the show's gotta go on.'

The next year, speaking with *Q*'s Danny Eccleston, a still-bruised Noel lifted the curtain on their departures a bit more. 'I think the way [*Standing on the Shoulder of Giants*] was made did have a lot to do with their dissatisfaction. Maybe they worried they couldn't do it live. What they played wasn't much cop anyway. I haven't spoken to either since the day my manager rang and told me that Bonehead had left.'

Bonehead's statement at the time said he wanted to spend more time at home with his two young children, a position he's never really felt the need to add anything more to. He reunited with Liam to play as a member of his solo band and for the entirety of his *Definitely Maybe* anniversary tour in 2024. Guigsy, meanwhile, has never given an interview about leaving Oasis, becoming something of a recluse. Given, however, that he stepped back from touring for a period in 1995 due to nervous exhaustion, it's perhaps understandable that he chose the start of a fresh album/tour cycle to step back. For both a new-ish father and a worn-out bassist, the prospect of another lengthy world tour in the full glare of Oasis-world may well have seemed less attractive than life back in the slow lane. Neither had envisioned anything remotely as full-time and large-scale when they were rehearsing back at the Boardwalk in 1993.

There's also possibly a message about Liam in the tweaked final chorus of 'Let's All Make Believe', a downbeat rejoinder to 'Acquiesce': *'Let's all make believe, that all mankind's gonna feed our brother/Let's all make believe, that in the end we won't grow old . . .'*

This was a time of turmoil in Noel Gallagher's life, with both his home and workplace in churning flux, but the biggest mystery about 'Let's All Make Believe' is not contained within its lyrics. It's why this sombre torch song was relegated to a B-side. It's an aberration as great as 'The Masterplan' being the support act to 'Wonderwall', but unlike that song this wasn't in competition for an album place against such quite high-calibre material. 'Let's All Make Believe' is equal to anything on *Standing on the Shoulder of Giants*.

This point was reinforced seven years later, when the February 2007 edition of *Q* magazine – then the biggest-selling music magazine in Britain – devoted an issue to its list of 'The 500 Greatest Lost Tracks: The Best Songs You've Never Heard'. There at number one in the poll of *Q* staff and writers was 'Let's All Make Believe', above Dylan, The Beatles, and everyone else. 'Not just one of the best songs Noel Gallagher has written, but also his most revealing,' read the blurb. It went on to declare that, had it been included on *Standing on the Shoulder of Giants*, it 'would've earned the album another star'. Thus making *SOTSOG* a five-out-of-five-star album. In other words: a classic.

Which would have been surprising news to Noel Gallagher, given *Q* magazine's schizophrenic relationship to *Standing on the Shoulders of Giants*. In 2000, its review awarded the album four stars out of five. In 2006, it was placed No. 46 in a magazine poll of 'the 50 worst albums of all time' (all time!), described as the 'low point of their fallow years'. In 2007, the same magazine was, however, saying it was one song away from a classic.

No doubt, Noel found these two extremes both ridiculous. 'I always say journalists aren't the fucking world,' he said a decade later. 'They don't decide – the people decide.'

Nevertheless, his own relationship to *Standing on the Shoulder of Giants* would prove ambivalent, at best, as revealed in the cover interview he gave to *Q* in April 2000, to preview the album's imminent release. 'If this was the last record I was ever gonna make, then I'd be thinking, *Oh dear*,' he revealed. 'In the final analysis, this is just another record by another band in the "O" section – just before The Osmonds.'

The new millennium unveiled a new Noel Gallagher, exhibiting unheard-of self-doubt, unhappy at home and work. This would not stand, as we were soon enough to discover. **TK**

'(As Long as They've Got) Cigarettes in Hell'

B-SIDE OF 'GO LET IT OUT'

The second Oasis song to feature 'cigarettes' in the title was certainly a different vibe to the first. This is Noel Gallagher looking around at life as a very famous, successful person and thinking, *Is this it, then?* Or, as the chorus here says, '*It ain't all that as far as I can tell*'. The same Mellotron flutes that decorate its A-side feature, as does the 'Something in the Air'-inspired descending chords that would fuel a couple more songs from this period. Oh, and the sound of a match being struck, a deep inhale/exhale and some coughing that verges on spluttering and sounds like the product of older lungs than those that made the single 'ahem' cough at the start of 'Cigarettes & Alcohol'. **HM**

Standing on the Shoulder of Giants

(ORIGINAL UK RELEASE: 28 FEBRUARY 2000)

1.	'Fuckin' in the Bushes'	3:18
2.	'Go Let It Out'	4:38
3.	'Who Feels Love?'	5:44
4.	'Put Yer Money Where Yer Mouth Is'	4:27
5.	'Little James'	4:15
6.	'Gas Panic!'	6:08
7.	'Where Did It All Go Wrong?'	4:26
8.	'Sunday Morning Call'	5:12
9.	'I Can See a Liar'	3:12
10.	'Roll It Over'	6:31

Written by Noel Gallagher (Tracks 1–4, 6–10) and Liam Gallagher (Track 5)

Producers: Mark 'Spike' Stent, Noel Gallagher

Bass guitar (Tracks 3, 6, 9, 10): Paul Stacey

Keyboards, additional guitar (Track 1): Paul Stacey

Sitar and 12-string acoustic guitar (Track 5): Mark Coyle

Harmonica (Track 6): Mark Feltham

Flute (Track 5): Charlotte Glasson

Recorded at Wheeler End, Olympic Studio, Supernova Heights, England and Château de la Colle Noire, France, between April 1999 and August 1999

'Fuckin' in the Bushes' contains samples from Murray Lerner's film *Message to Love: Isle of Wight 1970*. Used courtesy of Castle Music Pictures / Pulsar Productions. 'Go Let It Out' contains elements from 'I Walk on Gilded Splinters' performed by Johnny Jenkins. Used courtesy of Mercury Records under licence from Universal Music Special Markets, Inc.

'Fuckin' in the Bushes'

'To tell you the truth,' said Liam Gallagher in January 2000, 'I wanted to come back with "Fuckin' in the Bushes".'

In 2024, the idea of Oasis introducing their fourth album with an instrumental single – a single, in other words, without vocals from either Liam or Noel Gallagher – might seem, to use a phrase that did not exist at the turn of the millennium, batshit crazy. But in 2000? Not so much. *NME*'s single of 1999 had been Aphex Twin's vocal-less 'Windowlicker'. Prior to that, in 1996, there had been Underworld's pretty-much-instrumental 'Born Slippy': a huge hit that, in a totally different way, encapsulates the hedonistic mood of the nineties as much as 'Champagne Supernova'.

Primal Scream had trailed their 1997 album *Vanishing Point* with 'Kowalski', a song that, like 'Loaded', was based around sampled speeches with only flashes of vocals from Bobby Gillespie.

And the same year, the Chemical Brothers had their second number one with 'Block Rockin' Beats' – featuring just one line of a Schoolly D rap. It followed on from the noisy, abrasive 'Setting Sun', which was co-written and sung by Noel Gallagher. 'Hearing that first version on cassette,' Noel remembered much later, 'I would never in a million years have thought it would get to number one. Fucking no chance.'

Having a vocal sung by someone who had headlined Knebworth just six weeks before release definitely helped its chances. But 'Setting Sun' was a good example of the way that huge bands and superstar DJs were interacting around this time. The Chemical Brothers' Sunday Social nights at the Albany on London's Great Portland Street were regularly attended by the likes of Paul Weller, The Charlatans' Tim Burgess, Noel and lots of music heads who had come of age with *Screamadelica* and its breaking down of the boundaries between genres.

Although he'd been pegged by his detractors as a guitars-only-please luddite, Noel Gallagher was happily participating in this scene. In 1996, he remixed Beck's 'Devils Haircut', turning its slinky disco groove down and its distorted riff all the way up. The next year he was adding discordant guitar to drum 'n' bass pioneer Goldie's massively anticipated 'Temper, Temper'. In 1997, he was sampling the drums from Dr. Dre and Ice Cube's 'Natural Born Killaz' to build an instrumental titled 'Teotihuacan' that would be used on the soundtrack of *The X-Files* film, and much later form the basis of the 2004 single he wrote with Ian Brown, 'Keep What Ya Got'.

And then the year after that came 'The Knock (On Effect)': a remix he did for Unkle that took their original, added some drums from actual Led Zeppelin, plus a riff inspired by Led Zeppelin, and in the process provided the starting point for 'Fuckin' in the Bushes'.

After Oasis's imperial phase – 1995 to 1997 – two things were happening. The charts were being oversaturated with a third (or even fourth) wave of major-record-label-sanctioned guitar bands who, to be polite about it, were not very good. As is usually the case when something as radical-sounding as *Definitely Maybe* becomes a hit, the copycats had come in and made people bored. The new radical – not to be confused with the dire New Radicals – was coming from albums like DJ Shadow's *Entroducing* in 1996: the first record to be made up entirely of samples. It followed the likes of Massive Attack's *Protection* (1994), Tricky's *Maxinquaye* (1995) and plenty of other albums that no home you would want to go back to after hours seemed to be without in the twentieth century's last few years. Sampling was everywhere, and more and more bands were starting to dip their toe in the water: even if only to differentiate themselves from the dross that was straight-up guitar music at that time.

Prior to 1998, there was no way drum loops or samples would have been permitted on an Oasis album. There had in fact been a sample of NWA on 'D'You Know What I Mean?', but it was buried so deep beneath everything else that nobody noticed. But now Noel had a home studio in Supernova Heights and, having booted out the 24-hour Party People who had taken up permanent residence, had time to use it. It was here that he worked on the remix for Unkle, with the help of a multi-instrumentalist friend. Paul 'Strangeboy' Stacey had become the first extra musician to ever appear onstage with Oasis during the Be Here Now Tour, playing keyboards and triggering loops.

'We had a bit of downtime in the studio,' Noel remembered, 'so while we had the computers out . . . I sampled up this drum loop that I'd always liked, and then . . . we were just messing about really, and it just developed from there.'

The drum loop was the intro to Jimi Hendrix's 'Little Miss Lover'. Over the top, Noel played a riff that – like the one he'd just put on 'The Knock (On Effect)' – sounded like Led Zeppelin, but this time more direct and 'Immigrant Song'-y. Stacey added some further bits of lead guitar, and then, at a later date, some samples from the *Message to Love: The Isle of Wight Festival* documentary.

'We used to laugh at some of the characters in the film, so we sampled them,' said Noel. 'The beginning bit is the promoter, moaning at all the hippies who were kicking down the perimeter fencing. The little old lady you hear at the end is some eccentric toff who just gets right into the weekend and smokes pot, so she obviously loses the plot. It's the most radical track [on the album]. I imagine when people hear it for the first time, they'll go: "What the fucking hell have these lads been up to the last three years?"'

As it turned out, 'Fuckin' in the Bushes' instantaneously connected. With a new drum track recorded by Alan White – engineered to sound both metallic and titanic, the best-sounding drums they would ever have – it would remain Oasis's intro music at every single show from there on in, right up until the end, its first snare crash firing the starting pistol on the glorious, unhinged bedlam that would ensue in front of them each night.

'I fucking love it, man,' said Liam Gallagher in the same interview in which he suggested the song on which he did not appear at all might have made a single. 'It's just fucking rocking, man. You ain't gonna get a better rocker that that. That, right, to me, is the ultimate fucking rock 'n' roll song . . . me personally, I'll die happy being involved with a song like that. It's just fucking mental. It's rocking, man. I love it.' **HM**

'Go Let It Out'

SINGLE RELEASED 7 FEBRUARY 2000 (SEE PAGE 217)

'Who Feels Love?'

As the Be Here Now Tour came to a close in early 1998, Oasis finally took the year off that they would later reflect should have happened after Knebworth. 'I was trying to get out of the party party mode,' Noel said of this time. 'So I got a few bits and pieces, threw them in a bag, got my guitar, picked up the wife off the kitchen floor, got in a taxi, went to the airport and then to Thailand for about a month.'

'Who Feels Love?' would result from this trip. 'There was all these monks hanging out,' its writer remembered, 'and we ended up going around all these little villages, met some great spiritual people. Not that I think I'm affected by that in any kind of way, but it was a sense of well-being on my behalf one morning. The sun was shining and there was lots of animals knocking about.' Good, peaceful vibes in other words.

You would not have found the Oasis of previous years singing lines like *'My spirit has been purified'* or *'Now there's a million years between my fantasies and fears.'* Nor would you have encountered them using unorthodox tunings (open-G, if you must know) or tablas or sitar drones. Lots of people baulked at the idea of them sounding like this and, though 'Who Feels Love?' took pride of place as the second song in the set for the tour that followed, it was not a vibe that they would revisit. But, as a moment in time, it is fine. **HM**

'Put Yer Money Where Yer Mouth Is'

Noel Gallagher was quick – perhaps too quick given that people had only just bought it – to say that there are two 'shit' tracks on *Standing on the Shoulder of Giants*. The second was 'I Can See a Liar', which may include a rhyme with 'fire' in its chorus, but does at least have a chorus. 'Put Yer Money Where Yer Mouth Is' does not. Noel's assertion that it 'could have been better explored' was right: it's a decent verse – a more metallic take on The Doors' 'Roadhouse Blues' – with a fiery Liam vocal that just . . . doesn't go anywhere much after that, other than into some T. Rex-style 'aaaah's (courtesy of the legendary soul singer P. P. Arnold). Maybe it would have benefitted from being worked on by a full band, rather than being pieced together by writer and producer. **HM**

'Little James'

'I can write better tunes than our kid, no problem,' said Liam Gallagher at some point during Oasis's rise during the nineties. 'But right now I'm too busy getting off my cake.'

You can see why the younger Gallagher brother might have imagined the process of creating a song to be effortless. This, after all, was a kid who, in his early twenties, had watched the person he used to share a bedroom with bash out 'Supersonic' in the time it took for him and the rest of Oasis to nip out for a Chinese takeaway. Who had sat there, open-mouthed, as his brother premiered 'Live Forever' to him and his bandmates on acoustic guitar. Who knew, before anyone, about the seemingly endless stockpile of songs that Noel Gallagher was drawing from even as Oasis began recording their third album. Or even, in the case of 'Lock All the Doors', that Noel Gallagher was still drawing from as he was making his second solo album.

Prior to Noel joining the band in 1991, writing songs for Oasis had been the responsibility of Liam and Bonehead. The best of these is probably 'Take Me', a Stone Roses groove that has a great verse melody but never really progresses from there. Noel Gallagher would later say that he wanted to try recording and releasing it at some point, but it never happened. As a new millennium began, every song ever officially released by Oasis was credited to Noel Gallagher. There was, though, a fair bit of excitement at the prospect of Liam writing something: due mainly to his interviews, in which he came across as someone with a unique, different kind of brain and a way with a psychedelic, surrealist turn of phrase. When asked, for example, whether Oasis would have ever been successful without Noel, he replied: 'That's like asking, "Would Jesus have been a fucking pervert if he'd had a crisp packet on his head".'

Liam Gallagher was also not 'too busy getting off my cake'. He was living in London with actress Patsy Kensit, then pregnant with his first child, who he had married in April 1997, having met her two years earlier on a plane at the height of Oasis. (It was her jumper that he wore onstage for the second night at Knebworth, having forgotten to bring a change of clothes.)

In his last major interview of the nineties, with *Q* magazine, he presented a much calmer, more serene image of himself than the public was used to. Drinking only Red Bull, he detailed a daily routine of sobriety. 'A normal day? Get up about seven o'clock now. Downstairs, feed me cats. Then chase them around the home. I do that for about an hour.' In the evenings, he would eat dinner ('Chinese, normally'), play his guitar in the garden ('do the neighbours' heads in'), then watch films ('a western') and always be in bed by 10 p.m.

In between, Kensit's son would get up. Liam was enjoying spending time with him, 'watching cartoons, having a fight over the TV.' It would be James who would inspire, via those guitar-playing sessions in the garden, the first song on an Oasis album not credited to Noel Gallagher.

Liam claimed that 'Little James' took him all of three minutes to compose and, in the sweetest possible way, it sounds like it.

A simple, spontaneous lullaby over three chords, its lyrics – '*Live for your toys/Even though they make noise*' – would come in for some stick. But as pointed out by Ocean Colour Scene's Steve Cradock – who helped Liam demo the song – 'it's a song about and for a six-year-old child.' Cradock, along with Paul Weller, would hear the song before Noel did, Liam's thinking being that if his brother heard from other musicians he respected that it was a decent effort then he would be more inclined to take it seriously. This tactic worked. Noel approved of 'Little James' and it made it onto the fourth Oasis album. 'That's good for me, it gives me confidence,' Liam said. 'But I've got a lot to learn.' Thereafter, every Oasis album would feature at least three Liam-written songs, two of which ('Songbird' and 'I'm Outta Time') would also end up being released as singles.

Much, much later in 2017, when he was readying his first solo album for release, I asked Liam Gallagher why he felt he had to utilize professional songwriters. 'I class myself as a rock 'n' roll singer who writes the odd tune every now and again,' he shrugged. 'Ideally, you want to do it yourself. But I can't write those fucking big songs. I'm limited. My verses are up there, but I just can't do that next bit.'

This analysis is exactly right. Liam Gallagher's songs are generally short, sharp little curios that don't stick to conventional structures, that change all the time and are gone before you know it. No, they are not going to have entire stadiums with their arms aloft in the way that his brother's finest moments do. But they added a texture to Oasis albums that was not there before. 'Little James' was not his finest song, but it was an important step: marking the point at which Liam Gallagher got on his way as a writer and the dynamic within Oasis changed forever. **HM**

'Gas Panic!'

Noel Gallagher gave up drugs, forever, in the summer of 1998. No expensive stint in a rehab facility, no to-this-day-still course of therapy. No NA meetings for NG: just one final line sniffed in the basement of Supernova Heights, one last headache, one last look around at all manner of hangers-on he could not have named, and that was that. *Fuck this*, he thought, then moved to the countryside.

Not everybody has the character to do that. Certainly, as even a quick skim of the history of rock 'n' roll will make clear, plenty of no-longer-poor musicians with lots of free time and plenty of enthusiastic enablers around them have failed to do so. But even after a run that would put a large proportion of them to shame, Noel Gallagher managed it: immediately and seemingly without any fuss whatsoever.

Easy as it may outwardly have seemed, however, there had been the dark nights of the soul and the peeking-through-the-keyhole paranoia that come to anybody who takes it that far. You only have to listen to 'Gas Panic!' to hear that. The best song on *Standing on the Shoulder of Giants* is a bleak, ominous groove over which Liam Gallagher sings of '*sailing on a sea of sweat on a stormy night*'. His '*eyes are dead and my throat's like a burnt-out hole*.'

The lyrics to 'Gas Panic!' are some of the finest that Noel Gallagher has ever written. In his earliest, written-pre-Oasis lyrics, there had been flashes of this side of his head (such as '*I can feel the warning signs, running around my mind*' from 'Half the World Away'). Once they got moving, though, he knew what was needed were songs that encapsulated the excitement of dreams being realized, of rock 'n' roll fantasy, of the party that never ended. The party had for a long time seemed like it would never end. But now it was very evidently over.

The music of that era was often like this. Radiohead's *OK Computer* had arrived just a few months before *Be Here Now* in

1997 and by a year later many up-and-coming artists were citing it as their key inspiration. 'Gas Panic!' is quite close, in both sound and theme, to that album's 'Climbing up the Walls'.

One thing is for certain: there's no way that the earliest incarnation of Oasis could have played music like this anyway. The bass playing – by long-term associate Paul Stacey, in the period between Guigsy departing and Andy Bell arriving – is more complex than anything that had previously featured on an Oasis song: Led Zeppelin-esque runs that dance around the singing in the way that the lead guitar once would have.

The guitar playing, by contrast, is kept simple and abrasive, a two-note wah-wah solo adding to the powerful sense of dread.

'Roll with It', it is not. Oasis's very own 'Gimme Shelter', it is a hymn to the price that must be paid by anyone who lives the rock 'n' roll dream to its limits. HM

'Where Did It All Go Wrong?'

The Northern Irish footballer George Best was the most gifted British player of the 1960s, a skilful instrument of incredible flair and balance used by Manchester United to ruthlessly unlock defences and win trophies. But by the 1970s his career was nose-diving, wrecked by an insatiable love of wine, women and all the rest. His star had been in freefall for a few years, but by the end of 1973 he was heading swiftly for rock bottom: suspended by United and on the transfer list, he went missing. There's a possibly apocryphal tale that Best related about this period that takes place the morning after he'd had a very successful night on the roulette wheel in his Spanish hotel.

Bringing a room service breakfast up to Best, the bell boy read on the tray an outraged front-page tabloid headline demanding to know why George Best had squandered his talent and wrecked his career. The bell boy knocks on the door and is told to enter; it's open. Lying on the bed is a topless George Best, the current Miss

World in a similar state of undress draped across his chest and £15,000 in winnings strewn all around.

Taking in the scene, the bell boy asks, 'So, Mr Best, where did it all go wrong?'

Noel Gallagher knew exactly how George Best felt in the Spanish hotel bed: he used that pay-off for the title of this song, but 'where did it all go wrong' was not the punchline to an anecdote he wanted to regale chums with at the bar. It was the reason he wanted to close the bar.

As he always says, Noel Gallagher's best songs fall from the sky almost fully formed. But perhaps what he really means is that they come from somewhere real inside, that they flow most easily up from his subconscious. 'Where Did It All Go Wrong?' is one of his better songs and definitely comes from somewhere real.

In 1998, Noel returned from touring to Supernova Heights bereft of songs for the first time since Oasis formed. This made no noticeable difference to the entertainment schedule in his home. Most days he'd rise at three in the afternoon and wonder who these people sitting in his front room with the curtains closed were.

'It was, "Hello, who the fuck are you?" he told *Q*. 'That wanker DJ, Sasha, said the scene round my house was seedy. Well, I didn't see him complaining at the time.'

All of which was a good enough reason to quit drugs, as detailed in 'Gas Panic!'. 'I'd wake up in the night sweating, feeling like I was going to die. It was a dark time for me because I'd just started writing a record, but I was not feeling 100 per cent about myself. All the people around me were still doing loads of drugs.'

This scene was what Noel was writing about in the richly melodic, organ-driven 'Where Did It All Go Wrong?', specifically the line *'Do you keep the receipts/For the friends that you buy.'* Noel later said that he sang it rather than Liam because Liam struggled with the higher register of it, but this was also probably a song he had to sing. It's as close as he comes to soulful confession.

'Supernova Heights was great for the time, but then there came a point when I thought, *I need to get out of this*,' Noel explained to the *Belfast Telegraph* in 2019.

So Noel 'said to the wife, "Get your gear. Put it in the fucking car. We're leaving. The bar's shut."'

The plan was to move away from London, to the quiet of the green belt and write music, get to know his wife. 'I met her five, six years ago and I was whacked out of my head on drugs,' he said in 2000 about rural life in Chalfont St Giles, Buckinghamshire. 'So it's reacquainting yourself with yourself and the missus. It's quite nice.'

It didn't last. Soon enough, the people he'd hoped to leave back at Supernova Heights found their way to him again. 'Unfortunately, the party followed me out to the country,' he said in 2019. 'And what happened then is, they would just stay forever. It was at that point where I was, "I need to get rid of all these people".'

Getting to know his wife properly again had been disappointing. By 2001, he was divorced from Meg Mathews, but first he needed a way to clear the slate. Meeting music publicist Sara MacDonald at Space in Ibiza opened that path.

'Within two months of having that thought – *They've all got to go* – I'm thinking, *How do I do it? What do I do?* I met Sara, and that was the catalyst for everything. I was just like, "Well, I'll run away with her, then. That's what I'll do" And that's what I did.'

This is the origin of 'Where Did It Go Wrong?': the desperate need to shake off the people doing drugs in his living room.

'I didn't see those people for a good five or six years,' he said in 2019. 'We've since all reacquainted and become friends again. We were all too up in each other's faces twenty-four hours a day. I had [Supernova Heights] for two and a half years and it felt like I lived in there for a lifetime.' TK

'Sunday Morning Call'

More than once, around the time of its release, Liam Gallagher described the third and final single from *Standing on the Shoulder of Giants* as 'my favourite on the album . . . even though I don't sing on it.'

Not for the first or last time, the person who did sing it disagreed with his brother.

'What's the next one?' Noel Gallagher asked, as the video for 'Sunday Morning Call' was queued up for him to provide commentary over. 'Ah, fucking hell. I fucking hate this next tune. I really fucking hate it.' As the video cuts to him strumming its two-chord intro on an acoustic guitar, he just omits a deep, long sigh.

His hatred for the song was real: so much so that, when it came time to compile the first, complete Oasis singles collection – *Time Flies: 1994–2009* – every single single, as you would expect, is included . . . except for one. Anyone who bought the album hoping to hear 'Sunday Morning Call' would have to wait until two minutes after its final song, 'Falling Down,' had concluded. Only then, as an uncredited, secret track, would its very sad-sounding chords quietly start up.

Describing it – along with 'Where Did It All Go Wrong?' – as 'about certain real people who I know but who, obviously, remain nameless,' you can understand why Noel Gallagher doesn't remember 'Sunday Morning Call' or the time in which he wrote it with much fondness. Written when he was in the process of turning his back on the 24-hour Party People lifestyle, its still-nameless character is someone who wants to leave, but is still putting in the ungodly-hours calls and 'running you through their drug and booze hell, and they ultimately think that to sort all this out, they just write a cheque made payable to The Priory clinic, and six weeks later, everyone's going to come up smelling of roses.' What else can you say during such calls other than 'It's OK . . . it's alright' – as the refrain does here – even though you know what you say won't be remembered, and you just want it to be over?

Before 'Sunday Morning Call' was even released as a single in the summer of 2000, it had been retired from live performance, never to be heard of again by anyone other than the people who let their greatest hits collections play on after they have concluded. **HM**

'I Can See a Liar'

Even in the month before Oasis's fourth album came out, Noel Gallagher was telling interviewers he thought there were two songs on it that he didn't rate, no doubt delighting those tasked with publicizing *Standing on the Shoulder of Giants.*

'"Put Yer Money Where Yer Mouth Is" and "I Can See a Liar" – I was just messing about with the riffs in the studio,' he said ahead of release, in February 2000. 'But they sort of stuck.'

He was particularly down on the punchy 'I Can See a Liar'. 'I personally wouldn't have put that on the album. But Liam was like, "It's the fucking Sex Pistols, we've got to have some fast ones on there because it's a bit medium-paced," and I was like, "Fair enough."'

In the back of his mind Noel knew that 'Let's All Make Believe' would be relegated to a B-side by the inclusion of 'I Can See a Liar', because if his brother thought the album a touch slow then the pace would not be quickened with 'Let's All Make Believe'. 'There's a couple of songs that got shunted off onto B-sides of singles that should have gone on the album, but it's either the singer sulking or, you know, have some semblance of fucking normality in the studio – you've got to weigh up which one's better than the other. It's better not to have a singer sulking.'

By the time *Q* had him on their cover in late March 2000, a month after the album came out, Noel was happy to underline just which were 'the two shit tracks'. 'We weren't even gonna put "I Can See a Liar" on the album,' he said, just in case you hadn't got the message clearly enough, 'but Liam threw one of his bottom-lip fits.'

Readers of *Q* magazine domiciled in the United States would have been surprised, therefore, when on the night of 5 May 2000 they settled down to watch CBS's *Late Show with David Letterman*. That evening's musical entertainment was provided all the way from Manchester, England, by Oasis, and which song did the band – including Gem Archer and Andy Bell for their US TV debuts with Oasis – choose to perform? Not 'Where Did It All Go Wrong?', which just a month earlier had been released as a US-only single. No, they went with 'I Can See a Liar', Liam in a long Burberry mac, Noel in double denim, and the apparently 'shit song' standing on its two feet nicely, a snarling barb aimed at someone who no doubt suspected it might have been about them all along. It was the sixth time that 'I Can See a Liar' had been performed live by Oasis. It was also the last. **TK**

'Roll It Over'

On 3 and 4 June 2022, Liam Gallagher would make a triumphant return to Knebworth, playing to 170,000 people over two nights. (Unlike the first time, he remembered that there was a second show to do.) During the previous five years, he had made a point of digging deep into his former band's catalogue – often having consulted with fans on Twitter – and playing stuff far beyond the hits. The likes of 'Headshrinker' and 'Listen Up' had been revived and then, at his biggest ever show, it was the turn of 'Roll It Over': a song that Oasis had never played live.

'This is for all the old-school Oasis fans,' he announced before performing it. 'You should remember it.'

It's fair to say that *Standing on the Shoulder of Giants* is not fondly remembered by many. It is an album that represents a transitional phase for Oasis. It didn't sell in anything like the quantities that its three predecessors did. Coming between the departure of

Bonehead and Guigsy and the arrival of Gem and Andy, it's a record made largely by Liam, Alan White and Noel only (with a little help from Noel's friends). Its best moments – 'Go Let It Out', 'Gas Panic!' – are built around drum loops: something that wouldn't happen again. Very few of its songs sound like they are being played live in a room by a band. But 'Roll It Over' is the exception to this. Somehow, it reaches a kind of Pink Floyd epic-ness, the drums building to a crescendo and all manner of guitar parts jangling around it. It is like a less celebratory, more downbeat 'Champagne Supernova'.

As a document of how Noel Gallagher was feeling at this point, it could hardly be more explicit. '*Look around at all the plastic people, who live without a care*,' Liam sings in the second verse. '*They try to come and sit around my table, but never bring a chair*.' Five years on from moving to London and inviting the beautiful people back for a party that seemed like it would never end, the lights had gone up and their complexions had been revealed. **HM**

'Who Feels Love?'

SINGLE RELEASED 17 APRIL 2000 (SEE PAGE 227)

'One Way Road'

B-SIDE OF 'WHO FEELS LOVE?'

The collaboration between Paul Weller and Oasis did not end with 'Champagne Supernova'. Far from it. In the time between that and the release of 2008's 'Echoes Round the Sun', the first song credited to both Paul Weller and Noel Gallagher – 'We'd been trying to write something together for years,' said the latter – there had been plenty of guesting at each other's shows.

The year before Weller had released 'Echoes . . .', Noel had in fact covered one of The Jam's songs for the first time, with a little help from its writer. At a Teenage Cancer Trust show at the Royal Albert Hall, they duetted on a Jam B-side called 'The Butterfly Collector'. The Jam had a very similar attitude to B-sides as Oasis, i.e. you might as well just make them amazing.

Weller, though, had got there with this style of compliment a bit earlier, his first and only Oasis cover being recorded in 2003 as part of his *Studio 150* album of songs by his key musical influences. 'One Way Road' is the only song on the record that is written by someone younger than him. It is also a B-side but, by virtue of arriving after *The Masterplan* was compiled, not an especially well-known one.

Even in the *Standing on the Shoulder ...* era, Noel was still somehow assigning songs to B-sides that were the equal of their A-side. Or, in the case of 'One Way Road', which featured on the 'Who Feels Love?' single, far, far superior. You can see why Weller chose it above any other Oasis song: like his own 'Standing Out in the Universe', it nods (albeit far less blatantly) to the classic Thunderclap Newman post-hippy 1969 anthem 'Something in the Air', by way of 'Everybody Knows This Is Nowhere'-era Neil Young. It says what Noel was trying to say on the *Standing on the Shoulder of Giants* songs with his vocals, but in a much more understated way. Unlike many of that album's songs, 'One Way Road' was played live years after the dust had settled on that era of Oasis: a sign of how fondly Noel Gallagher – not to mention Paul Weller – thinks of it. **HM**

'Helter Skelter'

B-SIDE OF 'WHO FEELS LOVE?'

After just a couple of weeks' rehearsal, Gem Archer and Andy Bell had played their first Oasis show in December 1999 at a festival in Philadelphia. For that and the short run of US dates that followed, Oasis played just a thirty-minute set: Liam singing four songs before departing to leave Noel and the new-look Oasis to blast through a version of The Beatles' 'Helter Skelter' that bore a resemblance to the U2 version that featured on *Rattle and Hum*. The new members had been able to show off a bit on the opening 'Cigarettes & Alcohol' as it segued into a jam based on Led Zeppelin's 'Whole Lotta Love'. And when it came to the finale, Noel could focus on singing while Gem handled lead guitar and Andy played a dextrous bassline that would have been beyond Guigsy. The cover was phased out of the set by the time Oasis made their way into UK stadiums in 2000 – replaced by a version of Neil Young's 'Hey Hey, My My', also sung by Noel – but it was recorded live in Milwaukee that April: the first Oasis recording to feature Gem Archer and Andy Bell. HM

'Sunday Morning Call'

SINGLE RELEASED 3 JULY 2000 (SEE PAGE 235)

'Carry Us All'

B-SIDE OF 'SUNDAY MORNING CALL'

The B-side of the least well regarded Oasis single ever – according to their leader, anyway – suffers by virtue of landing in an era when Noel was consciously trying to move away from big, anthemic 'Don't Look Back in Anger'-style choruses of the type 'Carry Us All' has. It sounds very much like a trial run of 'Little by Little' and, had it arrived two years later in an era when Oasis were more unashamed about playing to their strengths of old, might have ended up with a slightly higher profile. HM

'Full On'

B-SIDE OF 'SUNDAY MORNING CALL'

Pretty much all of the *SOTSOG*-era Oasis material was written in the immediate run-up to the recording sessions for the album in France. But 'Full On' was being played in soundchecks by the Bonehead and Guigsy iteration of the band in 1997. You can tell it dates back to the *Be Here Now* times because it begins with squalling feedback, before launching into an old-style-Oasis barrage of guitar stomp. Only a Stooges-esque one-finger piano part and a kind of gothic effect put on Noel's singing – he sounds uncannily like Depeche Mode's Dave Gahan on the verses – give away the fact it was recorded in a slightly less chaotic era in the studio. **HM**

2002

More than 50 per cent of the UK now have access to the internet. President Bush makes his first ever State of the Union address, declaring North Korea, Iran and Iraq to be an 'axis of evil.' The Winter Olympics see the first ever disqualifications of athletes for drug-taking. One of the co-founders of PayPal, Elon Musk, founds the company SpaceX. Spider-Man *becomes the first ever film to earn $100 million in a single weekend, and Halle Berry the first Black woman to win a Best Actress Oscar. The third ever Coachella Music & Arts Festival is headlined by Björk and Oasis. Paul McCartney marries Heather Mills in Ireland. The euro becomes legal tender. The FIFA World Cup is the first to ever be hosted by two countries – South Korea and Japan – and is won by Brazil, who knock out England on their way to the final.* The Osbournes *debuts on MTV in the US, while the first series of* I'm a Celebrity . . . Get Me Out of Here! *is broadcast in the UK. U2 perform the half-time show at the Superbowl and pay tribute to the victims of 9/11. In December, having reviewed a 12,000-page weapons declaration document, the US announces its intention to invade Iraq.*

What happens in Vegas . . . Now fully installed, new recruits Gem Archer and Andy Bell watch their singer do his thing at the Hard Rock Hotel and Casino, Las Vegas, where The Who's John Entwistle will be found dead two months later. Photographed by Ethan Miller in April 2002.

'The Hindu Times'

SINGLE

RELEASED 15 APRIL 2002

The 10 Years of Noise and Confusion Tour in late 2001 offered the chance for a much-needed reset for Oasis. The tour in support of *Standing on the Shoulder of Giants,* which had come to an end earlier that year, had contributed to the more 'and confusion' end of the spectrum.

Taking place largely in stadiums with two new members who had not been involved in the making of the record they were promoting, the SOTSOG tour had seen Noel leave the band for a few dates after a particularly bad fight with Liam in Barcelona. With the help of a guitarist named Matt Deighton, the show had gone on – meaning that no single human being has played every Oasis set – before Noel returned for the UK shows. At which point Liam turned up at Wembley Stadium as drunk as anyone has ever been on a stage, for a show broadcast live on Sky.

The idea was that after all this 'and confusion,' there would now be noise: a six-date tour of the UK taking in small venues (smallest: 1,900 capacity, 1/65th the size of Knebworth) where Oasis could get in people's faces and show that this was a band revitalized. And now very much a band, with four out of five members writing songs for the next album. Taking place the day after 9/11, a gloriously funny joint *NME* cover interview with Noel and Liam conducted by Sylvia Patterson preceded the shows. It seemed like they were getting on better than ever. Asked whether he had apologized to Noel for the Barcelona incident, Liam looked at his brother and responded, 'Did I?'

'I think you may have, in your own little way,' came the reply. 'You certainly didn't say the word "sorry".'

In between slagging off everybody in the way that only they

can – 'Eminem? Walking onstage at Reading with his bag of Anadins and a bottle of Bacardi that's actually water?' – there was further warmth. 'He's the best songwriter in the world, end of story,' Liam insisted. 'He should be given a knighthood. A knighthood!' Noel enthused of his brother.

Asked about the next Oasis album, Noel described it as 'fucking loud,' Liam as 'punk rock.' This, too, was to be the modus operandi for the tour, with the likes of 'Fade Away,' 'Columbia' and a full-band 'Morning Glory' returning. So any new material previewed would have to fit in with this. To highlight the fact that this was now a band of songwriters, one would be Gem Archer's Stooges-esque 'Hung in a Bad Place.' The only other, which left a more lasting impression on the tiny audiences who got to hear it, was 'The Hindu Times.'

In fact, the reception was so positive that 'The Hindu Times' would end up being the lead single from *Heathen Chemistry*. As a statement of intent, it was emphatic: a loud, short, sharp, uncomplicated Oasis song on which feel is prioritized over profundity. The previous single, 'Sunday Morning Call,' suddenly felt like a million years ago. Here was Noel communicating in nonsense lyrics featuring 'light that shines on' and 'sunshine,' all sneered by a singer who sounded as fired up as ever. The title came from a T-shirt that Noel had seen. It clocked in at under four minutes: the first Oasis single since 'Roll with It' to do so. It went straight into the UK charts at number one.

By the time 'The Hindu Times' arrived, The Strokes' first album, *Is This It,* had come out, reshaping rock 'n' roll in its image. Suddenly every new band was wearing skinny ties and taking their cues from the American art-punk of the seventies rather than the British bands of the sixties who had so shaped the early Oasis songs. Oasis were free to be themselves, free of the pressure of still being the current generation-defining band with all eyes on their next move, free to do what they wanted to do. On 'The Hindu Times,' you could hear it. The freedom. **HM**

'Just Getting Older'

B-SIDE OF 'THE HINDU TIMES'

Dating back to mid-1998, you won't get a more blunt expression of how Noel Gallagher was feeling at that time than here. We meet a character who is staying in and no longer feels the inclination to make conversation *'with the friends that I don't know.'* At least by the end of the song his question – *'Am I cracking up or just getting older?'* – has become an answer. And as a one-off line of poetry, *'I'm halfway up to the bottom of another bottle of my next best favourite friend'* is pretty great. **HM**

'Idler's Dream'

B-SIDE OF 'THE HINDU TIMES'

Uniquely for an Oasis song, this features no guitar of any kind: only a piano and Noel Gallagher's voice. By the *Heathen Chemistry* era he was, rather than just writing songs, utilizing B-sides for their traditional purpose, i.e. to try out things that could never fit on an Oasis album. And, if this is an experiment, it's a highly successful one. 'Idler's Dream' presages some of the things Noel would do as a solo artist: a song that keeps you guessing as to where it's going right until the end, and is one of Oasis's most truly underrated moments. **HM**

Heathen Chemistry

(ORIGINAL UK RELEASE: 1 JULY 2002)

1.	'The Hindu Times'	3:46
2.	'Force of Nature'	4:51
3.	'Hung in a Bad Place'	3:28
4.	'Stop Crying Your Heart Out'	5:03
5.	'Songbird'	2:07
6.	'Little by Little'	4:52
7.	'A Quick Peep'	1:17
8.	'(Probably) All in the Mind'	4:02
9.	'She Is Love'	3:09
10.	'Born on a Different Cloud'	6:08
11.	'Better Man'	33:02
12.	'The Cage'	4:50

Written by: Liam Gallagher (Tracks 5, 10, 11), Noel Gallagher (Tracks 1, 2, 4, 6, 8, 9), Gem Archer (Track 3), Andy Bell (Track 7)

Producer: Oasis

Performers: Alan White, Andy Bell, Gem Archer, Liam Gallagher, Noel Gallagher

Additional musicians: Paul Stacey (keyboards; Tracks 1, 2, 6, 11), Mike Rowe (keyboards; Tracks 4, 5, 8, 9, 10), Johnny Marr (guitar; Tracks 8, 10)

Recorded at Wheeler End and Olympic Studios

'The Hindu Times'

SINGLE RELEASED 15 APRIL 2002 (SEE PAGE 245)

'Force of Nature'

It sounds like Iggy Pop's 'Nightclubbing' because it started life as Iggy Pop's 'Nightclubbing'.

'Force of Nature' dates back to the *Standing on the Shoulder of Giants* sessions in Château de la Colle Noire, in Montauroux, south of France, and a request Noel Gallagher received from near-neighbour Jude Law in Primrose Hill to provide a song for a gangster film he was making called *Love, Honour and Obey*, which featured some of Britain's most recognizable actors and least convincing gangsters. 'Fucking awful,' agrees Noel. 'Straight to video.'

With the commission in mind, Noel headed over to France a week early alongside an engineer and set up his gear to record this new song for Law's gangster film. He had the idea that the rhythm should sound like 'Nightclubbing', so rather than waste time mimicking it, he sampled and looped it. It sounded great.

'But we couldn't get clearance 'cos it had a bit where Iggy takes a breath or goes "ugh".' Rather than junk the idea, Noel engineered a solution. '[We] found what drum machine was being used and matched the sounds.'

The crunchy blues of 'Force of Nature' finds Noel acidly addressing *'a bird released'* in a brutal chorus, a person who's being binned *'for smoking all my stash/But burning all my cash . . . the sun's going down on the days of your easy life'*.

Noel was adamant, however, that these words were not about the dog days of his first marriage to Meg Mathews. 'I don't like talking about my ex-wife because I'm more mature than that,' he said later, a bit peeved to be asked something so clearly personal. 'Some people think "Force of Nature" is about her, as its lyrics are about someone taking my cash. It's not. Whatever I have to say, I'll say to her and not the press.' He added that he'd written the song a couple of years before the divorce (which was when he was probably most irritated by the revolving-door nightclub taking place in his house, but let's leave that point moot).

Was this perhaps why Liam was not tasked with providing a vocal, even when so in his range of passionate disdain? Not so, apparently. It had been earmarked as the first single from the album and, with that in mind, Noel asked Liam in to sing 'Force of Nature'. First, though, Liam listened to Noel's demo.

'Liam went, "That's one of best vocals I've ever heard", Noel told *NME*. 'I was like, "Cool. That scuppers the plan for the first single then."'

Noel, it turns out, was no fan of Oasis singles with his lead vocal, flying in the face of all previous evidence, most obviously 'Don't Look Back in Anger'. 'I don't like singing at all,' he said about 'Force of Nature'. 'I only started doing a couple of acoustic songs in the middle of the set to give Liam a rest. In America, it'd go down a storm. I come back to England thinking, *I'm having a bit of this*, Bob Dylan, you know. Then I read the reviews and I was going, *Actually, it would be a bit shit to see one of the best bands ever and the ugly one comes on and goes, "Hello, I'm going to sing you a song now."*'

Even so, Liam didn't sing 'Force of Nature', though not because it was too personal for Noel. 'But of course the story about it being about your ex-wife is quite titillating,' admits Noel. TK

'Hung in a Bad Place'

Colin 'Gem' Archer – always, always Gem, derived from seventies football great Archie Gemmill – only had one song on each of the three Oasis albums to which he contributed. Yet all were deemed significant enough to feature every night on their respective tours. The first of these was 'Hung in a Bad Place', a straight-up, scuzzy rocker that perfectly reflected the personal tastes of its composer.

Born in Hunwick, Durham, Gem had been plugging away in music since the mid-1980s. The Edge had released a couple of singles. He next joined a group called The Contenders, then formed Whirlpool. While auditioning drummers in 1987, Gem was seriously impressed by a fifteen-year-old kid who came along to the auditions. He would have got the gig easily, but it was decided he was too young to go on tour. Gem rang the kid's father and told him not to worry: his son was fantastic and would go all the way. Gem was right. The kid's name was Alan White.

Whirlpool signed to Food Records in 1991, making them labelmates of Blur, whose success they did not match. Members of Blur – along with lots of tastemakers – did, however, turn up to watch the first London show by Heavy Stereo – featuring Gem as singer, guitarist and songwriter – at the Africa Centre in Covent Garden. Somewhat inevitably given that a) this gig took place a month after *Some Might Say* had gone to number one, and b) they were signed to Creation, played glam and late-sixties-influenced rock 'n' roll and had a singer who sang with a similar kind of throaty rasp to Liam Gallagher, Heavy Stereo were, at the time, being hyped as the new Oasis.

They went on to play the *NME* New Music Tour in early 1996 and their debut album *Déjà Voodoo* followed in September of that year. On the guestlist for the London show in support of the record were Noel Gallagher and Paul Weller – both already fans who left further impressed by what they saw. *Déjà Voodoo,* though, failed to connect with the public the way it should have. 'I loved the first four singles, but they really George Bested their album – the life was mixed out of it,' said Noel (who of course himself had, with Oasis, at one point been in severe danger of George Besting the recording of a debut album).

By 1998, Gem was in the middle of recording 'the best music of my life' and touring with Heavy Stereo in support of Weller, when tragedy struck. His mother was seriously ill. All activity with his band was put on hold while he moved into her house in Newcastle to help her through it. One morning, he was watching *The Big Breakfast* when they announced that Bonehead and Guigsy had left Oasis. 'I thought, *Shit! They'll split now*,' he remembered. 'I was a real fan, and I'm not just saying that. For me Oasis had breathed life back into rock 'n' roll.'

Little did he know that plans were already afoot to solve Oasis's problems. 'Noel had rung my place in London where it was my son's birthday party,' Gem said. 'His auntie answered the phone and was going, "So you reckon you're Noel Gallagher?" Eventually he spoke to my wife and then rang me at my mum's. I told him I had to stay near my mum, but he invited me down afterwards to Olympic Studios, where they were mixing *Standing on the Shoulder of Giants*, to hang out.'

Within days, he was being asked to join Oasis. He asked his Heavy Stereo bandmates for their blessing, which they gave, and as the new millennium started he was onstage touring the album he had heard being mixed at Olympic. A far more accomplished and versatile guitar player than Bonehead, Gem immediately made a huge difference to the Oasis live setup. Every night on that tour, they would open with 'Go Let It Out' – its climactic guitar solo being played by the new member rather than the man who wrote it. He was able to add the intricate parts to other songs that Noel had overdubbed in the studio.

By 2001, Gem was installed as a full-time member, appearing in the group photographs and interviews, and contributing one of only two new songs previewed on the 10 Years of Noise and Confusion Tour. The buzzsaw guitars of 'Hung in a Bad Place' pilfered The Stooges' 'No Fun' with the same lack of shame that Noel Gallagher had displayed while borrowing from T. Rex's 'Get It On' for 'Cigarettes & Alcohol'. It also ran any Oasis song close on the nonsense poetry front. '*It's hasta mañana, you're on your own banana skin feet now*,' Liam snarled in its first verse. '*I can swing through the trees, Tarzan on harmonies for free*' in its second.

This new guy was going to fit in just fine. **HM**

'Stop Crying Your Heart Out'

By accident or design, the release of 'Stop Crying Your Heart Out' was extraordinarily well timed. It was clearly one of the better songs on *Heathen Chemistry* – with one of Liam Gallagher's best ever vocals and a classically, instantly anthemic Noel Gallagher chorus melody over descending chords – and therefore clearly destined to be released as a single. It was just a question of when. You did not need to be Nostradamus to predict that the England football team would crash out of the 2002 World Cup earlier than they had hoped. But even so . . .

Two weeks prior to the England football team indeed crashing out of the 2002 World Cup earlier than they had hoped – Brazil, quarter finals, freak accident free kick – 'Stop Crying Your Heart Out' was released and was all over the radio. Those hastily assembled television montages of weeping, hard-done-by fans across the nation had their soundtrack, and it became the anthem of a (once again) grieving nation.

This, though, would be far from the end of the lifespan of 'Stop Crying Your Heart Out'. Oasis may have retired it from live performance by 2005, but four years later it was to have an unlikely rebirth that would help it ascend to almost 'Wonderwall' levels of ubiquity.

In 2009, London singer Leona Lewis released her second album, *Echo*. On its release her debut, *Spirit*, had overtaken Arctic Monkeys – and prior to that Oasis – as the fastest-selling UK debut album of all time. She was the first winner of *The X Factor* to be considered a serious artist who might have a longer-lasting career than her predecessors. She worked with the highest-calibre professional songwriters: from Ryan Tedder (Lewis's own 'Bleeding Love', Beyoncé's 'Halo', Taylor Swift's 'Welcome to New York') to Mike Elizondo (innumerable hip-hop classics including 'The Real Slim Shady' and 'In Da Club') and the titanic Max Martin, who currently has twenty-seven Billboard Hot 100 number-one singles to his name, which is seven more than The Beatles managed.

All of *Echo*'s tracks are credited to at least two people . . . except for one that is credited only to Noel Gallagher. 'The idea to cover "Stop Crying Your Heart Out" came from Simon Cowell,' Lewis recalled. 'He said, "Why don't you try this song?" and we both loved it, which is probably why he keeps getting people on *The X Factor* to sing it!'

When Lewis returned, conquering hero style, to appear at the 2009 *X Factor* final, it was 'Stop Crying Your Heart Out', rather than any of the other expensive-professional-songwriter-written songs, that she performed. Immediately, her version entered the UK's top thirty and the second single from *Heathen Chemistry* began its unexpected second life.

Lewis was not exaggerating Cowell's enthusiasm for getting future *X Factor* contestants to perform it. The following year, in 2010, both Harry Styles and Liam Payne sang it on their journey to becoming members of One Direction. For years afterwards, it became almost impossible to watch an episode of the show without seeing some poor hopeful emote their way through it. In November 2020, with the world in and out of lockdown, it became the official single for the BBC's Children in Need appeal – the likes of Cher, Bryan Adams, Robbie Williams, Nile Rodgers, Kylie Minogue and many others singing their lines over Zoom in the accompanying video.

But why 'Stop Crying Your Heart Out'? Why not 'Wonderwall', or 'Don't Look Back in Anger', or 'Champagne Supernova'? Maybe because it exhibits a more clear, direct, universal sentiment than any of those songs. It's about not dwelling on something that is bringing you down, about finding the strength to move forward. Perfect, in other words, for someone who is about to have their dreams shattered live on Saturday night television, or someone wondering if they'll ever be allowed to leave their house and see their friends and family again.

The Oasis version is the best ever example of Noel and Liam's vocal talents working together, call and return style. When Noel breaks, in the second verse, from exactly mirroring what his brother is singing to instead responding to the line '*Why you scared?*' with '*I'm not scared*', it packs a powerful emotional punch. When you go back to the original, it is clear that this is a song best served by two people singing it together. HM

'Songbird'

If ever you wish to while away an hour watching old Oasis electronic press kits on YouTube, the journey from the defensive, sullen duo selling the world *Standing on the Shoulder of Giants* in separate interviews to the goofy, united new gang recommending you tune into *Heathen Chemistry* two years later is instructive. Something huge shifted positively in mood between the two periods.

Beyond the change of personnel being as good as a rest for the Gallaghers, perhaps the key to the vibe shift was the new loves that had recently entered the lives of both brothers, as evidenced on two songs each wrote for *Heathen Chemistry*. Noel had Sara MacDonald clearly in mind with 'She Is Love'. Liam, meanwhile, composed the sweet pop lullaby 'Songbird' for Nicole Appleton, with whom he'd had a son, Gene, in 2001.

'I was in France in this massive mansion, recording,' said Liam, describing the creative process behind it. 'I went out one day, sat under a tree, had a bit of a biblical moment.'

And *voilà!* 'Songbird' was born. 'It took three minutes, and I wrote all the words there and then.'

Liam liked to say the whole thing was easy to nail – 'I just came into the studio playing it on two strings' – but Andy Bell had a slightly different interpretation of 'easy'. 'How it works is this. Liam comes into the studio and strums an acoustic guitar every day for six months, and he'll be singing without any words, just going "la, la, la" over and over again. Then eventually the words start to come and he's got a line or two. Then, after about a year, he's got the song.'

For Andy, 'Songbird' reinforced the sunnier sense he had about being a member of Oasis now. 'This is what I like about Oasis at the moment, even as a fan: they're back to being what they're best at, being uplifting.'

Liam wanted the world to see this side of him, too, that 'it's not all dark in Liam World. I like beautiful things.'

Noel thought his brother's song was 'amazing, one of our best songs – it doesn't matter who wrote it.' Nevertheless, Noel played a key role in its manifestation as an acoustic pop number. 'It was sounding like a 1964 "Love Me Do" vibe, all mouth organs, quite fast. We hit a brick wall with it,' he explained.

Noel sent everyone out of the studio for lunch for half an hour, stripping all the guitars, drums, harmonica and bass.

'Liam had said, "I don't want it to be acoustic, it'll be fucking shite." Everyone went to the chippy, came back and I was, "See? Now it's 'Norwegian Wood'." I have to take credit for that.' Despite everyone loving 'Songbird', it was performed infrequently live by Oasis, chiefly, according to Noel, because Liam didn't want it included. 'I have to push to get it in the set because Liam won't have it. "Do you think it drags on a bit?" It's two minutes and one second long!'

One band who were very happy to play 'Songbird' live was Coldplay. Frontman Chris Martin absolutely loved it.

'I think it is the most beautiful song in the world,' he said. 'It makes me cry – such a heartfelt, beautiful song. Liam Gallagher always gets some bad stuff but it's like Beethoven in that film about Beethoven. His girlfriend says how could I not love him because he writes such beautiful music. Anyone who can write something like "Songbird" is basically alright by me.'

Unfortunately for Chris Martin, neither Coldplay nor specifically Chris Martin was basically alright with Liam Gallagher in the noughties. Above all, he was not a fan of Martin's style. 'He looks like a geography teacher,' Liam decided. The band did not come off much better. 'They look like The Tweenies.'

Generally, Liam was not a fan of people covering Oasis songs. 'I heard the Foo Fighters do "Lyla" once and it sounded like it was being murdered,' he said in 2008. He wasn't keen on Ryan Adams's version of 'Wonderwall' either: 'too fucking pansy.'

Soon after *Heathen Chemistry* came out, in August 2002, Coldplay played New York's Bowery Ballroom. For the encore, Chris Martin sat at the piano solo and performed a heartfelt 'Songbird.' In the audience, up in the balcony, were Liam and Noel Gallagher. Noel stood and cheered when the first chords rang out. Liam, on the other hand, forbade Coldplay from covering 'Songbird' again. 'I told Chris Martin, "Don't ever fucking sing that song,"' he said later.

Chris Martin laughed it off. 'I don't care what Liam says he'll do to me: I love his song!' Coldplay continued to periodically cover 'Songbird'.

Time passed. Once, a few years later in *Q* magazine, Liam compared Chris Martin to a vicar. More time passed. Then, in 2017, Liam was about to do a gig in Germany when word reached his partner and manager Debbie Gwyther that Chris Martin wanted a word with Liam.

'I'm like, "Does he want a fucking scrap or summat? I'm not in the fucking mood right now, man."'

Chris Martin did not want a scrap. He wanted a chat about the One Love Manchester concert he was helping to curate to commemorate the victims of the Manchester Arena bombing on 22 May, specifically wondering if Liam could perform. So Liam and Chris got on a Skype call together.

'I think he wanted to do "Imagine",' Liam told Hamish. 'And I'm like, "Look, I'm not doing 'Imagine', it ain't happening." He went, "Oh go on, it'll be great." I was, like, "I'm sure it fucking will be great, I'm fucking great and you're fucking great and I'm sure it would be great but it ain't happening." So he goes, "Oh, would you do an Oasis tune?" and I said, "Yeah of course, man."'

So, on 4 June 2017, Liam Gallagher joined Chris Martin and Johnny Buckland to perform 'Live Forever'.

Watching at home elsewhere in Manchester, Bonehead spat his tea out. A few hours earlier he'd heard some Oasis being played in soundcheck, so he'd called Liam and asked where he was. 'Germany,' replied Liam. Oh, maybe it's your kid then, suggested Bonehead suspiciously. 'Well, it ain't me,' insisted Liam. 'I'm in Germany.'

But here he was with Coldplay in Manchester, delivering a heavy, beautiful 'Live Forever' to not a dry eye.

Before he left the site after his turn, Liam grabbed Chris Martin. He had some amends to make.

'I went, "Listen, I'm sorry about all that shit, that I keep fucking slagging you off and all that, I'm sorry about that. You know I don't fucking mean it."'

Chris Martin is a stand-up guy, though. He doesn't care. 'He's going, "Nah, nah, nah, no worries, we love it, mate, carry on!" He was cool. But I've not heard back from him since. He's fucked me right off now.' TK

'Little by Little'

If the two ballads ('Where Did It All Go Wrong?' and 'Sunday Morning Call') that Noel Gallagher wrote for the fourth Oasis album were not fondly remembered by their author, the same cannot be said of the pair he delivered for the fifth.

Both Gallagher brothers had claimed that *Heathen Chemistry* was a loud, punk rock, back-to-basics album. Which in part it was. But in truth it was an album that would be defined by and best remembered for its ballads. 'Stop Crying Your Heart Out', obviously. And then the Noel-sung 'Little by Little', another song that dates back to 1998, when Noel was asked to write some songs for *Love, Honour & Obey*.

Unusually, this was not a song that he had earmarked to sing himself. The plan had been for Liam to tackle its skyscrapingly big chorus. But it was not to be. 'It's a shame 'cos that would have made it extra, extra special,' Noel said. 'When it came to him [recording the vocals] you could see he was going, "I'm not going to fucking get it." And we were all willing him to get it. I went in and did a version and you could see he was sat at the desk going, "Fucking bastard. He's got it."'

Because it had been recorded with Liam in mind for the vocals, Noel went for a much more aggressive than usual delivery in the extremely loud guitar-driven middle section, in the same way he had on 'Force of Nature'. On the verses, though, he went for a softer baritone more typical of his singing style. The lyrics are noticeably zen: the product of the month-long trip he took to Thailand in 1998 that also berthed 'Who Feels Love?'.

'"*True perfection has to be imperfect*": I love that line,' he said. 'I think it's very Zen Buddhist; I must have been smoking pot that time.' HM

'A Quick Peep'

'The Psychedelic Giraffe,' as he was nicknamed in the early days, joined Oasis in early 2000, shortly after Gem Archer had been recruited on rhythm guitar. Andy Bell did not turn up in time to be in the video for 'Go Let It Out,' but by the time the Standing on the Shoulder of Giants Tour began he was stood stage right, playing his distinctive black Burns bass guitar, towering 2 inches over the next tallest member of the band, and a full 4 inches over Liam Gallagher. Hence the nickname.

When he got the call, Andy was set to join much-hyped British band Gay Dad as touring lead guitarist (that band's singer, Cliff Jones, had previously been a music journalist who had written an August 1994 cover story about Oasis for *The Face* magazine that dubbed them 'The Sex Beatles'). Like Gem Archer, Bell was a Creation labelmate of the band, having been a founding member, singer, guitarist and songwriter of Oxford shoegaze sensations Ride. Ride's 1992 single 'Leave Them All Behind' had been the label's first top-ten hit in the UK.

Ride were darlings of the indie scene, but by 1994 were on the point of breaking up. Their final show (before they re-formed years later) was at Brighton Centre in December of that year: playing support at what was, at that time, Oasis's biggest show to date. Ride's third album, *Carnival of Light*, had been released just two months before *Definitely Maybe*. It was clear which band was on the way up and which was on the way down.

When Ride finally called it a day in early 1996, Bell immediately formed Hurricane #1, a band who, no two ways about it, sounded quite a lot like Oasis. Their singer, Alex Lowe, perhaps not used to the tactics of the British music press, was goaded into slagging off Oasis. A quite silly back-and-forth war of words ensued. 'Hurricane #1?' Liam joked with Ted in 1997. 'Never heard of them. Isn't that some indie band with the guy from Erasure in them?'

Andy Bell joining Oasis on bass surprised a lot of people. Long regarded as one of the most gifted guitar players of his generation – you could make a decent argument he was better than either Noel or Gem – the bassline of 'Supersonic' was, no offence to Paul 'Guigsy' McGuigan, not going to be much of a challenge. He was also a talented songwriter, taking on the Noel Gallagher role in Hurricane #1.

Now, though, he was in a band with the actual Noel Gallagher: best in breed when it comes to writing songs that sound like Oasis. From the word go, Bell's brief was to bring songs to the table that offered something different. Enter, seven songs in to *Heathen Chemistry*, a curious little thing entitled 'A Quick Peep'.

Andy Bell would go on to write more significant Oasis songs – 'Turn Up the Sun' would serve as the opener to *Don't Believe the Truth* and every show played in support of it – but his first was to be a quiet, brief, discreet entrance. Sounding quite a lot like Fleetwood Mac, 'A Quick Peep' was instrumental, clocked in at one minute fifteen seconds – the shortest Oasis song to date – and featured some dextrous acoustic guitar-playing courtesy of its writer. If not much else, it definitely delivered on sounding nothing like anything Oasis had ever done before. **HM**

'(Probably) All in the Mind'

Finally, the dextrous, genial guitar-playing of a long-term Oasis associate was to feature on one of their songs. Although to describe Johnny Marr as a mere associate is to drastically understate the role he played in their rise. It is not an exaggeration to say that there's a good chance no one would have ever heard of them were it not for him.

As Marr listened to a playback of '(Probably) All in the Mind' at Wheeler End studios, thinking about what he could add to this light, dreamy slice of Noel Gallagher psychedelia, his former guitar tech Jason Rhodes – now working for Noel – handed him a guitar. The custom black 1978 Gibson Les Paul looked and felt familiar, as well it might: it was one of his. He had played it during the recording of The Smiths' *The Queen Is Dead,* and even written 'Bigmouth Strikes Again' on it. It had ended up in Noel Gallagher's possession when he had broken another of Marr's loaned-out Les Pauls defending himself against someone who had jumped onstage and punched him during a gig in Newcastle in early 1994. The very next day, this other, black Les Paul had shown up with a note attached to it.

'This one's a bit heavier, in weight and sound,' it read. 'If you get a really good swing on it, you'll take some fucker's head off. Love from Johnny.' It immediately became Noel Gallagher's main guitar, played live on Oasis tours for years to come, long into the days when Noel could have afforded to buy any guitar in the world.

Marr's role in helping out Oasis involved much more than a steady stream of Gibson Les Pauls, however. First – and most importantly of all – there had been the inspiration he had provided to the Smiths-obsessed, teenage Noel Gallagher, in terms of both great guitar-playing and great clothes and great haircuts, all of which he copied to some extent. So you can imagine how he felt when, sat at home one day, the phone rang and it was his guitar hero telling him he had heard and liked the Oasis demo tape, and suggesting that they meet up for a drink.

'I was coming out of a record shop, having just bought [one of Marr's post-Smiths bands] The The's *Dusk,*' Noel later recalled. 'I bumped into my friend Ian, and he saw the album and said, "Oh, my brother's in them."' Noel had no idea who Ian's brother was. But once he found out, and Ian offered to give his brother Johnny an Oasis demo, he made sure that he did.

Marr, Noel said, 'was the first person outside of the band to show any interest whatsoever.' In 1992, he came to watch Oasis play in front of an audience that just about stretched into double figures. Noting that Noel was taking a long time to tune his inexpensive guitar up in between each song, he offered to lend him a couple. Then he passed on the demo tape to his manager, Marcus Russell. He brought an enthused Russell along to a show at the Hop & Grape in early 1993, who immediately offered to manage the band. Then, when the recording of *Definitely Maybe* was not working out as planned, he put forward Owen Morris to mix it into its glorious final form.

So that's '. . . and the rest is history', times three.

Another of Marr's bands – The Healers, in which he sang as well as played guitar – opened for Oasis on the UK leg of the Standing on the Shoulder of Giants Tour in 2000. But unlike Noel Gallagher's other hero – Paul Weller, who is on 'Champagne Supernova' – he didn't make it on to an Oasis recording until *Heathen Chemistry*.

To say that '(Probably) All in the Mind' is not the equal of 'Champagne Supernova' would be more than fair. It has never and never will be performed live and was forgotten about fairly soon after the album that contained it was released. But, in some ways, that suits Johnny Marr's character: an egoless guitarist who, in whatever band he is in, has always served the song rather than playing showstopping solos – which, by the way, he could, if he wanted, play as well as anyone who has ever picked up a guitar – and has never loudly boasted about all the help (and Les Pauls) that he gave Noel and Oasis when no one else cared. Whatever they needed was fine. A sprinkling of magic on an album track? No problem. Just hand him that heavy, black guitar over there. **HM**

'She Is Love'

There are many, many millions of songs written about being in love. It is the food of music. But there are few more direct than Noel Gallagher's song for the woman he fell for in a nightclub in Ibiza in 2001, Sara MacDonald, his future wife.

'All I know is I'm in love/With someone who loves me too,' he sings in 'She Is Love,' a rainbow of a song that mentions the word 'love' fourteen times. This was a departure. 'In the past, I've definitely shied away from using the word "love" in songs, but I'm an older gentleman now,' he said at the time. 'I'm thirty-five. So I really couldn't give a toss if people think it's soppy. That song's real, it's how I feel about her.'

It was written on a sunny Sunday afternoon in a hotel room near Buckingham Palace, where Noel was living having split from Meg Mathews. 'Warm day, fuck all on the telly. I'm in love with my girlfriend. I wrote "She Is Love", a song about how lovely I think she is, in about ten minutes.'

When his friend Johnny Marr heard it for the first time, he told Noel it sounded like it had taken even less time to write. He estimated Noel cooked it up in five minutes. 'That's a compliment,' said Noel, his theory about the good stuff just dropping from the sky proven once more.

Noel took his swiftly recorded demo to the studio where he unveiled the song to his colleagues so they could record it. He started playing the chords on repeat for several minutes to bewildered looks. 'I said, "Just give me five minutes." I sang it once, put the harmonies on; our keyboard player put three solos on – Mellotron, Hammond, pump organ – all three were shockingly bad, but when we put them together it sounded perfect. As we lived with it, we thought, "That's the song."'

There was one other person who needed to hear it, of course. 'I showed Sara the words and she went, "Play it to me."'

This was not the desired outcome. He told her he'd rather not, thanks. She insisted. 'I had to play it with my back turned to her,' he said, revealing a hitherto unknown shy side, but hers was the only opinion that really mattered. 'I really don't give a fuck what people think of it. It means so much to me. I'll always remember that day.' Noel had one more revelation about the song while playing it live for others over the coming years. 'You write it, put the kettle on, sing it into a tape recorder – fast-forward six months and there's sixty thousand people singing it to you.'

Noel's love song for his girlfriend was out in the world, being reflected back to him. TK

'Born on a Different Cloud'

If the Liam Gallagher-written Oasis songs have one thing in common, it is usually brevity: get in, do what needs doing, get out. But 'Born on a Different Cloud' is different: a kind of Pink Floydian epic that stretched over more than six minutes, with lots of sprawling guitar atmospherics and not much in the way of vocals taking up more than a third of that time. There's a verse, a bridge, no chorus but still a middle section. All very strange and eccentric. 'A Manc Odyssey,' in the words of its writer.

When asked, following the birth of his son with Patsy Kensit, Lennon, whether there was a 'Little Lennon' coming – a reference to 'Little James,' about Kensit's first child – Liam said that there was, and that it was called 'Born on a Different Cloud.' '*It's no surprise to me, that you're classless, clever and free*,' it goes at one point. '*You're the hero that's still unsung*,' at another.

So it could be about Lennon. But 'Born on a Different Cloud' feels like it is as much about its *sui generis* creator as it is his son. No normal songwriter would sit down and structure something like this, a song that ticks by its own clock. HM

'Better Man'

Somewhere, Gem Archer has a photo of 'Better Man' being recorded in Wheeler End in late 2001, shortly after George Harrison died.

All the players are standing in a line: Gem on one guitar, Johnny Marr on another, Paul Stacey on the piano, Andy Bell on bass, and Noel playing his 'little Ringo drumkit, with a Beatles drumskin.'

They recorded it live, jamming out the two chords that Liam had put together with the spare, aspirational words he'd written, originally as an acoustic composition. With that line-up, though, it didn't stand a chance of surviving in an acoustic form. 'When I heard it, I thought, *That's an Oasis song*,' said Noel. 'It's the blues, innit? With Gem and Johnny on guitars, it was really hard for me to find a bit in the song, you don't want three guitarists on a song, so I got my drumkit and bashed it out. Fucking great.' Liam had wanted to write a song with as few words as possible to reinforce the message of him trying to improve himself, though the lower register he chose to sing in is the one that suits him best. 'I wanted a groove more than a song, something like "I Don't Wanna Be a Soldier" by the Plastic Ono Band,' he said. 'Not too many words, just hitting like that.'

And a big, smoky groove is what he was provided with, though it flourished live most of all, becoming a staple of the set over the next two years. By then, Noel had found his spot beside his brother back on guitar, though. TK

'The Cage'

You could argue that The Clash started the hidden track phenomenon when 'Train in Vain' – which ended up as their biggest single – went uncredited at the end of their 1979 album *London Calling*. But the truth is that situation only occurred because it was added to the record once the sleeve had already gone to print. The trend for secret tracks only really took off in the CD era: where you would leave an album silently ticking away after it had finished until another song unexpectedly – or expectedly, given everyone was doing it – sprang up from the speakers.

Nirvana were early adopters, including the noisy, wilfully ugly 'Endless Nameless' at the end of the highly commercial, millions-selling *Nevermind* to remind everyone that they were still an underground punk band at heart. Oasis did not need to offer such apologies – their albums loudly and proudly showed what they were about – and, in their earlier incarnation, they did not have the personnel for improv. That changed when Gem and Andy joined. On their fifth album, following a full half-hour of silence after 'Better Man', Oasis finally delivered a secret track.

'The Cage' – as it would become known – is a kind of Pink Floyd-y, early Verve-esque groove and the sound of what was pretty much a new band playing off each other for the first time with no real expectations. **HM**

'Stop Crying Your Heart Out'

SINGLE RELEASED 17 JUNE 2002 (SEE PAGE 252)

'Thank You for the Good Times'

B-SIDE OF 'STOP CRYING YOUR HEART OUT'

If 'A Quick Peep' had been a short, somewhat eccentric, instrumental introduction to Andy Bell's writing within Oasis, then his next song to make the cut was more conventional and all the better for it. In November 2003, he played 'Thank You for the Good Times' during an acoustic set in his then-hometown of Stockholm as support to his former Ride bandmate Mark Gardener. With his far softer vocals, it's a completely different feel to the Oasis version: proof of Liam's ability to make any song sound like his own as soon as he sang it. **HM**

'Shout It Out Loud'

B-SIDE OF 'STOP CRYING YOUR HEART OUT'

As unashamedly Neil Young as Oasis ever sounded, this is another underrated song that continues the long-held tradition of being vastly superior to quite a lot of the album in whose era it belongs. You can also hear strong echoes of 'If I Had a Gun . . .', one of the standout tracks on the first High Flying Birds album, at this point a decade off being released. The biggest clues as to what Noel Gallagher might sound like as a solo artist were on the B-sides of the *Heathen Chemistry* period. **HM**

'Little by Little'/'She Is Love'

SINGLE RELEASED 19 SEPTEMBER 2002 (SEE PAGES 258 AND 262)

'My Generation'

B-SIDE OF 'LITTLE BY LITTLE'/'SHE IS LOVE'

On 20 January 2000, Oasis's new line-up made their UK broadcast debut on BBC Radio 1's *Evening Session*. It was also to be the first time listeners were treated to their cover of The Who's 1965 mod anthem, 'My Generation'.

For this, the band had the gods of radio to thank. Either that, or they fixed the results of an *Evening Session* poll whereby listeners had to choose a cover for Oasis to complete their five-song set with. The other candidates were 'Sympathy for the Devil' by the Rolling Stones, Motorhead's 'Ace of Spades', Nirvana's 'Come as You Are' or, perhaps most challengingly, Blur's 'Country House' and 'Angels' by Robbie Williams.

On air, Noel professed himself disappointed with the final results. 'I was looking forward to doing "Country House",' he claimed, 'which would have entailed me going to the toilet with some laxatives, reciting the lyrics off a big lyrics sheet, and flushing the chain in rapid succession. There was talk of us doing "Angels", and Liam was going to sing it with about fifty meat pies in his mouth.'

Oasis covering 'My Generation' made complete sense. Of all the bands they'd been compared to, the one that drew the cleanest line of descent was not The Beatles nor the Sex Pistols (or a combination of the two), it was always The Who. Like Oasis, The Who were founded upon playing very direct, concise, catchy songs written by a guitarist who was a frustrated band leader who could not, nevertheless, function in the band without his pugilistic, handsome frontman with the powerfully recognizable voice. The tension between Townshend and Daltrey propelled the band forwards, just as the fraternal fizz did with Oasis. The Who too made their name by unapologetically adapting their influences into something brand new. Noel Gallagher recognized all this.

'The thing about The Who, you think, *Fuck The Beatles and the Stones!*' he said years later. 'The Stones were a blues covers band; The Beatles were a piano-pop band. The Who were something for the British people to be proud of, them and the Sex Pistols. The Beatles were such gods, but Pete Townshend's songs were so easy to play, D-G-A. If I was sixteen in 1966, I would have been a massive Who fan. Especially the clothes and that.'

Listening to Oasis debut their cover of 'My Generation', it was obvious why they'd waited until the new millennium to pay homage to Shepherds Bush's most famous sons. 'Andy [Bell] did that bass break on "My Generation" note for note,' said Noel, remarking on the technical advancements now available to him. 'It was brilliant. All of a sudden, we've also acquired this new drummer – Alan's turned into Keith Moon! As much as I loved Guigs, he was pretty naff on the bass, and that frustrated Alan because he had to sit on the beat all the time. Now he's a whirling dervish.'

Fifteen years later, Liam agreed to sing 'My Generation' again for a broadcast, this time on TV. It was during a rare period of insecurity for the singer. In October 2014, he'd announced the end of his post-Oasis band, Beady Eye, after two albums. His own solo career was still a couple of years away. He was, as he would later describe it, 'out of the bubble' provided by management and daily itineraries.

But on 12 June 2015, Liam Gallagher stepped from the shadows for a one-off broadcast on Channel 4 to celebrate the twentieth anniversary of *TFI Friday*. Accompanying him onstage to perform was Bonehead for a rare appearance, sharing guitars with the

Lightning Seeds' Ian Broudie. Zak Starkey sat behind the drums, the only man alive who's performed as a member of both The Who and Oasis. Taking care of that tricky 'My Generation' bass solo was Jay Mehler, who'd go on to be a mainstay of Liam's solo band.

Most unusually, however, the lead vocals were shared between Liam and The Who's Roger Daltrey, each taking care of a verse. Daltrey's were typically coarse and rootsy, Liam's clear, smooth and true. The contrast between the two styles was apparent for anyone watching, though surprisingly it was Liam, exhibiting a kind of confident desperation, whose performance rang most true. In that fleeting reappearance in the public eye, all were reminded just who was missing from contemporary music. It couldn't hold. TK

2003

Shortly after the birth of Greta Thunberg in January, 2 million people are flooding the streets of London in protest against the Iraq war. One hundred and twenty-two Labour MPs vote against Tony Blair's government in a debate over the conflict. Less than a month later, British soldiers join troops from the United States and invade Iraq. Beyoncé releases 'Crazy in Love'. In April, Blair holds a one-day summit with Russian president Vladimir Putin. Finding Nemo *is released in cinemas, and later will become the biggest-selling DVD ever.* Peep Show *and* Little Britain *are shown on UK TV screens for the first time.* Harry Potter and the Order of the Phoenix *is published in June, selling 5 million copies overnight thanks to thousands of children waiting outside bookshops at midnight and beating* The Da Vinci Code *to become the year's bestselling book. Jude Bellingham is born and Manchester United sign an eighteen-year-old Cristiano Ronaldo. Chelsea FC are bought by Roman Abramovich for £150 million. Supersonic aircraft Concorde makes its final commercial flights after twenty-seven years. George W. Bush visits the UK in November, greeted by scenes of more huge protests against the war. In December, Mick Jagger is knighted, aged sixty, having spent most of the year on tour with the Rolling Stones.*

Noel Gallagher displays a pair of *NME* Awards at Po Na Na, Hammersmith, in February 2003, shot by Dave Hogan. The statue, with two fingers rather than one, is unique, made especially for the occasion.

'Songbird'

SINGLE RELEASED 2 FEBRUARY 2003 (SEE PAGE 255)

'(You've Got) The Heart of a Star'

B-SIDE OF 'SONGBIRD'

If 'Stop Crying Your Heart Out' could be emoted by an endless succession of *X Factor* hopefuls then . . . why not this too? It's a mix of Noel at his most everyman-anthemic *('Come on, come on, my brothers and sisters')*, aspirational (*'You're never gonna get it on, and be someone, stuck in that crowd')* and confessional (*'Maybe I could justify the bad things in life that I've done'*). It's a lovely, simple arrangement, with the acoustic guitar backed only by a brass band. And ripe for rediscovery and reinvention as a torch-song pop single. HM

2005

President Bush is inaugurated for a second term, Tony Blair a third. The final Star Wars prequel, Revenge of the Sith, *is released in cinemas, as well as Christopher Nolan's* Batman Begins. *The first ever video is uploaded to YouTube. Live8, a series of ten simultaneous concerts around the world, takes place with the goal of Making Poverty History. Four days after the London leg and twenty-four hours on from the city being awarded the 2012 Olympics, a terrorist attack on the British capital kills fifty-two people. Chelsea FC win their first top-flight title in fifty years, while a seventeen-year-old Lionel Messi scores his first goal for Barcelona. Hurricane Katrina hits the coast of the United States, causing severe damage and more than 1,000 deaths. Live on air during the televised benefit concert that followed, Kanye West tells the American public that 'George Bush doesn't care about Black people' and Green Day release 'American Idiot', a song (and then corresponding album) aimed at the same president.* Time *magazine's Person of the Year is 'The Good Samaritan', by which they mean Bill and Melinda Gates and Bono.*

Causing trouble at the *Q* Awards, 2005, with poor Robbie Williams and Chris Martin in the firing line. Shot by Mick Hutson.

'Lyla'

SINGLE
RELEASED 16 MAY 2005

Somewhat sadistically, Oasis developed a habit of introducing new drummers via the medium of a headline set on the Pyramid Stage at Glastonbury. Alan White had done it in 1995. And in 2004, after a very similar amount of time to rehearse – two months or so – it was the turn of Zak Starkey to do the same. White had departed Oasis early that year after a dispute about band meetings – or rather not showing up to band meetings.

In contrast to White, when he took to the Pyramid Stage, Starkey had plenty of experience of previously playing to outdoor crowds of such a size. Since 1996, he had been the drummer for The Who, filling the not-insubstantial shoes of Keith Moon (and the less substantial but still-not-insubstantial shoes of The Faces' Kenney Jones, who had joined after Moon's passing). In 2000, he had found time to moonlight with Johnny Marr's band The Healers, whose debut shows included a number of support slots with Oasis. By November of that year, he was back onstage with The Who at the Royal Albert Hall, when they were joined onstage for 'Won't Get Fooled Again' by Noel Gallagher. So his and Oasis's paths had crossed more than a few times.

And then there was the small matter of who his father is. 'If he can get us his dad's autograph,' joked Noel, 'then he's in.'

Zak's father is of course Richard Starkey, better known as Ringo Starr, drummer in that band from Liverpool from whom Oasis sought more than a little bit of inspiration over the years. Zak's father had given him a beautiful four-piece champagne sparkle drum kit for his eleventh birthday. After that, he gave him one drum lesson: less out of inattentiveness, more because his young son was, even then, well on his way to becoming a fantastic drummer with his own distinct style.

‘I think we kind of George Best-ed it the last time we headlined,’ Noel Gallagher said just ahead of their slot in 2004. ‘So this time will be great, I think. Then again, we’re not doing ourselves any favours because Zak’s first gig will be to 150,000 people.’

As it turned out, through no fault of Starkey’s, it wasn’t great. Liam Gallagher later blamed his switch to in-ear from onstage monitors. It was unfeasibly muddy. They hadn’t played live in a while, let alone with a new drummer and a couple of songs to bed in. Quite soon afterwards, it was being talked about very negatively by fans (who by now of course had messageboards to post on) and went on to be one of Oasis’s less well-thought-of moments.

Basically, they kind of George Best-ed it. Again. And then there was, following aborted sessions with dance duo Death in Vegas (see ‘Turn Up the Sun,’ page 281), a sixth album to make from scratch, for which Starkey would be involved. It went well and they soon had plenty of songs recorded. Somebody in an office somewhere, though, decreed that none of them were single-worthy, and so a Noel demo of ‘Lyla’ – ‘annoyingly catchy and sounds like The Who,’ according to its author – was bolstered by a new drum track from Zak plus a fresh vocal from Liam and readied as the lead-off single from *Don’t Believe the Truth*: a turn of events that did not sit well with Noel Gallagher.

‘If it was up to the band, that wouldn’t be the single,’ he said. ‘Don’t get me wrong: I think it’s a brilliant song. But it was the powers that be, whoever they fucking are, that decided that “Lyla” was the first single. It’s a fucking scandal that as the leader of the group I don’t get to pick what Oasis fans hear first.’

The severing of ties with Sony – who, since the demise of Creation in 1999, had been Oasis’s label – had begun. Yet, in the meantime, ‘Lyla’ did more than OK. It went straight in at number one, though that was to be expected. But it was when Oasis debuted it live, with the tumbling crescendo of Zak Starkey drums that characterize its outro, that its true magic revealed itself. The simple, poppy chorus was bellowed back at them at deafening volume by a crowd pogo-dancing up and down as one. It was to take pride of place as the second song on the setlist at every show they played, right up until the end in 2009.

Which is not to say the powers that be were right. But . . . **HM**

'Eyeball Tickler'

B-SIDE OF 'LYLA'

Speedfreak punk blues was, thanks to the White Stripes, pretty en vogue at the start of the millennium. And Gem Archer was certainly capable of bringing that to the Oasis table, knowing he had a singer who could rasp his way through this kind of material with the best of them. And who else could infuse lines like *'I got my drip drab velcro moustache, keeps them all at bay/Get yours someday'* with such feeling? **HM**

'Won't Let You Down'

B-SIDE OF 'LYLA'

It's not divulging any secret sauce to suggest that Liam Gallagher's songwriting was influenced by the solo work of John Lennon. Tucked away on the CD single of 'Lyla' is a prime example of this, even if it's not the best of Liam's output, partly because of a strangely reedy vocal and a dusty old production. Over an echoey acoustic thrash, Liam begins the song promising loyalty and love to someone who is otherwise *'surrounded by clowns.'* By the chorus, he's suggesting they get on it together: *'Let's get out of our minds/Won't waste your time/Give it a try!'* Who could refuse? **TK**

Don't Believe the Truth

(ORIGINAL UK RELEASE: 30 MAY 2005)

1.	'Turn Up the Sun'	3:59
2.	'Mucky Fingers'	3:55
3.	'Lyla'	5:10
4.	'Love Like a Bomb'	2:52
5.	'The Importance of Being Idle'	3:39
6.	'The Meaning of Soul'	1:42
7.	'Guess God Thinks I'm Abel'	3:24
8.	'Part of the Queue'	3:48
9.	'Keep the Dream Alive'	5:45
10.	'A Bell Will Ring'	3:07
11.	'Let There Be Love'	5:31

Bass: Andy Bell

Drums: Zak Starkey (Tracks 1, 3–11), Terry Kirkbride (Track 2)

Guitar: Gem Archer

Guitar, vocals: Noel Gallagher

Vocals: Liam Gallagher

Written by: Andy Bell (Tracks 1, 9), Gem Archer (Tracks 4, 10), Liam Gallagher (Tracks 4, 6, 7), Noel Gallagher (Tracks 2, 3, 5, 8, 11)

Producer: Dave Sardy (Tracks 1, 4, 6–11), Noel Gallagher (Tracks 2, 3, 5)

Recorded at Olympic Studios, Strangeways, Capitol Studios, Wheeler End, between December 2003 and January 2005.

'Turn Up the Sun'

Like the album it opened, 'Turn Up the Sun' started off heading in one direction but eventually wound up many miles in the opposite location.

In January 2004, Oasis were about to start work on a new album, with Richard Fearless and Tim Holmes of experimental electronic duo Death in Vegas producing. Two years earlier, Liam had added vocals to 'Scorpio Rising,' the standout number on the duo's third album of the same name. The psychedelic menace of the song and the clean, rhythmic production suited Liam's delivery perfectly: perhaps Death in Vegas could help Oasis similarly?

Before work started, Noel realized that it was ten years 'to the day' since Oasis had begun excavations for *Definitely Maybe* in Sawmills studio in Cornwall. So partly out of sentimentality it was decided to head back there for album number five. 'We thought, *The stars could not be more aligned,*' said Noel. The Gallaghers remembered the studio as being palatial. 'We walked in and . . . "It's fucking cold in here."'

'The studio was shit,' said Liam, more succinctly. 'That was Noel's fault. He wanted to get all nostalgic. As soon as I walked in, I knew it wouldn't work.'

More disappointment was to follow. 'About two weeks in it became apparent we didn't have the songs – only half an album really,' decided Noel.

In total, they spent around a month trying to make the bones of *Don't Believe the Truth* fit together from the bits they had with Fearless and Holmes. 'It never really happened in the end,' said Noel. 'I tried to make it as psychedelic and experimental as I could, but we just didn't have the songs. It was really hard to have the meeting with Richard and say, "We're not taking it any further." He was convinced it was going in the right direction. He kept saying, "You're fucking insane! It's going to be amazing!" It was difficult but we shook hands in the end. It was too soon.'

'It wouldn't have sounded anything like Oasis,' said Andy Bell. 'But it would've been an amazing Death in Vegas record. They had some kind of head-trippy thing in mind.'

In something of a 180-degree shift, American producer Dave Sardy (who'd recently scored a big hit with Australian good-time rockers Jet's debut LP) was drafted in to work with Noel on production in LA after a short break. He made one significant suggestion. 'He said a few things about my songwriting I'd forgotten,' explained Noel. 'He said, "The thing about your songs is, why write another verse when three choruses will do?"'

Noel was taken aback by this observation. He could only agree. 'Who listens to verses anyway? Verses are shit. He was also better at massaging Liam's ego, getting the right performance. Every time I say to Liam, "You might want to try to back off on that," the words he hears in his head are, "Your two sons are lesbian Nazis."'

'Turn Up the Sun' began its own life as a lament, a winter-time blues, born in Andy Bell's Swedish home. It was a literal plea for some warmth. 'The lyrics make perfect sense when you realize they were written by Andy Bell who lives in Sweden,' observed Sardy.

'It was really downbeat,' recalled Bell in 2020. 'It was like a La's demo, one of those tracks they did like "Over", very lo-fi and hushed. I really liked it, but I didn't know what I was going to do with it.'

What he did was give it to the other members of Oasis and put it to the back of his mind, until he turned up late for rehearsals one day. As he walked in, he recognized what the others were playing. 'They gave it this huge rock 'n' roll makeover. It blew my head off. They made it what it became.'

Noel, however, always had it in mind for *Don't Believe the Truth*. 'From the first time I heard it, it was always going to be the opening track.' In fact, he said, for a while it was the album's working title.

The intro and outro, all chiming guitar play, bear some resemblance to its frosty Swedish origins, but the rest of the song – the meat – was pure Oasis. 'It's just a behemoth,' said Sardy. 'Recorded sixty-five times, three thousand tracks, just a wall of sludgy aggression.'

There had been one other significant change in the song, something completely altered to its character. In the song that Andy Bell wrote, the first line was *'I carry a sadness everywhere I go.'*

'In rehearsal that got changed to *"I carry a madness everywhere I go",'* Bell revealed. 'It fits it so much better with Liam singing that. I think it was Liam's idea. That was the effect they had on the song. It makes it Oasis.'

'Turn Up the Sun': born in Sweden, made in Burnage. TK

'Mucky Fingers'

'I had to write "Where Did It All Go Wrong?" to get to the point now where I can write "Mucky Fingers" and go, "Wa-hey, it's back!"' Noel said around the time of *Don't Believe the Truth*. 'That's all part of the story. It's all part of the life of Oasis.'

Something was certainly different. The fact that, collectively, Oasis had been listening to Dylan's *Highway 61 Revisited* during the making of *Don't Believe the Truth* was most evident on its second track: a song with a similar kind of clattering production and a noisy harmonica part played by Gem Archer. There were shades, too, of the Velvet Underground.

'Mucky Fingers' is powered by a primitive, 'Waiting for the Man'-style chug-chug rhythm and a cheap piano that Andy Bell bought on eBay for £50. Long-term guitar tech Jason Rhodes was dispatched to a block of flats somewhere to pick it up from the seller, who lived five floors up.

The lyrics, meanwhile, make it pretty clear where Noel Gallagher is at. *'Fed up with life in the city,'* sings the now-grown-up kid who once 'dreamed of moving to London' and then did in the euphoric middle section, *''cos all the phonies have blown my mind.'* In 1999, he had finally sold Supernova Heights – 'the biggest tourist attraction in Belsize Park' – to actress Davinia Taylor, then moved to Chalfont St Giles in Buckinghamshire. 'It's a bit isolated out here, yeah,' he said at the time, 'but it's fuckin' fresh air, innit? I can actually walk round the garden without somebody sticking a camera up my arse. If I want to play my music double, double, double loud, then I can.'

'Mucky Fingers', in sentiment and sonics, was a world away from the original Oasis sound. But just like 'Lyla', it fitted nicely into the live show: sandwiched most nights between 'Live Forever' and 'Wonderwall'. Noel played it frequently with the High Flying Birds many years later, too: a song on which he sounded more joyous than he had in a long time. **HM**

'Lyla'

SINGLE RELEASED 16 MAY 2005 (SEE PAGE 277)

'Love Like a Bomb'

There are few introductions in British cinema quite as striking as Julie Christie playing the free-spirited Liz in the 1963 British comedy-drama *Billy Liar*. The world's first view of Christie is as Liz hops from the cab of a lorry she has just hitched a ride in, then, humming a tune, she swings her handbag and skips down a drab Northern high street, making faces in the window of C&A. This is a young, carefree, liberated woman, the kind rarely viewed onscreen previously.

'Oh, she's crazy,' marvels Billy Liar, awestruck from afar. 'She just enjoys herself.'

Perhaps this was the moment Liam Gallagher had in mind when he composed 'Love Like a Bomb'. Or maybe it was Christie a few years later, winning an Oscar in the Swinging London of *Darling*, or starring in the epic *Doctor Zhivago* . . . it was definitely her, though.

'All I see with "Love Like a Bomb" is Julie Christie,' said Liam upon *Don't Believe the Truth*'s release. 'That's the woman in it. I wanted the sound to be a bit Elvis.'

Performing the same role that 'Songbird' had on *Heathen Chemistry*, 'Love Like a Bomb' is a blast of warm sunshine, a swirl of acoustic guitars and Liam sweetly singing '*You turn me on, love's like a bomb, blowing my mind'* from what sounds like the very bottom of his heart. 'It's meant to be pastoral and uplifting – in a lad kind of way,' said its co-composer, Gem Archer. 'Liam plays guitar like he's going to saw it in half.' Martin Duffy, the late keyboard magician of Felt and Primal Scream, was enlisted for a sparkling piano break that elevates the song to an even higher plane.

Once again, Liam had wrong-footed all his colleagues with the gentle outer range of his writing capacity. 'It was quite surprising to me,' said producer Dave Sardy. 'It's kind of light, which is not what you think of with Oasis. It's actually rather pretty.'

Andy Bell agreed. 'It's a beautiful Liam tune. He shows a side of himself in his songs that he doesn't often show in his public life.' TK

'The Importance of Being Idle'

In the era before streaming rendered the UK Singles Chart meaningless, it was typical for the single preceding a band or artist's album to chart high. After that album had been released, less so, fans of the band being unwilling to spend £3.99 on a CD or 7-inch featuring a song they already owned plus a couple of extra tracks. (And yes, the idea of anyone, anywhere, spending that much – double that with inflation in today's money – on a CD or 7-inch featuring three songs really does now seem like an idea from a parallel dimension.)

By virtue of being notorious for tossing away ridiculously great songs as B-sides (see: half of this book), Oasis were better placed than most to buck this trend. But they still struggled. Even 'Wonderwall,' despite selling 3.5 million copies in the UK, never made it to number one. Neither did 'Stand by Me' (which followed *Be Here Now*), 'Who Feels Love?' (*Standing on the Shoulder of Giants*), 'Stop Crying Your Heart Out' (*Heathen Chemistry*). 'Lyla,' too, as expected, had topped the chart on its release a few weeks before *Don't Believe the Truth*. But by this point nobody really expected its post-album-release follow-up to do the same.

No wonder Noel Gallagher was 'so fucking made up' when 'The Importance of Being Idle' did: an indication that this was a song that was connecting with people Oasis might not ordinarily be connecting with.

'I was lying on the couch at home, two years into making the album,' said Noel of its writing. 'We'd scrapped it twice and Liam was on the phone going, "What the fuck are we going to do?" I was saying, "Look, it's all gonna be alright, don't worry about it." Everybody was trying to throw as many ideas into the mix as possible as to how we could make this album. And I was like, "It'll all come right in the end, stop panicking." All the songs were great, and it happened. That song is about that period.'

The title comes from an August 2000 book of the same name – or *The Importance of Being Idle: A Little Book of Lazy Inspiration* to give it its full title – by Stephen Robins. Proudly billing itself as a 'call to arms for would-be loafers everywhere to turn their hands to absolutely nothing whatever', it succeeds with the help of witty quotes from, to name but a few, Aristotle, Dickens, Chaucer, Bertrand Russell and Beau Brummel ('I like to have the morning well aired before I get up'). And, if its author ever plans on releasing an updated edition, Noel Gallagher could be included too.

Noel had previously, in 'She's Electric', 'Bonehead's Bank Holiday' and 'Digsy's Dinner', done funny. But 'The Importance of Being Idle' is the first time he had done witty. Every line – right up to the chorus's climactic '*I can't get a life if my heart's not in it*' – is a zinger: the way with words that had made his interviews essential reading even for people who didn't like his music finally appearing in song. It's self-deprecating, relatable, true . . . a song that the Noel Gallagher of *Definitely Maybe* could never have written, and all the better for it. By then he was a father moving into his late thirties and, rather than falling into the rock 'n' roll trap of trying to act like you are still eighteen years old forever, was writing about who he was.

Musically, it's a mixture of The Kinks' 'Sunny Afternoon' and, in the case of the intro, The La's 'Clean Prophet'. This would not be the first or last time that Noel would take direct inspiration from either band, but 'The Importance of Being Idle' is maybe the most unmistakably 'me' song that Noel has written. It would go on to be played at every Oasis show from the moment it was released onwards, and every solo show that he played after the band split. His first solo single, 'The Death of You and Me', bore more than a passing resemblance to it: a song on which one of the UK's greatest ever songwriters found a new way of going (lazily) about his business. **HM**

'The Meaning of Soul'

There's footage of Zak Starkey sitting in the basement studio of the famous Capitol Records building in Los Angeles hitting a packet of Wheaties wholegrain cereal placed on top of his snare drum with a pair of wooden spoons, as Oasis journeyed from studio to studio, slowly piecing together their sixth studio album, after the aborted Death in Vegas sessions. This is the rhythm you hear on the rollicking Liam Gallagher-written 'The Meaning of Soul'.

'We were trying to get a sound reminiscent of Elvis Presley's drummer D. J. Fontana on records like "Hound Dog",' explained Starkey.

This is the other side to Liam's songwriting of that time. On one hand, he was the pastoral moondancer of 'Songbird' or 'Love Like a Bomb'; on the other, he wanted to write in-yer-face rockabilly numbers, like 'The Meaning of Soul'. And with each side, he liked it to be short and sweet, no messing around with big intros/outros or showy solos. 'It's done in two minutes again,' said Gem. 'Doesn't mess around, as raw as possible.'

'Music wasn't that important to me ten years ago,' Liam explained, thinking about where this new creative outlet for him came from. 'Because Noel was writing them all. But I'm happy now. A lot of the stuff in me head is getting put out in the music, getting my frustrations out.'

Such was the enthusiasm for the song that even Noel had trouble recalling who played what: both he and Gem play bass, both play harmonica; Andy Bell played some guitar, as did Liam. 'Only Zak played the spoons, though.'

As for what the meaning of soul might be, nobody's sure that's answered within the song. 'I'm just having a rant, I suppose, not thinking about it too deeply,' Liam decided. 'It's not an anthem, it's spit in yer face.'

Andy Bell perhaps came closest to unveiling its 'ferocious' provenance. 'It's like Liam after five brandies,' he said, 'of which I have first-hand experience.' **TK**

'Guess God Thinks I'm Abel'

On which Liam Gallagher went Biblical. Not the 'biblical' that he would endlessly declare audiences/songs/sandwiches to be once he got a Twitter account. But actually Biblical.

As early as 1994, he was referencing the Good Book's most notorious pair of feuding siblings. 'I read something in the Bible, right,' he said in an early interview, used to set up the narrative of the *Supersonic* documentary. 'There was Adam and Eve, yeah, they had these two sons, yeah. These two sons had a fight one day, one fucking stabbed the other and that.'

'That's you two,' the interviewer responded.

Ten years later, with the sessions for *Don't Believe the Truth* progressing nicely, everyone else working on the sixth Oasis album assumed for a long time that the best of the three Liam Gallagher-written songs to feature was entitled 'Guess God Thinks I'm Able'. Then came time to actually write the track listing down.

'It's not fucking "Able",' Liam Gallagher said. 'It's "Abel".'

For those who skipped religious studies class, a quick refresher on what goes on with the actual Cain and Abel. Cain, the firstborn son of Adam and Eve, is a farmer who offers up his crops to God. Abel, his younger brother, is a shepherd who offers up the firstborn of his flock to God. God favours Abel's offering over Cain's, which enrages Cain to the extent that he murders his brother. God punishes Cain by banishing him to the Land of Nod, where he is doomed to spend the rest of his days wandering around alone.

So in the Gallagher version, Noel murders Liam, but gets sent off to exile for doing so.

It should be noted that, in the above 1994 interview, Liam finished his retelling of the story with, 'So Adam says, "Look, geezer, fuck off to the Land of Nod." The Land of Nod?! Where the fucking hell is that? My religion is The Beatles.' But a lot then happened in the next ten years; any human upon whom such good fortune had been bestowed could well become convinced that someone up there likes them.

During an interview at the time of *Don't Believe the Truth*, Liam insisted that he had 'always gone to church. I don't do confession. I've got nothing to confess. I'm practically a fucking saint. I'm not a God-head. I just think. I spend an hour with The Big One.' In the same piece, his brother was asked, separately, whether he believed Liam had really become a believer.

'I think he's shit scared of religion,' he said. 'I think he throws his chips in with the Lord occasionally just in case there's some truth in it.'

Liam was asked about 'Guess God Thinks I'm Abel,' and whether it was referring to the warring brothers of the Bible. 'It's meant to be. I thought I'd do it just to mess with people's heads . . . as well as my own.'

If this was the intention, it worked. 'He wrote [the title] out and we were all kinda looking at each other, going, "Hmmm,"' said Noel. 'I had to go back and listen to it, and then I was just sat down thinking about it and the story of Cain and Abel.'

'I'm thinking, "Well, that's very religious and biblical and it's a bit deep." But the first line of the song is "*You could be my lover*" which . . . you'd have to speak to Liam about. He has a religious fixation with Abel and Jesus, I think. It's very strange.'

If it is to be taken as a song about the relationship between its writer and Noel Gallagher, then 'Guess God Thinks I'm Abel' certainly supports the love/hate theory that most outsiders have. '*You could be my enemy/I guess there's still time,*' Liam sings at one point, while the verse previous notes, '*You could be my best friend/We stay up all night long.*' Most heartwarmingly – and pertinently – of all, there's a climactic sort-of-chorus that runs, '*No one could break us/No one could take us/If they tried.*'

Described by Noel as someone who 'doesn't live by the same timetable as the rest of us', the songs Liam was at this point writing had begun to take on this quality. The beauty of 'Songbird' had been its utter simplicity. 'Guess God Thinks I'm Abel', though, is structured in a way that feels completely spontaneous: shifting into new sections completely unrelated to the last. Nobody who had sat for hours and hours studying the craft of songwriting would come up with something like this. The full band kick in, loudly, for the last twenty seconds, then they're gone. In line with what Noel said, this is a song that is ticking by its own clock, written by a man who does the same. HM

'Part of the Queue'

In 2006, Noel Gallagher released an album on his Sour Mash label called . . . *The Corner of Miles and Gil*, the fifth LP of jazzy psychedelic rock by Liverpool's Shack, who Noel described as 'the second-best band in the world'.

There were plenty of similarities between Oasis and Shack: both were Beatles- and Bacharach-influenced groups from the north west of England, and neither could exist without the combustible fraternal bond and creative dynamic provided by their singer and guitarist. Before then, in 2005, Oasis unveiled a further similarity with the release of 'Part of the Queue'. 'It's Shack-doing-Love,' Noel admitted, referencing Arthur Lee's visionary sixties folk-rockers, which it partly was. It was also The Stranglers, of course.

'It's "Golden Brown" with bongos via Manchester,' agreed Gem, though the bongos were actually provided in LA by superstar percussionist Lenny Castro, responsible for the slaps on Toto's 'Africa', among many other well-known hits.

The subject matter, meanwhile, was a path that had been trodden before by some of Noel's great songwriting lodestars, such as The Jam on 'In the Crowd' and 'Shopping,' or The Clash with 'All Lost in a Supermarket': i.e., feeling alienated by big-city consumerism. In Noel's case, the song was inspired by feeling frustrated while he waited in a non-moving shop queue, buying either cigarette papers or milk, depending on the interview. What, wondered some long-time readers of Noel interviews, had changed since he'd declared in 1994 that, 'I want to write about shagging and taking drugs. I don't want to write about going down the supermarket.'

'It's about living in London,' countered Noel, describing the city he returned to after his break-up with Meg Mathews and when confronted with this quote by Tim Jonze in *NME*. 'When I moved here it was a magical place. I lived in Camden from '94 to '97 and it was the centre of the universe for music. These days, every cunt's got a business card, every cunt's got a man-bag.' **TK**

'Keep the Dream Alive'

'Andy is just great,' Noel said to me in 2008. 'He'll play you stuff and you go, "I have no idea what's going on in your head and how you think that is going to sound in any way remotely interesting on an Oasis record," then the next thing he plays you is so fucking hitting the nail on the head it's unbelievable. You just have to go "Where the fuck are you coming from?" Seven out of his ten songs you don't see it, you don't get it, and then the other three are incredible.'

As it turned out, Andy Bell would have the two most Oasis-sounding songs on the sixth Oasis album. 'Keep the Dream Alive' was the second – a reverb-drenched, echoing homage to the first Stone Roses album, all jangling guitars and swirling drums.

'I can't sing this like Liam, nowhere near,' Andy commented when he performed a 'busker' version of 'Keep the Dream Alive' on YouTube during the lockdowns of 2020. 'LG's vocal on the recorded version is right up there with his best for me.' Maybe so, but seeing the song in this form did show that he was just writing songs rather than trying to write Oasis songs. If anything, in this guise, it sounded like something that his first band, Ride – in which he was also co-lead vocalist – could have put out. Only when Liam got his teeth into it did that change. **HM**

'A Bell Will Ring'

In the Oasis divorce of 2009, Liam Gallagher took custody of live drummer Chris Sharrock, who arrived in 2008 when Zak Starkey left (mainly to due to schedule conflicts with The Who), along with Andy Bell and Gem Archer, quickly enlisting all three for his Beady Eye. It was Gem Archer whose absence Noel Gallagher felt most keenly.

'I miss Gem,' Noel said in 2011. 'We used to be a great team; we did all my demos together. He's a brilliant guitarist and bass player. If anything was unfinished, he would say, "We can make this better".'

A year later, after touring with a new stand-in guitarist, Noel's position on losing Gem had further hardened. 'I should have had custody of Gem. I'm fucking jealous that he's in Beady Eye and he's not in the High Flying Birds, I've gotta say. He's my mate.'

Without diminishing his skill as a guitarist and writer, it was this last comment that is most revealing. Gem Archer was universally loved in Oasis. He was everyone's mate, largely because he was such a supportive, good-natured, even-tempered presence. No song that he contributed to Oasis better demonstrates his personality within the band than the paisley pop of 'A Bell Will Ring'.

'My favourite lyrics on the album are "A Bell Will Ring",' said Andy Bell. 'It's an unbelievably positive lyric. It's a typical Gem philosophy.'

This translates nicely to the upbeat, circular chime of the guitars on the song, a tune and delivery highly reminiscent of the 1966 work of The Byrds and, most obviously, The Beatles. 'It's the song that most sounds like *Revolver*,' confirmed Noel. Which probably explains one titbit Gem had learned about it, probably from Zak Starkey: it's Ringo Starr's favourite song on the album. TK

'Let There Be Love'

Noel Gallagher is, to say the least, no fan of jazz music. 'Please print this,' he told me in 2009. 'I fucking HATE jazz. Jazz is four people onstage having a better time than the 400 people in the audience. That's what fucking jazz is.'

One man who would take issue with this typically understated opinion is Noel's former idol, now close friend, Paul Weller. Weller has been as vocal about his love of John Coltrane and Charles Mingus as he has about John Lennon and Ray Davies. Jazz had seeped into the records he made with the Style Council, and then his solo career: not least on the 1994 single 'Hung Up,' which would go on to help Noel Gallagher finish one of his longest-gestating songs.

'I saw him playing it one night, do you know that tune of his, "Hung Up"? It's some fucking weird jazz chord. I said, "Show me that chord." And it took me eight years to write a song around it.'

The writing of 'Let There Be Love' began in 1998. It was demoed soon after, with completely different lyrics, all sung by Noel, under a working title of 'It's a Crime,' and then taken to the sessions in France for *Standing on the Shoulder of Giants*. It did not make that album, nor the one that followed it. But by *Don't Believe the Truth*, it was ready: even becoming the third and final single from the sixth Oasis album, with vocals now split between Liam on the verses and Noel in the Weller-jazz-chord inspired middle section. Bar 'Acquiesce,' it's the only time that this would happen on an Oasis song.

'Let There Be Love' would never be played live – it served as house-lights-up music for the tour around *Don't Believe the Truth* – but, like 'Stop Crying Your Heart Out,' it had an afterlife that went to unexpected places. In 2023, the most popular member of K-pop titans BTS – a boyband who managed to fill Wembley Stadium with 60,000 English people singing back to them in Korean – was readying his first solo album. The twenty-five-year-old Jungkook went on the BBC's *Live Lounge* to promote it, where, as is customary, he was to perform one of his own songs plus a cover version of his choosing. He chose 'Let There Be Love', and in doing so proved that generation after generation across the world were discovering Oasis for themselves, and an Oasis that stretched far beyond 'Wonderwall' at that. **HM**

'Can Y'See It Now (I Can See It Now!!)'

DON'T BELIEVE THE TRUTH BONUS TRACK

A curious quirk of the Japanese music market means that they require all western albums to feature a bonus track of some kind. The reasons for this are somewhat complicated, economic and frankly a bit too boring to go into here. But, in simple terms, it boils down to encouraging fans to buy an edition manufactured in Japan rather than one imported from the UK.

Over the years, Oasis normally solved this problem by adding B-sides from whichever album's singles. But, when it came to *Don't Believe the Truth*, there was, for the first and only time, a track that was not available anywhere else: an almost-instrumental piece – Noel sings the title a few times at the end – that repeats the chord sequence of 'Mucky Fingers' but dispenses with the song's Bob Dylan influence and slows down to a full-on Velvet Underground chug.

'Can Y'See It Now (I Can See It Now!!)' did finally get a wider release in 2009 when it popped up on *Brand Neu!*: an album celebrating the enduring influence of the krautrock legends of the same name and their much-copied motorik drum beat. Neu! are the sort of band beloved of insufferable 'I'm into more obscure music than you are' musos, so the inclusion of an Oasis track made them quite angry. They had a useful champion, however, in the shape of Neu!'s

Michael Rother, who said in interviews that, while some of the bands on the compilation 'don't impress me that much,' he did enjoy what was going on here. **HM**

'The Importance of Being Idle'

SINGLE RELEASED 22 AUGUST 2005 (SEE PAGE 285)

'Pass Me Down the Wine'

B-SIDE OF 'THE IMPORTANCE OF BEING IDLE'

If Noel could do criminally underrated B-sides, then why couldn't his brother too? This might just be the best song Liam Gallagher ever contributed to Oasis: a kind of bohemian ode to drinking on through to the early hours *('Let's go see the sun burst/Wait 'til I go numb first')*. The middle section – *'To all the mothers/Well come on now, don't be shy'* – is simply glorious. **HM**

'The Quiet Ones'

B-SIDE OF 'THE IMPORTANCE OF BEING IDLE'

A rare Gem song that is not a firing-on-all-cylinders rocker and lives up to its title. Strong shades of The Beatles' 'I Will' and a nice, understated Liam vocal. **HM**

'Let There Be Love'

SINGLE RELEASED 28 NOVEMBER 2005 (SEE PAGE 293)

‘Sittin’ Here in Silence (On My Own)’

B-SIDE OF ‘LET THERE BE LOVE’

Did Oasis like The Beatles? Yes. Did Noel Gallagher have any compunction in leaning on his influences? Absolutely not, never (and especially not for a B-side). Does ‘Sittin’ Here in Silence (On My Own)’ sound very similar to ‘Sexy Sadie’ from the White Album? Of course. And does this maudlin two-minute number feature the only xylophone solo on any Oasis song? Very possibly. **TK**

‘Who Put the Weight of the World on My Shoulders?’

GOAL! SOUNDTRACK

With characteristic bluntness, Noel commented that Oasis got involved in the soundtrack for the 2005 film *Goal!* – in which an illegal immigrant rises to football stardom – ‘because of the money, not for love of football’. Still, while the movie garnered reviews that could politely be described as mixed, the soundtrack was not to be missed: chiefly because it contained three new Oasis tracks. There was a garage-y rework of ‘Morning Glory’, a shuffling take on ‘Cast No Shadow’ and, most excitingly, this Noel-sung brand-new song, produced by Unkle, who teamed up the tender melancholy of ‘Who Put the Weight . . .’ with a suitably cinematic string arrangement. **HM**

'Damon Albarn? He went fucking bald trying to be me!'

On the frontline with Oasis #5

Looking back in time with Noel Gallagher, November 2006

I was in the *NME* office one day having not long started writing for them, when I overheard some people much more senior than me discussing who they should send to interview Noel Gallagher about the first ever Oasis 'best of', *Stop the Clocks*, that was coming out at the end of 2006.

It should be me, I thought. So I sent the editor an email saying that it should be me. 'Why should it be you?' came the reply. Suddenly in a job interview situation potentially far more important than any job interview I had ever sat through, I speed-wrote an enormous list of all the amazing questions I would ask, and how I'd been there as a fan from the start – in 2001, I'd queued for eighteen hours to get a ticket to see Oasis on the 10 Years of Noise and Confusion Tour – and wouldn't it be better, given it was a reflective, looking-back sort of an album, to have a die-hard fan doing it?

Unbelievably, the editor agreed. And so, a week later, I was being driven by the band's press officer to Wheeler End. 'You look nervous,' she said.

I was. I started babbling about what a fan I was, about hearing 'Live Forever' for the first time and so on and so forth. But in that situation, a press officer is hoping – a bare minimum – that the interviewer isn't going to start hyperventilating at the sight of their hero, which at that point I don't think I could have guaranteed.

As anyone who has ever read an Oasis interview might surmise, interviewing Oasis is on one level not the most taxing of assignments. Even on a bad day, you're pretty much just pressing record on your Dictaphone and letting the quotes come forth. But in some ways, that makes it more pressured: the bar has been set so high (see: any of my co-author's encounters) that you need it to be really good. *Stop the Clocks* struck me as a decent shot at this, and I had in my possession a collection of classic Oasis *NME* covers for Noel to comment on, which would surely be gold. And more to the point, easy.

'This is Hamish,' the press officer said as we went upstairs to where Noel was sat. 'He once queued up eighteen hours to get an Oasis ticket!'

Noel Gallagher looked at me with a slightly worried look in his eye – a smattering of the 'Jed, I'll level with you: I'm really scared' from *I'm Alan Partridge* – but I switched on the tape and off we went.

Within about two minutes – around about the time he described watching *NME* band of the moment Klaxons as 'like torture' – I knew it was going to be fine. He started talking about how text messaging was 'genius' because now you could bail on plans and not have people detect that you just couldn't be arsed to meet them. Fortuitously, too, Liam had recently made the cover of *Hello!* magazine for the wedding of *EastEnders* actress Tamzin Outhwaite, which I was going to bring up but didn't need to because Noel did.

'A pink fucking pinstripe suit! With a white vest! Fucking hell!' he raved of his brother's outfit. 'I was in our offices doing something and it just jumped out at me across the room, like, "What the fuck is that over there?" Only he could get away with the pink suit: colossal, man. Just . . . colossal!'

He was spot on about Arctic Monkeys ('They're great, but their public persona is a bunch of grumpy old men even though they're nineteen, d'you know what I mean?'); his relationship with Liam ('I'm always trying to say to him, "The core of Oasis is three fundamental things: you, me and the songs. Without one, it all just falls down." I wish he'd accept that'); and had more than one brilliant story, the best of which was being pulled aside by some misanthropic US customs because there was a problem with his documentation. 'I'm going, "Just phone anyone in England! Anyone! Email them a photo!"'

'All the fantasy's gone out of music,' he said at one point. 'Because everything is too fucking real. Every album comes with a DVD of some cunt going, "Well, we tried the drums over here . . ." Give a shit, man! It makes people seem too real, whereas I was brought up on Marc Bolan and David Bowie and it was like, "Do they actually come from Mars?"'

When the covers were brought out – most of which I had bought as a teenager – it was just great. On the famous 'Blur versus Oasis' one: 'Shit cover. The thing about that whole "Roll with It" versus "Country House" thing was that they were both shit songs. I thought I'd written the hit of the summer, Damon thought he'd written the hit of the summer, then Supergrass come along with "Alright" and just 'ave it! Thing is about [Damon] is that he still thinks I hate him, which fascinates me. He thought he was the king of London, and I was like, "No, I am the fucking king of London!" He was desperate for all that "spokesman for a generation" shit – he went fucking bald trying to be me!'

He loved the 'Morning Glory' era one of him and Liam ('I tell you, I can pinpoint exactly when I started using cocaine excessively by the clothes'); was less keen on the *Be Here Now* big exclusive ('The single worst cover shoot we ever did. Look at me! I look like Windy Miller out of fuckin' *Trumpton* [*sic*]!'); and very, very funny about the Liam solo one from Glastonbury 2004 wearing a bright white parka. 'This is one of those occasions where he comes out of his trailer and you're just like, "What the fuck is he doing?" I'll go to him, "You're not wearing that, are you?" I mean, I know you're trying to make a statement, that it's Glastonbury, everybody's dirty and you're wearing white, but fucking hell . . . looks shit with a skinhead, that's all I'm saying.'

There was some music, too, but not too much. He saw my question about why there were no songs at all from *Be Here Now* on the 'best of' and was ready. '"D'You Know What I Mean?" was on it for a bit but it upset the flow of the album, and I wasn't going to put a *Be Here Now* track on it for the sake of it. Perversely, I kind of like the fact that there's a whole new album for people to discover. That's who it's for: the kids in the future. It's supposed to be a concise introduction to Oasis.'

Buzzing on the way home, I wrote the interview up immediately and sent it in. The editors said that they loved it, but that there was one problem: it had been decided that Liam should be on the cover, too, so could I knock up a side panel with some of his old quotes. Oh, and if you speak to the press office, don't tell them what we're doing, because they don't know.

This is the end of the world, I thought (I was twenty-five years old): *Noel is going to hate it, and me.*

But, of course, he couldn't have given a shit. Even better, when I turned up at the premiere of 'Lord Don't Slow Me Down' a few weeks later, he came over and told me he'd loved it, and asked if I was coming to the party later. I was not on the guestlist, but somehow got in with a little help from some friends. The rest of that night is a blur of a kind I have rarely experienced. An *NME* colleague said that I was in a corner with Noel toasting me – 'You have the youth!' – and dancing to 'Cigarettes & Alcohol' with him when it came on. As the lights went up, I somehow found myself ballroom dancing with Noel into the back of a car, blinded by the lights of the paparazzi flashes. 'To Ringo's house!' he shouted at the driver. And off we went.

Around 5 a.m., I realized I was not going to be able to make it to work the next day and so texted someone – Noel was right: texting *was* genius – to say that I was ill. But there was one problem. There was a paparazzi photo of me, looking somewhat worse for wear, with Noel, that for some reason had been splashed big on the gossip pages of one of the London morning papers.

'Ill, huh?' someone at work texted me. I didn't reply. *Shit.*

Stick to the story, I thought. You can be out late and still be ill, can't you? The two are not mutually exclusive, are they? But I was scared. If I lost my job then, hey, it would have been worth it – I had a story that discredited the 'never meet your heroes' maxim in some style – but I really, really didn't want to lose my job, even if my next assignment was interviewing Keane. But the *next* day I sheepishly entered the *NME* office . . . and everyone got up and applauded.

I like it here, I thought. *Can I stay?*

2007

To much fanfare, Apple CEO Steve Jobs unveils the first iPhone to the world and, a month later, microblogging site Tumblr is launched. A total lunar eclipse is visible from the Americas, Africa, Europe and Asia. British three-year-old Madeleine McCann disappears in Lagos, Portugal, the subsequent case becoming the most heavily reported in British history. Tony Blair resigns as prime minister and leader of the Labour Party, with then-chancellor Gordon Brown replacing him. The Live Earth concerts are held in nine major cities across the world, with the aim of raising environmental awareness. Britney Spears is pictured on the front page of US tabloids having her head shaved. Rihanna releases 'Umbrella'. One Victoria Borwick is defeated in the Conservative Party's London mayoral selection by one Boris Johnson. Javier Bardem stars in No Country for Old Men *and the first episode of* Mad Men *airs. The year ends with Led Zeppelin reuniting for a one-off show at London's O2 Arena: a preposterously star-studded affair attended by – among many others – Paul McCartney, Naomi Campbell and Noel and Liam Gallagher.*

Closing the show at the 2007 BRITs, Earl's Court,
where Oasis had just received the lifetime achievement award.
'Seeing as we don't get nominated for this shit any more,
I guess this'll have to do,' Liam tells the crowd.

'Lord Don't Slow Me Down'

STANDALONE SINGLE

RELEASED 21 OCTOBER 2007

If you want a documentary that presents life on the road in a phenomenally successful band as a hellish, stressful existence, then you should watch Radiohead's *Meeting People Is Easy*. If you would prefer a film that instead makes you think it must be the best job in the world, then Baillie Walsh's *Lord Don't Slow Me Down* from 2007 is for you.

Aside from one heated argument between Liam and Noel, it takes you behind the scenes of an Oasis tour on which the band seem to be having the time of their lives, twenty-four hours a day. Shot in beautiful black and white, Liam quaffs oysters on a speedboat, Noel belly-laughs his way through strange interview questions, Gem and Andy perpetually look like they've won the lottery, which they kind of have, except this is even better. If you win the lottery, you don't get to play a heated game of Frustration! with the Gallagher brothers.

It was a film that deserved a new song. Noel went into the vault and came out with a tune from the *Don't Believe the Truth* sessions that he described as 'one of the best things, like The Who, The Yardbirds and the Jeff Beck Group combined . . . and it's got two drum solos on it!'

Uniquely for an Oasis song, there are versions with both Liam and Noel singing. The Noel version was the official release – with the dubious honour of being the first ever download-only Oasis song – but in truth there's little between the two. It's more about the vibe: a rough-and-ready, bluesy stomp that's out the door in just over three minutes and is a lot of fun during that time.

'I'm tired, and I'm sick,' Noel (or Liam on the later-leaked version) sings. On the evidence of the film of the same name, nothing could be further from the truth. **HM**

'Who do you think started the fucking sing-along?'

On the frontline with Oasis #6

Glastonbury and the (attempted) cancellation of Noel Gallagher, August 2008

In the modern world, we are of course familiar with the idea of someone saying something off the cuff and that something then being taken in isolation and used to hang the person who said that something out to dry in the digital town square. But back in mid-2007, with Twitter just a twinkle in the eye of Silicon Valley, it was less prevalent. Lots of people were just starting to get their heads around Facebook and shutting down their MySpace page. But two years on from Tom Cruise jumping up and down on Oprah's sofa becoming the first ever viral moment – not that it was referred to as a viral moment at the time – news outlets were starting to see how moments could become stories much more quickly than they previously had.

Enter Noel Gallagher. 'I'm sorry, but Jay-Z?' he had told BBC News back in April. 'No chance. Glastonbury has a tradition of guitar music and even when they throw the odd curve ball in on a Sunday night, you go, "Kylie Minogue?" I don't know about it. But I'm not having hip hop at Glastonbury. It's wrong.'

The context of these comments (remember context?) was that Glastonbury had not – as unthinkable as this might seem in the modern era – sold out anywhere near all its tickets that year. In 2007, the Pyramid Stage bill had been topped by Arctic Monkeys, The Killers and The Who. Noel was being asked at the end of an interview why he thought that might be and answered in his usual outspoken fashion. Having said lots of far worse things, he did not think he had anything to worry about.

And then all hell broke loose.

Suddenly, every news site, music or otherwise, was running with a headline along the lines of 'NOEL: HIP HOP IS WRONG FOR GLASTONBURY'. By the time Jay-Z stepped onstage on the Saturday night, he was well aware of what a scandal this had been built up into and came out with a guitar draped around his neck, the clip of Noel playing on a loop, and started his set by miming along to 'Wonderwall'. Before he had even begun, the press had their picture and their narrative . . . and their villain.

Two months after all of this, I had been sent to the west London studio where Oasis were rehearsing to interview Noel for *NME*: his first interview since all of this. He knew what was coming. And so when I, somewhat sheepishly, asked him to make a comment about the furore he had unexpectedly created, he was ready.

'I'll say it once and I'll say it very clearly,' he said, picking up my Dictaphone. 'I wasn't saying I was better than Jay-Z as a person or rock was greater than hip hop as a thing or whatever it is. I said what I said, and it was wrong, or it was taken wrong, and now all this. And that's all I gotta say.'

This, I recognized, was a paraphrasing of John Lennon's comments in 1966, when he had claimed in an interview that young people were more infatuated with The Beatles than they were with Jesus. People back then had responded by organizing mass public burnings of Beatles records – meaning that John Lennon, wherever he is now, can lay claim to, among all the other things he pioneered, inventing the concept of being cancelled.

'That's all I gotta say,' Noel reiterated. 'Print that quote. The amount of attention that got was fucking ludicrous. Ludicrous! Print that quote – that's all I've got to say about it.'

But, of course, it wasn't.

'That's the broadsheets for you, man, you know what I mean?' he continued. 'I don't really get what all the fuss was about. I don't know. I was just kind of sat there and it takes on a life of its own. And then you're just like, "What the fuck is everybody going on about?"'

Noel Gallagher, of course, does not and did not hate hip hop.

There had been a sample of NWA underpinning 'D'You Know What I Mean?' And it stretched further back than that. 'I fucking went to see the Def Jam tour in Manchester in nineteen eighty whenever it fucking was, with Public Enemy, Run-DMC and the Beastie Boys!' he told me. 'But I'm not going to sit here and list all the records I own, because I don't fucking have to. It's just like, if people in *The Observer* and *The Guardian* wanna get on their high horse about it, there's not a lot I can do about it.'

Did it not piss him off? I asked. The idea of anyone who doesn't profess their love for every kind of music being cast as some kind of bigot?

'It really pisses me off. All these spotty herberts whose mams and dads voted for Margaret Thatcher all those years are now sitting on some moral fucking highchair. It's like, "Get to fuck, man!" There's no point in dwelling on that side of whatever comments I made, that's kind of . . . I wouldn't want to carry that on. But the thing about people being very right-on is that it's just . . . suffocating. It's suffocating and boring. Nobody can like every kind of music. Don't get me started on classical music. Don't get me started on heavy metal. It's just bollocks. But you know, hey-ho. My single went back in the charts. Jay-Z's profile went through the fucking roof. Everyone's a fucking winner.'

As it turned out, he had actually met Jay-Z before, when Oasis had appeared on the same bill at a festival in Japan. There is even video footage of this encounter – 'Is Jay-Z playing?' Liam beams as he sees a sign on a dressing room door, 'Love him!' – during which the band pose for a photo with him and he offers a 'My man!' handshake to Noel.

'And he's fucking cool as fuck!' Noel smiled. 'And I have a mutual friend in Chris Martin. He knows that I was misrepresented, as I guess he was, so let's fucking move on. And Glastonbury's full of those moments. Arctic Monkeys getting up with Shirley Bassey, that kind of thing. What do they call it? I think Jo Whiley calls them, "Seminal Glastonbury moments". That's what Glastonbury's all about, right? Plus it's a fucking great song.'

I had been at Glastonbury to watch the set, and 'Wonderwall' had certainly done what 'Wonderwall' tends to do in those kinds of scenarios. 'Well,' said Noel, 'I was saying to a guy the other day – some spotty herbert – he goes, "How do you feel about it, maan?" And I went, "I was there!" He goes, "You were there?" and I said, "Who do you think started the fucking sing-along?"'

'But I mean, people are so desperate, because there's fuck all going on at the minute,' he continued, getting back into slightly-more-serious mode. 'I think people are so desperate to write something about it. It got a bit out of hand, but there you go. For my own part I can sit here and say that I never dissed that fucking guy. I never would. But there's no point in going on about it because you end up sounding like Heather Mills – "I said this! I meant that!" To be quite honest, I really don't give a fuck. I'll have a beer with him one day and it'll all be fine.'

It was all fine. The next year's bill was headed up by Neil Young, Bruce Springsteen and Blur – and sold out instantly – but the modern era of Glastonbury, where any artist from any genre could headline without any controversy, was in the post. And Noel Gallagher himself would become an enthusiastic, regular attendee even when not performing. Asked what he thought of Kanye West's headline set in 2015, for example, he commented that 'For the first half an hour, it was as good as it gets.' (Like a lot of people, he had lost interest when it had descended – or rather ascended, given that West was elevated hundreds of metres above the crowd on a crane – into a 'Bohemian Rhapsody' sing-along.)

A coda to the interview I did came in 2009, when I interviewed Jay-Z for *NME*. Well, I say, 'I interviewed Jay-Z.' In reality, I had somehow orchestrated one of the magazine's sporadic 'when *x* met *y*' covers, and so was just sitting in. But given that the *y* to Jay-Z's *x* that day was Ian Brown – Chris Martin had had a hand in giving Jay-Z a Stone Roses explainer and telling him he should do it – it was bound to come up.

'That was something new for me,' Jay-Z said when it did. 'It was almost like we were conquering a territory. We came over and there were these tents, it was like war, you know!? There was all this banter, about hip hop shouldn't be here, and then, at that point, I was like, "Man, should I not be here?" I was like, "What have I gotten into?"'

'The people in control of the press and the media,' he continued, 'they all made it seem like it was a real thing, but once I played the short film at the beginning – about the people saying, "You shouldn't play Glastonbury" – when the crowd responded like "Nooooo!", that was when I was like, "Wooo!"'

I had been to see Jay-Z at the Roundhouse the week before, and he had finished his set with 'Wonderwall'. I wondered whether he was a fan?

'Well, that is the irony of it! At my bar called the Spotted Pig, that is, to this day, our theme song. The song, when everyone has had enough to drink . . . that is the song of the night! "OK, put 'Wonderwall' on now!" Because we know the place goes off, you get everyone singing. It is brilliant, you have a fantastic time. So, you know, it was like, "Man, it is weird how it works out." But it worked out.'

It certainly did. Glastonbury had been changed. 'Wonderwall' had been bought by the few people left on the planet who had somehow not at that point bought 'Wonderwall'. Everyone was indeed, once the dust had settled, a winner.

2008

A financial crisis begins in the United States and leads to the Great Recession, the worst economic downturn since the Great Depression. Music streaming service Spotify is launched, and work on the Large Hadron Collider is completed. The Dark Knight *is in cinemas, with its star Heath Ledger having tragically passed away in January.* Grand Theft Auto IV *is released worldwide, making $310 million during its first day – becoming not only the highest-grossing video game of all time, but also the highest-grossing entertainment product ever. The Marvel Cinematic Universe launches with* Iron Man, *starring Robert Downey Jr, while* Mamma Mia! *becomes the highest-grossing film in UK history. Apple launch the App Store, with 500 different apps initially available to download. Spain win UEFA Euro 2008, a tournament for which England did not even qualify. In November, Barack Obama is elected the 44th president of the United States, becoming the first Black man to do so.*

Announcing what will turn out to be the final Oasis shows – until 2025, at least – on the Wembley Stadium pitch in October 2008 (*left to right*: Gem Archer, Noel Gallagher, Liam Gallagher, Andy Bell). Shot by Samir Hussein.

'The Shock of the Lightning'

SINGLE

RELEASED 29 SEPTEMBER 2008

The launch of the seventh Oasis album was all nicely planned out. There would be a small Thursday night fan gig at their rehearsal studios, then on the Friday morning the live dates would be announced just as Noel Gallagher arrived at BBC Radio 1 to guest on Chris Moyles' *Breakfast Show* in order to premiere the new Oasis single.

A straightforward schedule that could only really be scuppered if the writer of said new single, instead of going to bed, went out after the fan gig and ended up pressing on through to his radio engagement. Which he did. Cue a quite spectacularly drunken radio appearance that could go toe to toe with the time Liam and Noel turned up on Steve Lamacq's show in 1997 and the former offered out every living member of The Beatles and the Rolling Stones.

Had things gone to plan, Noel would likely have been calmly discussing how krautrockers Can and Neu! had influenced 'The Shock of the Lightning' and how it fitted in on *Dig Out Your Soul* and guitar sounds and that sort of thing. Far more entertainingly, the UK's morning commuters instead got a litany of insults aimed at Robbie Williams ('He's officially on strike, isn't he? On strike from being brilliant'); Mark Ronson ('Wants to write his own tunes instead of ruining everybody else's'); Kaiser Chiefs ('I done drugs for eighteen years – three hundred and sixty-five days in a row for eighteen years – I never got that bad that I would go "You know what, I think the Kaiser Chiefs are brilliant!"') and anyone else unfortunate enough to have a playlisted single that morning.

There were stories about meeting Jeremy Kyle ('He actually said to me with a straight face, "When are we going to get you and your brother on the show?" He wasn't joking!'). When asked about the single, all Noel said was that it 'took me ten minutes to write that. No, eight minutes.'

Much like 'Lyla' on *Don't Believe the Truth*, the lead single from *Dig Out Your Soul* had been added at the last minute. It sounded a lot like Stereolab's propulsive classic 'French Disko' but with a big, cartoon drum solo in the middle played by Zak Starkey and lyrics like *'Love is a time machine/Up on the silver screen'*, which one critic with a straight face suggested might be about watching *Back to the Future*. It wasn't. It was Noel throwing words that sounded good together.

Because of the way the charts were compiled was changing, 'The Shock of the Lightning' became the first Oasis lead-off single since 'Supersonic' to not go in at number one. But no matter: it was a back-with-a-bang type affair, much like the radio interview given at the time of its unveiling. 'I don't really remember a great deal about that interview to be honest,' Noel said during a more sober appearance on Zane Lowe's show a few days later. 'I have no recollection of actually being in the studio. All I know is what I said was printed in the paper the next day . . .' HM

Dig Out Your Soul

(ORIGINAL UK RELEASE: 1 OCTOBER 2008)

1.	'Bag It Up'	4:40
2.	'The Turning'	5:04
3.	'Waiting for the Rapture'	3:03
4.	'The Shock of the Lightning'	4:59
5.	'I'm Outta Time'	4:10
6.	'(Get Off Your) High Horse Lady'	4:06
7.	'Falling Down'	4:20
8.	'To Be Where There's Life'	4:35
9.	'Ain't Got Nothin''	2:14
10.	'The Nature of Reality'	3:47
11.	'Soldier On'	4:50

Written by: Andy Bell (Track 10), Gem Archer (Track 8), Liam Gallagher (Tracks 5, 9, 11), Noel Gallagher (Tracks 1–4, 6, 7)

Bass, electric guitar, keyboards: Gem Archer

Drums, electric guitar, keyboards: Noel Gallagher

Drums, electric guitar, electronics, tambura: Andy Bell

Vocals: Liam Gallagher

Drums: Zak Starkey (Tracks 1, 3)

Producer: Dave Sardy

Recorded at Abbey Road Studios, London, England, 2007

Mixed at the Village Recorder, Los Angeles, CA, USA

'Bag It Up'

Early on in 2007, I asked Noel Gallagher if he had any sense of what the next album, which Oasis would begin to record later that year, would sound like.

'All the tunes I've written recently have been on the kind of acoustic side, you know?' he said. 'But I really fancy doing a record where we just completely throw the kitchen sink at it . . . We haven't done that since *Be Here Now*. I'd like to get, like, a 100-piece orchestra and choirs and all that stuff.'

'I think since *Standing on the Shoulder of Giants*,' he continued, 'we've been trying to prove a point of just bass, drums, guitar and vocals and nothing fancy. But I kind of like fancy! I'd like to make an absolutely fucking colossal album.'

When *Dig Out Your Soul* finally arrived, it was evident, on first listen, that he had had a change of heart. There were no 100-piece orchestras. No choirs. The opening 'Bag It Up' did sound colossal: but colossal in a different way. The guitar that opens it, and the album, is some of the rawest, most rough-and-ready guitar to ever feature on an Oasis song. Like 'Lyla', it is initially propelled along by a simple, pounding kick drum. It has a primal feel that is similar to the White Stripes' 'Seven Nation Army': a song that, by then four years on from its release, was well on its way to becoming the unlikely stadium-chant monster that it remains to this day.

Like much of the seventh album, it doesn't feature a huge, soaring chorus of the type that characterizes so many Oasis songs. It has no big guitar solo. Instead, it's a short, sharp blast of acid rock with a structure directly inspired by 'Baron Saturday', from the Pretty Things' 1968 album *S. F. Sorrow*. Noel and Oasis had begun hanging around with Kasabian quite a lot: Noel appeared onstage with them for the first time in 2006, and they would act as main support on the tour documented in the 2007 documentary *Lord Don't Slow Me Down*. One night on tour, Kasabian's very own

Noel-style mastermind, Serge Pizzorno, had put 'Baron Saturday' on. Noel wrote 'Bag It Up' shortly afterwards, then demoed it, along with two other songs, at Gem Archer's home studio. It set the tone for *Dig Out Your Soul*: the least Oasis-sounding Oasis record that there would ever be.

Recorded at Abbey Road with the tabloids having long moved on from tracing Oasis's every move ('Brilliant,' Noel told me nearer the album's release. 'You cross the zebra crossing and there's all the Spanish tourists – "Morning, can we have a quick picture?" – and you go in there, have a quick cup of tea in the canteen and then you clock in and do your thing'), *Dig Out Your Soul* was the result of an unusual setup. 'The dynamic of the group was me playing guitar, Gem playing bass and Andy on keyboards. Zak [Starkey] played the drums and that was it unless required, so Gem doesn't play a lot of guitar on it, Andy doesn't play a lot of bass and that seemed to work a little bit.'

The whispers, before anyone had heard it, was that this was to be a record that focused on grooves rather than songs. But this came about naturally, with all the members of Oasis writing separately. 'None of us discuss what kind of songs we're writing because that would be ridiculous,' Noel insisted. 'We don't go into the studio with a concept. We just go in and record the songs we think are the best and the rest will look after itself. But [producer] Dave Sardy came over for a meeting and said, "Have you got any songs with grooves?" So then the rest of the lads started digging out demos that were kind of in that vein.'

Noel had been quite candid about the fact that he had 'literally got nothing left to write about: I've wrote about being a youth, and I've wrote about being a rock star, and I've wrote about living life in the big city . . .' He had instead been looking back to his formative years.

'"Bag It Up" is about the time I used to do psychedelic drugs,' he said. 'You always remember your acid trips and mushrooms and glue-sniffing when you were a kid. It was kind of remembering all the old acid trips we used to have on the local golf course. That period of my life from fourteen to seventeen.'

This is certainly evident from lines like *'Someone tell me I'm dreaming/The freaks are rising up through the floor'*. Elsewhere on the album, there's quite a lot of biblical imagery. 'I know what you mean. All the fucking shit about religion, it's just like, "Woah!" I don't know where it's fucking come from. Quite mad, though.'

In the case of 'Bag It Up', there was another, very different, altogether more unfortunate coincidence. 'When I came home with the finished thing,' its writer remembered, 'I stuck it on and the missus goes, "'Bag It Up?' Isn't that a song by Geri Halliwell?" I'm straight on the internet and sure enough. I was like, "You've ruined my entire year."' **HM**

'The Turning'

A few months prior to the release of *Dig Out Your Soul*, I turned up to interview Noel and it had, as usual, been great: he was full of funny stories from the album's recording in LA, such as the time at a Marilyn Manson after show when Kenickie from *Grease* had pulled a knife on him, Liam and the rest of Oasis. Having finished up, I was about to make my way out until he said, 'Aren't you gonna watch us rehearse?' I would have loved to have stayed, but sadly I had a dentist appointment that I couldn't miss.

Just kidding.

Nobody knew that the set Oasis were running through in a west London studio that day would be for their last tour. They certainly didn't sound like a band near the end to me. Liam wasn't singing – 'I only sing on Wednesdays,' he told me – but I got to watch Noel, Gem, Andy and a newly installed Chris Sharrock ('He can play "Supersonic" properly!' beamed Andy) blast their way through a set of classics with some of the *Dig Out Your Soul* songs thrown in. 'The Shock of the Lightning' took pride of place three songs in, between 'Lyla' and 'Cigarettes & Alcohol'. 'To Be Where There's Life' and 'Waiting for the Rapture' slotted into the mix nicely.

As I was finally making my way out of the building – dazed by what I had just witnessed – I saw Noel sit down at the piano set up on the side of the stage and start to play the chords of 'The Turning'. This made sense: he'd talked in the interview about how, given it was one of the best, if not *the* best song on *Dig Out Your Soul*, they were looking to get it in the setlist for the tour. The problem was that, in its recorded guise, there were very few guitars on it, just lots of piano. Floating along on a beat similar to The Zombies' 'Time of the Season', it recalls the late-night car radio vibes of Doves – a band who had supported Oasis many times – until it exploded into the chorus, Liam elongating all the vowels in '*the rapture*' to menacing effect.

'The Turning' ended up never being played live. Maybe it was because Oasis couldn't quite get it right live. Or maybe it was just part of the problem of being a band with ninety minutes' worth of must-play material. When I watched them rehearse that day, 'Live Forever' wasn't in the set. That would obviously have to change when the stadium dates came around. Most bands don't have this kind of issue. Coldplay, say, only really need to play two or three songs from their first couple of albums. Whereas there are six songs each on *Definitely Maybe* and *. . . Morning Glory* that Oasis would not get out of the building without playing. The fact that I do not need to list them says it all.

As a songwriter, that's going to affect you. It's why Noel came up at the last minute with 'Lyla': because he knew it would work live among the bigger songs. I thought about 'The Turning' and other later, slightly different Oasis songs when I spoke to Noel immediately after the press conference to launch his solo career. I had asked him whether there was still road to be travelled with Oasis. 'You mean musically?' he asked. Yeah, I said.

'I think people had stopped listening,' he continued. 'People kept coming to the gigs, but people had stopped listening. It's like, if I was sat here today, doing a press conference for a new Oasis album . . . Well, I wouldn't be doing a press conference, would I? It would be like, "Oh fucking hell, Oasis have got a new album out, so what?" That's just the way it is when you go on for so long. Does anyone care about a new Rolling Stones album? They go and see 'em, don't they? The kids hadn't stopped listening, but I guess the press stopped listening. But I never felt we were at the end. Because half of this stuff, the High Flying Birds album, was written and demoed before that, so some of it was going to seep in there at some point. But it's all kind of in hindsight now. I mean, I didn't think of any of this stuff at the time.'

Two of his best solo singles, 'AKA . . . What a Life!' and 'Ballad of the Mighty I', were driven by piano rather than guitar, in the same way that 'The Turning' was. They became two of his biggest songs, both played at the majority of his solo shows. Suddenly, with only the Noel-sung Oasis songs plus maybe a couple of others – his solo acoustic version of 'Supersonic', for example – there was space for such things. HM

'Waiting for the Rapture'

Like *Heathen Chemistry*'s 'She Is Love', this is another song for Noel's then girlfriend, soon-to-be-betrothed and, over a decade later, ex-wife, Sara MacDonald. 'A love song inspired by the meeting of an angel in Ibiza,' he said unambiguously upon the release of 'Waiting for the Rapture'. It was pretty hard to misunderstand the message of the song, certainly: '*I still don't know what I was waiting for/Big love to fall down from the sky?/She took my hand and picked me up off the floor . . .*' Andy Bell described the directness of the song by saying, 'Noel can put things in a down-to-earth way that goes right to the core.' Lyrically it may have had plenty in common with 'She Is Love', but musically, as captured on *Dig Out Your Soul*, it lived in another galaxy. While 'She Is Love' is airy and light-headed, 'Waiting for the Rapture' is a big, guitar-heavy number that was one of only three songs from Oasis's last album ('The Shock of the Lightning' and 'To Be Where There's Life' the others) to make it on the band's setlist over the next year, which was something of a Greatest Hits. It had the requisite poise and volume to stand shoulder to shoulder with such exalted company.

Live and on record, it's essentially Queens of the Stone Age doing 'Roadhouse Blues' by The Doors. When, however, Noel did a solo version, on YouTube and also on BBC Radio 1 accompanied by Gem, the song shed its suit of metallic armour and revealed itself to be of an autumnal shade and filled with rueful reverie, so far away from the original as to be as good as a new song. And maybe somewhat better. TK

'The Shock of Lightning'

SINGLE RELEASED 29 SEPTEMBER 2008 (SEE PAGE 315)

'I'm Outta Time'

The Liam Gallagher-written song in the middle of *Dig Out Your Soul* was a big step forward for him. On the least Oasis-sounding Oasis record, it is the most Oasis-sounding song, with a chorus sung over the type of descending chord sequence that Noel Gallagher had used to great effect on all of his band's biggest songs, but which he had by then grown tired of. His younger brother, however, was just learning how effective this trick could be for a songwriter.

Liam Gallagher had the initial idea for 'I'm Outta Time' about three years before *Dig Out Your Soul* was recorded. As usual, the verse chords and melody came quickly. The lyrics, not complicated, had flowed too. In the past, that might have been that. Move on to the next one. But this time he knew it needed something, needed to go up, needed to soar. So he kept on messing about with it until something happened. 'When I finished that,' he said, 'I thought, *Yeah man, there's something in this writing business. I should keep it up and not throw in the towel.*'

Neither Liam nor anybody else knew at the time how apt the title of the second-last-ever Oasis single was. Had they continued on from that point, it's not hard to imagine a future in which Liam contributed a couple of classically Oasis-sounding songs to albums, leaving Noel to take his writing to new places. But it was not to be. As Beady Eye were hastily formed in the aftermath of the split – 'Beady Eye was just kind of a safety blanket for me,' Liam reflected to me after his second band had unceremoniously called it a day – their singer had gone back to his more impulsively written songs. By the time he went it alone, he was writing a little – 'Bold', solely credited to Liam, is one of the best moments on his first solo album – but was leaning heavily on what he called 'an army of songwriters'.

'It is what it is, mate,' he said to me when I asked him, in 2017, if he was worried how this would be perceived. 'I didn't write "Live Forever", but as soon as I sang it, I made it my own.'

The chorus of 'I'm Outta Time' is actually not a million miles away from 'Bold', rising to the kind of falsetto that Liam had not used since the earliest versions of 'Up in the Sky', and which he would go on to utilize on many of his solo songs, taking his voice to new places. His key inspirations, however, remained the same. 'I was playing it, and the outro goes round and round, it needs something,' he said. 'Obviously I'm a big John Lennon fan and it's got a bit of a Lennon vibe, so I thought, *Well, I've got to find a bit of him speaking.* So we went through all these old interviews, that's the first one I found, and it just sort of worked. It's not a tribute to John Lennon because if you sat down and tried to write a tribute to John Lennon it'd be fucking rubbish, but it's kind of a nod.'

The sample comes from a BBC interview with Andy Peebles that was recorded in December 1980. 'As Churchill said, "It's the Englishman's inalienable right to live where the hell he likes,"' Lennon says in it. 'And as I say to anyone who says, "Don't you get homesick?": what, do you think it's going to vanish? It's not going to be there when I get back?' Two days later, he was murdered outside the Dakota building where he lived in New York.

It fitted perfectly with the melancholy feel of 'I'm Outta Time', the most accomplished song that Liam Gallagher ever wrote. 'I think that was the one,' he said. ''Cos a lot of my songs, verses repeat and shit like that. And I don't have the big anthem chords. But I pulled that one off. I'm proud of that.' **HM**

'(Get Off Your) High Horse Lady'

'Let's not pretend I'm the world's greatest lyric writer,' Noel admitted to me in 2009, talking about what topics he had left up his sleeve. 'I always have to get the words to fit the tune – I'm not Morrissey or Dylan.'

An old song, written around *Heathen Chemistry* but resurrected for *Dig Out Your Soul* because 'the bass is so heavy', '(Get Off Your) High Horse Lady' could not be mistaken for the lyrical work of either Morrissey or Bob Dylan. There's a couple of lines about *'a fire in the sky'* but the rest is just the chorus repeated: '*Get off your high horse lady/I don't need a ride tonight/Lay down*'. A plea, in short, to avoid a row with your partner before bed.

The song itself is as close to the blues as Oasis ever came, sounding like J. J. Cale covering Tommy Tucker's 1963 mod blues anthem 'Hi-Heel Sneakers', a tune it almost identically resembles. Time has been kinder to this atypical Oasis song than contemporary reviews suggested. The bass line remains very good. No surprise it made a persuasive case for inclusion. TK

'Falling Down'

The final song on the first side of the final Oasis album also became their final single – and a single that its writer and singer would describe as 'the best-sounding of them all'. The first anyone heard of it was in remixed form – the first ever Oasis remix, no less – as a B-side to 'The Shock of the Lightning'. Noel Gallagher had worked with the Chemical Brothers before, contributing vocals to two of their most superb singles in the shape of 1996's 'Setting Sun' (one of the duo's two number ones) and 1999's 'Let Forever Be'.

These two songs, though, were far from his first two dalliances with dance music. Go back to the very first entry in this book, and you will be reminded that 'Columbia' borrowed its riff from Axe

Corner's 1991 single 'Tortuga'. Further back than that, too, in 1992 Oasis were covering Cartouche's 'Feel the Groove' as 'Better Let You Know'. Both of these are songs that Noel would have heard when he was a regular on the ecstasy-drenched dancefloor of Manchester's legendary Haçienda nightclub in the late eighties and early nineties.

'It was a forty-second walk from my house,' he said when he appeared on *Desert Island Discs* in 2015. 'I remember going there one night and, of course, never having done ecstasy, thinking, *This is nonsense. What is this music? There's no words. It's just a drum machine and I can't hear anything else.* And then taking ecstasy and going back and thinking, *This is the greatest thing I've ever heard in my life*. The music I still love to this day.'

Their detractors may have constantly lobbied charges of being guitars-only purists at Oasis. But from their very inception, dance music had fed, albeit subtly, into the mix of their sound. They just didn't put out a single that could feasibly be played in a club until the very end.

'Falling Down', like 'Columbia', is largely built around three chords that go round and round. Over the top you get one of Noel Gallagher's finest ever, most beautiful melodies. But its defining feature is its groove: a propulsive, hypnotic beat that, like the Chemical Brothers' 'Setting Sun', recalls The Beatles' 'Tomorrow Never Knows'.

In the midst of recording *Dig Out Your Soul*, Oasis had taken time out to contribute to the BBC's fortieth-anniversary celebration of *Sgt Pepper's Lonely Hearts Club Band*, for which thirteen different artists would cover the album's thirteen different songs. Rather than playing it straight, Oasis took inspiration from the 2006-released *Love* album, which mashed up Beatles tracks together. Lots of this album did not work. But one segment that did was the fusing of the rhythms of 'Tomorrow Never Knows' with the Indian vibes of George Harrison's sole contribution to *Sgt Pepper's* . . . The resulting Oasis version of 'Within You, Without You' in this style was – against admittedly not-stiff competition – by far the best contribution to the BBC programme. And also, in retrospect, offered hints as to where they might be going, then did go to great success with 'Falling Down'. Because it is the most remixable Oasis song ever, more versions were to follow as part of its release as a single on the B-sides. There is a superb, abrasive reworking by The Prodigy. And then, most significantly, there is the *A Monstrous Psychedelic Bubble Remix* by Amorphous Androgynous.

At twenty-two minutes, it is the longest piece of music Oasis ever released by well over ten minutes. It is also the most totally and utterly out there, with all manner of twists and turns and a whole segment sung by a female vocalist.

'I fully expect 50 per cent of you not to have the attention span to deal with something like that,' Noel wrote in his *Tales from the Middle of Nowhere* tour diary. 'But the rest of you, I hope, will be blown away. It's a staggering piece of music. Monumental even. All superlatives will apply.'

Noel Gallagher had first come across Amorphous Androgynous via their *A Monstrous Psychedelic Bubble Exploding in Your Mind: Volume 1* album. 'I've had it on in the dressing room for a month now,' he wrote in December 2008 in *Tales* . . . 'It's one of the best things I've ever, ever heard. Go and find it NOW! It'll blow your tiny little minds.'

In August of 2009, it was even announced that he would appear at one of the collective's live shows in London. A week later, Oasis split up. His appearance, which would have turned the event into a media circus, was cancelled.

But he stayed in touch with Amorphous mastermind Garry ('Gaz') Cobain. When it came to announcing his solo career in July 2011, the press assembled at Notting Hill's Electric Cinema were told that there were not one but two albums imminent. The first, *Noel Gallagher's High Flying Birds*, would be more song-based, while the second, in collaboration with Cobain, would be more experimental. As time went on, however, Noel grew increasingly dissatisfied and frustrated by the mixes that were coming back to him and the project became a fiasco. During a show at London's Roundhouse that November, someone in the crowd shouted out at him, asking him where the Amorphous album was. 'Well, I haven't finished it,' came the response. 'Would you buy it unfinished? Really? For a tenner?'

By 2015, having been asked repeatedly about it, Noel Gallagher declared that the album was, to borrow the title of one of his later solo songs, dead in the water. 'There's no bootleg because I own the master and I destroyed it,' he told *Noisey*'s John Doran. 'My manager's not even heard it. I wouldn't play it. It was so underwhelming to me that I never played it to anybody. I'm not going to put records out to please people and their imagination, then have them hear it and go, "Actually, it's a bit shit". I know it's shit. That's why it's not coming out. And that's the end of it.'

The record is survived by a couple of mixes that ended up as B-sides, one, 'Shoot a Hole into the Sun,' serving as the intro music for High Flying Birds live shows. Two songs on Noel's second solo album, *Chasing Yesterday* – 'The Mexican' and 'The Right Stuff' – had their production partially credited to Amorphous Androgynous. They were, however, nowhere to be seen on a companion album of *Chasing Yesterday* remixes.

One producer who *did* feature on that album, however, was David Holmes. He would later successfully work with Noel on the dance music-infused *Who Built the Moon?*. Released in 2017, it was his third and most critically acclaimed solo album, earning him his first Mercury Music Prize nomination since *(What's the Story) Morning Glory?* in 1996. More importantly, it was a record that – finally, thirty-odd years on from those Haçienda days – made good on the promise of 'Falling Down.' **HM**

'To Be Where There's Life'

'With Oasis, you'd put songs on the table and Noel would go through them,' Gem Archer told me. 'I do understand Noel's thing of always having the overall picture of the album. Like with *Dig Out Your Soul,* I put five songs on the table but none of their faces fit. So I came up with "To Be Where There's Life". It came, he said, 'out of thin air. I played this instrumental for Noel and he said, "Have you got any words?" I said no, but then I just had one of those good weekends; sometimes it can take weeks, but this took a couple of days.'

Among those lyrics was the line '*Dig out your soul, 'cos here we go*' which of course ended up giving the seventh Oasis record its title. Appropriate, given that 'To Be Where There's Life' – its heavy, almost dub bassline played by Gem rather than Andy – is the song on the album that most fulfils the record's stated brief of being groove-based. HM

'Ain't Got Nothin''

It was 2 December, the last night, as it turned out, of Oasis's German tour of 2002. Liam Gallagher, Alan White, tour DJ Phil Smith and Liam's security detail were enjoying some drinks in the lively bar of their fancy Munich hotel, Bayerischer Hof.

Details thereafter are hazy. 'We were sitting at a table under a balcony and Steve [Allen, Liam's security] has just pulled me by my neck under a table,' Liam told me in 2016, still raging about the incident. 'Next minute, some geezer on the balcony has dropped a massive table over the balcony on us. That's when it went off.'

There had, perhaps, been words exchanged earlier with some Italian and German 'businessmen' who were also in the hotel bar, about attention being paid to one of their female companions. 'I don't know what's gone down,' Liam said. 'Everyone was a bit pissed, but nothing to do with me. I was just having a lager and next thing I know I'm covered in Steve and glass and it is kicking off like you would not believe. That table would have killed us if it had hit anyone.'

According to Liam, this was a somewhat more hectic and violent incident than a typical barroom brawl. 'People were getting smacked with table legs, metal bars, all sorts.'

The fight moved out of the bar area and that's when dozens of police arrived. 'I might have kicked a copper at some point in the lobby,' Liam admitted. After that, he was knocked unconscious and awoke in a police cell minus his two front teeth. Liam is sure 'the police pulled them out with pliers.'

The police, meanwhile, maintain that he was running, tripped on the stairs and knocked himself and his teeth out. Liam remains unconvinced. 'I didn't have a fat or cut lip, which I definitely would've if I'd fallen on my face, but I just had these perfectly removed teeth! I woke up in a prison cell, handcuffed, no teeth and no other marks on me. What's that about?'

We may never know the truth of what really went down that night in Munich. But we do know that Liam was eventually fined €5,000 two years later, with the threat of jail hanging over him until then. In the interim, he wrote 'Ain't Got Nothin'', a song that furiously pleads his innocence. 'I wrote it,' he said, 'because everyone – the police and even people I thought were on my side – said we started it, and we fucking did not!' Despite Liam telling the press that 'Ain't Got Nothin'' was 'gonna be a hit' and it featuring on demos for *Don't Believe the Truth*, it lay dormant for five years until finding its rowdy way onto *Dig Out Your Soul*.

Liam's new teeth reportedly cost him between £9k and £20k, but he didn't forget the part his old front pairing had played in his heartthrob status. A week after the Munich incident, Oasis played in Cardiff and Liam dedicated 'Live Forever' to his former front teeth. TK

'The Nature of Reality'

In 2007, Andy Bell was in spiritual crisis, enduring what he described as 'a transitional phase in my life.'

Separated from his wife, he was travelling between Stockholm where she lived with their two young children and London, where he had recently bought a new home. 'I was becoming divorced from my first wife, but not yet attached to my second and final wife,' he said a decade later. 'I was trying very hard to have a "John Lennon lost weekend" and succeeding pretty well.'

Eventually, this wore him out, both physically but, more significantly, spiritually. He sought help and courageously described that process to *Q* magazine in 2008. 'I got divorced. And I went through therapy,' Bell explained. 'It felt like my life was empty of love at the time and the way I dealt with that was by becoming a staunch atheist, having been brought up as a Christian. It was a very religious upbringing. So I read Richard Dawkins's *The God Delusion*, and decided I wanted to be an intellectual – scientific, logical and rational.'

In this period of therapeutic change, Bell wrote 'The Nature of Reality'. 'It's me deciding there's no mystery. Later on, I stopped having the therapy and ended up falling in love again.' From here, he rowed back on his atheism. 'I wouldn't say I'm religious, but I'm definitely spiritual. Now, as far as I'm concerned, it's all about love. We don't know what love is, but we know that it's all there is.'

Bell felt the song too personal to include on an Oasis record, but Noel insisted, feeling its grungy thump too good to skip away from. The album needed some heavy guitars. The trade-off was that Bell would act as the song director, rather than band bassist.

'I taught Noel the guitar parts and then let him roll with it,' he said. 'Gem played bass on it. I don't play on it at all. I wanted to make sure that it sounded right in the control room.' **TK**

'Soldier On'

One of the biggest advantages of Gem Archer and Andy Bell joining Oasis for Liam Gallagher was that he had people who could help him get down his ideas for songs. Ocean Colour Scene's Steve Cradock had helped him demo his first Oasis song, 'Little James,' but when Gem and Andy arrived he had people he was in a band with who were up for meeting up, often, and getting the thoughts and melodies and chord structures down on tape in a more complete form than he would have the patience for on his own. 'He wants to write, but it takes him a while,' Archer reflected. 'You have to say, "Put your finger there on the guitar" . . . but he gets great songs out of it.'

'He's got his own style,' Andy said, 'and he's basically invented his own chords all the way along.'

'I'm into writing songs,' Liam told me, 'but I'm not going to freak out and go, "Whoa, these songs . . .!" I know there's all this spiritual nonsense that people go on about, but I'd be more worried about losing my voice than losing my ability to write a fucking song.'

Liam's attitude to songwriting – imagine it, get it out, move on to the next one – meant that from about 2002 onwards there was a huge vault of demos that no one could keep track of . . . least of all him. 'The thing about Liam is,' Noel said to me around the same time, 'that you've not even heard the half of it. If he could even be bothered to finish some of the songs he started . . . Honestly they're amazing. I've got demos of his at home with about forty tunes on them.'

The process for *Dig Out Your Soul* was that all four Oasis members would bring songs to the table and they would gradually narrow them down. But how are you supposed to do that when you don't remember even half of the ones you've done? Answer: leave it to others. 'Soldier On,' for example, would be lost, buried on some CDR somewhere, were it not for some other nosey musicians/Oasis fans: The Coral.

They had been at Wheeler End in Buckinghamshire, a beautiful studio that Noel had a long lease on. He'd been impressed by it when he was introduced to it by Paul Weller in the nineties and, having recorded much of *Standing on the Shoulder of Giants* in France, came to Wheeler End to finish the record. It then became a permanent base for Oasis, and Noel would often let bands he liked – such as The Coral – use it when they weren't there.

This meant that there would be a lot of Oasis's stuff around the place. And not just guitars, or coats. While The Coral were searching around in the studio for some ProTools plugin or other, they came across a hard drive titled 'New Oasis stuff'. So, of course, they next checked that nobody was looking and did what anyone would do in that situation.

And it was fortunate that they did. 'I was doing the Electric Proms with them,' said Noel, 'and [Coral singer] James Skelly, a bit sheepish, asks me, "Are you gonna do that tune 'Soldier On'?" Now I don't remember it, Gem doesn't remember it, Liam certainly doesn't remember it, but the other lads in The Coral are going, "You've gotta record this tune, it's fucking boss!" So I ransack this hard drive, can't find a track called "Soldier On". We get to Abbey Road and we're chatting away, and Andy Bell goes, "Soldier On"? Brilliant! I've got a CD of it in my bag.' Turns out he recorded it with Liam, but Liam still doesn't remember it. "Well," says Andy, "you were pretty fucking pissed."'

So into the mix of *Dig Out Your Soul* it went, a slow, somewhat ominous piece of almost dub-psychedelia with a rumbling bassline that ended up as the album's finale. Similarly to the way that, even when they were at each other's throats, McCartney would give his all to Lennon's songs, Noel added a melodica part and some harmonizing to Liam's mantra-like ending. And so the last song on the seventh Oasis album faded out with Liam and Noel Gallagher singing, in unison, about soldiering on and on.

Soon after that, they split up. **HM**

'The Boy with the Blues'

DIG OUT YOUR SOUL BONUS TRACK

There were plans for this Liam-written song to be a standalone release of some kind. '"Boy with the Blues" could be as big or small as you want it to be, it could be like a gospel track or something,' Noel enthused to me in 2006. It would have fitted in well with the plans he had at that point for a 'colossal sounding album, with two orchestras and stuff'. Once the idea for the seventh Oasis album shifted, though, it was – despite all the bells and whistles and strings and choirs – left on the cutting-room floor, to be released as a bonus track in the *Dig Out Your Soul* box set. The drums on it are provided by Jim Keltner, the legendary American session drummer who had played with all the Beatles bar McCartney, not least on the *Imagine* album. Doubtless some stories were coerced out of him. **HM**

'I Believe in All'

DIG OUT YOUR SOUL BONUS TRACK

Another Liam number left out from the final *Dig Out Your Soul* line-up, relegated to the Japanese version of the album until rescued for the box set alongside 'The Boy with the Blues'. It's a curious omission, as it fulfils Noel's stated aim for *Dig Out Your Soul* to be 'a rock 'n' roll album with grooves', though the groove here is more 1950s bop than contemporary dancefloor. Perhaps it was felt that only one song on the LP could mention 'a fire in the sky', and Noel had cornered that market with '(Get Off Your) High Horse Lady'. **TK**

2009

On 3 January, a cryptocurrency called Bitcoin is launched. James Cameron's Avatar *is released in December and becomes the highest-grossing film of all time. Manchester City finish their first season under the new ownership of Abu Dhabi United Group, who purchased the club for £400 million. Michael Jackson dies on the same weekend as Glastonbury, triggering a worldwide outpouring of grief. Noel Gallagher leaves Oasis, after a backstage altercation with Liam in Paris. A co-ordinated campaign to download Rage Against the Machine's 'Killing in the Name' and make it an* X Factor*-thwarting UK Christmas number one is successful. The band keep their promise and announce a free, one-off victory show in London.*

Liam sports a black parka from his new Pretty Green clothing range at the Rock Werchter festival, Belgium, July 2009. Just fourteen shows and one backstage fight later, Oasis will be no more.

'Falling Down'

SINGLE RELEASED 9 MARCH 2009 (SEE PAGE 325)

'These Swollen Hand Blues'

B-SIDE OF 'FALLING DOWN'

By the time of *Dig Out Your Soul*, Oasis were serving up remixes as B-sides – a Twiggy Ramirez remix of 'I'm Outta Time', anyone? – but their final single had a fittingly great original song. Pinching its title from Pink Floyd's 'Nobody Home' – and its line about masturbation – 'These Swollen Hand Blues' is a delightfully strange coda to Oasis that's as un-Oasis-sounding as they ever got. HM

'I'm a tiger! Welcome to the fucking jungle.'

On the frontline with Oasis #7

Forty-eight hours in Amsterdam, January 2009

On the morning of 21 January 2009, Noel Gallagher delivered a new post for his enjoyable online tour diary, *Tales from the Middle of Nowhere*. It read:

> Q *magazine are with us for a couple of days. At least it'll alleviate the boredom. I like doing interviews. I find myself having opinions on things I truly couldn't care less about. I wonder what they'll ask me about this time? Blur re-forming, I suppose. We'll find out soon enough.*
>
> *In a bit.*
>
> *GD.*

Behind the stage of Amsterdam's Music Hall, past the punch bag and flight cases, down a corridor lined with brooding house security, up two floors in an elevator, past Liam's personal security guard Steve Allen eating chocolate pudding, beyond Oasis's other security stationed by the band's dressing room and behind the Manchester City flag, it was a pleasure to discover Noel in the form of his life after the first of their two nights in Amsterdam.

As the *Q* reviews editor, I'd commissioned myself to write an on-the-road feature with Oasis, mainly because I really wanted to go see them play, ideally in a European country where fans were less likely to spend the night lobbing beers through the air. I also hadn't interviewed either Gallagher since doing Liam for *The Observer* six years earlier ('Do I recognize you . . .?'), and the closest I'd come to

Noel were drinks in pubs after recent award dos. I missed it. Here was a perfect opportunity to scratch both itches.

Shortly before I left, though, rumours had been filtering through that all was not well with their tour. Shows had been cancelled, due to Liam's temperamental throat. The brothers, it was also said, were no longer speaking, instead travelling by separate buses, preparing in separate dressing rooms, Gem Archer acting as a go-between. There had been bad vibes before, of course. But the juju was apparently worse than ever.

Yet here was Noel, full of bonhomie, Heineken in hand, reminiscing with his guitar tech Jason Rhodes about the first time Oasis came to Amsterdam in February 1994. Or rather, the first time he and Jason came, as the rest of the band had been arrested on the outbound ferry after getting caught up in a disturbance between West Ham and Chelsea fans in the disco (photographer Kevin Cummins, also on the ferry with the band, is adamant, however, that only Chelsea fans were aboard). It's a story we have touched on earlier in this book, of course, but now Noel added new detail. Liam was stopped as he ran by the roulette table, he said, and grabbed the roulette ball.

'Guigsy says that the copper told Liam he was going to arrest him. Liam goes, "You and whose fucking army?"' recalled Noel. 'Except he never got as far as the word "whose". In one movement they had him on the floor with his arm behind his back.'

The next morning, Noel was escorted down to the hold to collect the van's keys. 'They were behind these plastic shutters. As the shutters came up so they could pass the keys, Bonehead shouts, "You gotta call Marcus!", but the shutters start coming down again and the copper leans down into the gap and says, [affects sinister Euro cop voice] "Say goodbye to your little friends."'

'Disaster,' Noel reminisced, fondly. 'But me and Jason got to Amsterdam with the float. It wasn't a washout.'

No such organizational pratfall could banjax the Oasis juggernaut and its twenty-seven crew members in 2009, even though calamity had struck on 7 September the previous year when an audience member had rushed onstage in Toronto and pushed Noel with sufficient force to break three of his ribs. Now, all crew had to wear Oasis tour jackets and woe betide anyone onstage without one. At first, they were given Oasis T-shirts, but the crew found them a touch figure-hugging. 'We crossed out Oasis and wrote Take That on them,' said one crew member. 'We'll give them as presents to their crew when we cross paths with them.'

The brothers still had the capability to sabotage a gig easily enough, too, of course. The first night's show had been a bit of a highwire act, with a very subdued Liam swigging onstage from honey and lemon and crunching his way through the eleven packs of Lockets we'd been asked to bring over. But they'd made it, and afterwards the mood in the band dressing room was one of relief as Noel, Andy Bell, Gem, drummer Chris Sharrock and various crew cracked open beers while mingling with a couple of Dutch long-hairs and a willowy blonde in a miniskirt that nobody could quite place. Liam was nowhere to be seen.

Noel, one sensed, was just happy to have some new people to talk to, telling tales of meeting up with Morrissey in LA while Morrissey drank from a pint pot of vodka, and watching Barack Obama's inauguration the day before: 'ruined by Aretha Franklin's hat – disgraceful, man.'

I wondered about Oasis's future. Would they, like the Rolling Stones, still be playing stadiums when pensioners?

'It won't happen because Mick Jagger carries the Rolling Stones,' Noel decided. 'Ronnie and Keith prop each other up and Charlie sits down. I can't see Liam doing it at sixty-four. Not that he runs about or anything, but at some point, he is going to lose the ability to balance that tambourine on his head.'

An early night seemed to do the trick for Liam Gallagher, as he was back to balancing his tambourine on his head like a mutton-chopped seal the next evening, his voice also in full working order as he snarled and swooped his way through a heavy, grungily psychedelic greatest hits set, the highlight of which was an especially rueful 'Slide Away,' Liam dedicating it 'to all the lesbians out there.'

Afterwards, the mood was ebullient in the main Oasis dressing room, with everyone popping open bottles and clinking glasses, including, unusually, Liam, who circled the throng in his heavy woollen coat while keeping an eye on the vacant seat to my left as if stalking prey. Eventually, he sat down. On the other side of the room, Noel peered through the crowd and raised an eyebrow at me.

An earlier encounter with Liam that evening before the show had not gone particularly well. As I chatted with Noel in Liam's warm-up room ('I don't know what warm-ups he does in here, probably squat thrusts'), Liam had thrown open the door and slammed his bag on the floor.

'*Q*? Why even bother coming over here? You don't like our record, fuck off! Putting us on the cover fifty times, if you don't like the record then do one. Dickhead!'

'Don't worry about that,' said Noel after Liam had stomped off. 'I have to put up with that every day, usually over something like the fact that sugar can also come in cubes.'

Now, though, Liam turned and smiled.

'How you doing?' he asked.

Very well, how are you?

'I'm a tiger,' said Liam. 'Welcome to the fucking jungle.'

We talked for a little while, about wearing his heavy wool coat on stage ('not a problem if you're really cool'), about his outburst earlier, for which he almost apologized. His mood had been improved by his performance, about which he'd been stressed. 'I need to sing, me. If you take away my singing . . . I'm . . . I'm fucking lost.'

The doctor in Germany had told him he needed at least a week off, so he'd cancelled a couple of shows. 'And I did a shit one last night, but it was alright tonight. I like a drink, I like the odd cig, but I prefer singing, so I can't smoke. My voice is more important than a cigarette.'

Nevertheless, three hours later at 3 a.m., Liam was sitting in the Tara Irish pub in Amsterdam determinedly working his way through everyone's cigarettes. We'd arrived just as the bar was closing, but seeing the Gallaghers and entourage enter, the owner announced that we could have a lock-in for as late as we desired. This was foolish. The next day was a day off for Oasis. Spirits were high, and on tap, and nobody had anything to get up for.

All of Oasis other than Andy Bell had come along, as well as tour DJ Phil Smith, two apocalyptically drunk young members of support act Twisted Wheel, Oasis's security team, and Noel's friend Matt Morgan, who at the time was Russell Brand's writing partner and sidekick, but in recent years has worked with Noel on radio and podcasts. He'd come over with a mate on a whim, and the three of them immediately commandeered the pool table.

On the other side of the bar, Liam watched the trio in some agitation. 'Who's Noel with?' he demanded of Gem. 'Who's he with?'

'That's Matt Morg—'

'I know who he is! I've met him but I've never been introduced. "Who are you with, Noel?" "Oh, just a couple of guys." Couple of guys?! I don't know any guys, me. I've never hung out with any guys in my life.'

I pointed out that Liam was actually hanging out with a couple of guys at that moment.

'No, mate,' he replied. 'The only guys I hang out with are in the band. Everyone else I hang out with is a geezer.'

'What's the difference?'

Gem rolled his eyes. 'You can ask what someone is like and be told, "Oh, it's just some guy." But if you like them, he's a geezer. "What's he like?" "Geezer".'

'And Noel says those two are guys,' added Liam, conspiratorially.

None of this proved a barrier to a good time, it turned out. By 5 a.m., the party had gathered onto one table when suddenly Liam returned from a comfort break with a message for all. He pointed at each person present, repeating the same message: 'You know it, you know it, you know it, you know it, you know it . . .'

'Know what?' asked Gem.

'That I'm Jesus.'

At which all erupted in laughter. All except Noel, who picked at the label on his beer bottle with a shake of his head. Liam's security man Steve Allen sat down next to me. Moments earlier he'd been miming the guitar and singing along to The Jam standing on the pool table. 'Knackered,' he explained, then pointed out that we were witnessing a rare phenomenon. 'Liam and Noel never go on the piss together on tour,' he said. 'It just doesn't happen. It's good to see it going on.'

Suddenly, Liam was back. 'Can you feel the Dutch vibrations?' he demanded of all. 'It's pineapple time!'

Noel had heard enough. 'I really don't know what you're talking about,' he replied. At which Liam clicked his heels, downed his medicinal glass of port and beckoned to Steve that they were offski. 'I need to be fresh for my run in the morning,' he could be heard explaining as they stepped out into the daylight.

As they marched off, Matt Morgan turned to Noel. 'Is he a bit mental, your brother?'

'Of course he's mental,' replied Noel. 'Just look at his hair.'

That afternoon, a new post from Noel's tour diary appeared on the Oasis website.

Urgh! My head hurts today. Had a bit of a smash-up last night. Where? But an Irish bar of course. I got left with the bar bill – which I've just found in my pocket. It reads as follows:

29 pints of Guinness
16 pints of Strongbow
6 pints of Jupiler (whatever the fuck that is!)
4 pints of Heineken
3 Gordon's gin
5 Sauza Tequila
12 Bacardis
11 vodka Stolis
14 Jameson whiskey
10 Bushmills malt

16 bottles of Coke
7 bottles of tonic
4 7-Up
. . . and this is the killer: 1 glass of port and a packet of cheese and onion crisps!!?? (I'm blaming the guy from Q*)*
All came to a colossal €708.40. Bargain.
In a bit.
GD.

Back in the office, I realized I'd forgotten to ask Noel for his thoughts about the recently announced Blur reunion. Nobody editing the piece mentioned the omission. It didn't seem to matter, for some reason. Besides, in nine months Noel would have an entirely different reunion to answer questions about – queries that would dog him for the next fifteen years.

'I shouldn't be in this position. This is not me at all . . . it's a pain in the arse!'

On the frontline with Oasis #8

Liam unleashes Beady Eye and Noel goes it alone, July 2011

Around lunchtime on Wednesday 6 July 2011, I entered the somewhat bougie surroundings of Notting Hill's Electric Cinema. Just under a hundred members of the world's media were assembling for a press conference by Noel Gallagher. It was the first time he would be speaking in public since the statement on 29 August 2009, in which it was confirmed that, 'with heavy heart and a sad face', he had been 'forced to leave the Manchester rock 'n' roll pop group Oasis'.

This re-emergence into the public eye could not really have been any more different to his brother's. While Noel immediately disappeared into the shadows following the split, Liam had launched himself at full pelt into a long succession of interviews. These were ostensibly to promote his clothing label Pretty Green. But while the conversations may have started on the subject of parkas, being the uncontrollable ball of passion that Liam is, they normally ended up being about the end of Oasis and Noel. In the immediate aftermath of the split, right up until the announcement of Beady Eye – featuring Liam, Gem Archer, Andy Bell and Chris Sharrock – in May 2010, he had been everywhere.

This meant that the gruesome details of Oasis's final hours backstage – a fight in a Paris dressing room, ending with Liam brandishing a guitar over Noel like an axe – had been recalled plenty of times by one half of its attendees. So Noel, as he put it to me in the bar upstairs after his press conference, only had to tell his side once 'and then it's out there and I don't have to talk about it again. I've given . . . well, I won't say I've given my version of events – I've told the truth about what happened. We can all move on now. That was the main purpose. It was to announce the two records, yeah, but it wasn't to say, "Ta-dah! I'm back!" I just don't want to keep going over Paris a hundred times: it's fucking boring. So it was, "Let's get it out of the way."'

Filmed and left on YouTube for all to revisit, Noel's press conference had been a success. 'Let battle commence,' he had grinned as he sat down in the centre of the stage, but in reality, it was not a combative occasion. 'We had a bit of a sweepstake on how long this would take,' he said as the first question about Liam arrived three minutes in. And he gave a long monologue about Paris ('At the end of the day he doesn't like me. He doesn't like me in a violent way. For me, there's no point in being in a band with people you fight with. What's the point?'). But other than that, the questions pretty much concerned the music that was coming and the plans that he had when it came to playing live. 'I thought it was a bit tame, actually,' he told me later, with a hint of disappointment.

It all felt quite understated and modest, which again was in stark contrast to Beady Eye's promotional strategy. By the time they had released their first single 'Bring the Light' that November, they had been talked up to the skies by their singer for months. Liam Gallagher, it was clear, knew no other way. When I met up with the band in Milan in April 2011 – by which time their album *Different Gear, Still Speeding* was out – I had asked Liam (who had, he said, 'not had a drink since New Year's Eve' in the interest of staying focused) whether he thought Beady Eye could be as big as Oasis.

'Fuck being as big as Oasis, man,' he responded immediately. 'I want to be as big as The Beatles. I want to be *bigger* than The Beatles. That's what we're dealing with and whether we do or not – and we probably won't – who cares? It's just the fucking name of the game. So yes, we want to sell a shitload of records, play stadiums and inspire shitloads of kids all over the fucking universe. Deep down that's what I want to do.'

When I caught up with Noel Gallagher later that day, though – over nothing stronger than cappuccinos – his outlook on the future seemed a very different one. 'I don't see me ever being able to stand on stage in a stadium, like a jobbing fucking minstrel with an acoustic guitar, and pull it off for an hour and a half. I just don't think I've got that in me.'

This surprised me. Really, I asked? 'I don't think the demand will be there,' he continued. 'I could probably do an arena in Manchester. Probably. I've not been in this position since *Definitely Maybe*, where it's just like, "We'll put this album out, don't know what's going to happen." Anything is possible and I'm not setting any limits on it. But I can safely say: I won't be in any way approaching being as big as Oasis were. Never.'

'To now go out on a stage, with new songs and – for want of a better term – sell them to people is a pain in the arse! I shouldn't be in this position. This is not me at all. I was the guy, stage left, doing the backing vocals, playing the electric guitar, and that's me. I'd perfected that role. Now I've got to go and do something else. But I'm not . . . you know . . . I'll give it the best shot I can.'

He had, too, been spooked somewhat by the chart performances of Beady Eye's singles. 'To be quite honest, it was a bit of a wake-up call for me. 'Cos I was like, right, well, fucking hell, maybe that's what's out there for me. So on the day [Beady Eye single] "The Roller" went in at thirty or whatever . . . a lot of people I know were like, "Fucking hell, I bet you're happy with that!" And I was like, "Not really," because I was quite shocked. I thought it would do what Oasis singles do. So obviously, someone who puts my records out has got some fucking work to do!'

Written by Gem, 'The Roller' had been demoed by Oasis as far back as 2002, around the time of *Heathen Chemistry* – 'I always thought it was going to be a mega, mega hit for Oasis,' Noel told me – and plenty of the titles on this just-announced solo album were familiar too. 'Stop the Clocks' and '(I Wanna Live in a Dream in My) Record Machine' had been set to feature on *Dig Out Your Soul* until, Noel had claimed, 'it came time for Liam to do the vocals, and he'd fucked off to get married without telling anyone.' In more recent times, though, Liam had insisted his brother was holding back the better songs for a solo record all along.

'Well, Liam talks a lot, doesn't he?' Noel said when I brought this up. 'Ask Andy and Gem is what I'd say. Those songs have been recorded on two separate occasions, for two albums, and vocals were never completed. I've re-recorded them now in a different key to suit my voice. And they are the two most Oasis-sounding songs on the album. But whatever he says is bullshit.'

Noel Gallagher's High Flying Birds would go on to sell nearly 3 million copies worldwide: an extraordinary feat in an era in which streaming was well on its way to eating the music industry's lunch. And by the end of the year, the tour in support of its release was completely sold out. Noel had been right about filling an arena in Manchester. But there were a further thirteen shows of a similar size – not least at the O2 Arena in London – at the start of 2012, and plenty more after.

The next time I interviewed Liam at the end of that year, his assessment of how Beady Eye had gone was both brutal and honest. 'Maybe it was too quick after Oasis,' he told me. 'You can blame it on this, you can blame it on that . . . but at the end of the day people just didn't fucking buy it. They didn't get it. It didn't connect. So back to the drawing board.' There was to be a second album in 2013 – the more sonically adventurous *BE* – but it fared similarly to the first and by October 2014 Liam Gallagher was taking to Twitter to announce that 'Beady Eye are no longer. Thanks for your support x'. His period in the wilderness had begun.

Noel, meanwhile, was firing on all cylinders, the doubts about being able to play Oasis-sized venues just a distant memory. 'I meet fans all the time who say, "I'm coming to see you at the O2",' he told me when I interviewed him just prior to the release of his second solo album, *Chasing Yesterday*, 'and it's like, "Well, if you're coming to see anything, don't bother coming to see, because there's nothing to see." But what I have got is songs that people like to sing. And I think that's more important. So if my promoter was to ring me up tomorrow and say, "I think you could do Wembley Stadium," then fucking right! It's time to reclaim that fucking stadium. There's been too much shit going on there recently.'

As it turned out, of course, both Gallagher brothers would get to play stadiums, solo, on many occasions. And by 2017, both of them were finally getting what they ultimately wanted: Liam his own blockbuster album *As You Were* and a triumphant return to Knebworth; Noel the chance to make a record like *Who Built the Moon?*, which found him utilizing completely new ways of writing and garnered great reviews from people who might not ever have liked Oasis.

'The Noel versus Liam thing?' Liam had said to me back in Milan. 'I'm a bit saddened by it, that some people feel like they need to pick sides. Like I wouldn't go and see the Roses and be like, "I fucking hate John Squire but I'm into Ian Brown" or whatever.' He was right. In the years between 2009 and 2025, it turned out there was plenty of room for both.

'I believe that Oasis will sail again and that it'll be glorious.'

On the frontline with Oasis #9

To the pub and pictures with Liam, August 2016

At the other end of Warren Street, a familiar voice rang out.

'Ted!' Liam Gallagher shouted from inside the doorway of a coffee shop 100 yards down the street. Apparently he knew my name after all.

'Coffee?' he called. 'Flat white?'

It was a beautiful summer's day in London, and all was incredibly well with the world. In some kind of seemingly far-fetched fever dream, I was midway through the perfect date with Liam Gallagher.

The day before, 2 August 2016, I'd walked into a near-empty pub in north London's well-heeled Highgate just after lunchtime to be greeted by Liam, who was sitting with his new partner/manager Debbie Gwyther and her twin Katie at a table on the other side of the room. 'What'll you have?' he shouted across the boozer. 'My card's behind the bar.' By anyone's estimations, these were ideal drinking conditions. And so, we tucked in.

I was the acting editor of *Q* magazine, which is almost exactly the same as being the editor but on the features editor's wage. While my bosses deliberated whether they were going to give me the title (and wage), they regularly asked who my dream cover star would be (even though I was picking the cover stars anyway). The answer was always Liam Gallagher. That applied in 1994, as it also did in 2024, but it applied perhaps even more so in 2016 because we hadn't heard from him in print for a couple of years, since Beady Eye had split after two commercially disappointing albums in 2014. Since then, very little other than tabloid tittle-tattle about the end of his marriage to Nicole Appleton. By coincidence, I'd known Debbie Gwyther longer than she'd even known Liam, and so I would politely beg her for that interview with him every few months or so. Then, one day, she called.

There was a new documentary film about Oasis coming out in the autumn, she explained, one focused upon the band up to and including Knebworth. It was made by the people who delivered the excellent *Senna*, and it was called *Supersonic*. Would I be interested in talking to Liam exclusively about it and whatever else was on his mind? Well, come on now . . .

In the pub, over pints, Liam explained what had been going on for the past two years. Since he'd dispensed with the intricate management scaffolding that keeps rock megastars afloat, he'd spent a while in freefall. He had tumbled 'out of the bubble' to such an extent that for a while he considered jacking it all in and moving to Majorca, living 'Sexy Beast-style'. Debbie, who had previously worked at Beady Eye's management company, put paid to that.

'She swooped me up when I was falling and sorted me right out,' he explained.

What that meant was that 'she just told me to stop being a dick-head. She got me out the house, introduced me to new people outside my world, got me doing new things.'

She also firmly reminded him that he was the greatest rock 'n' roll frontman of his generation, he was only forty-three and there was lots of mileage left on his engine. Perhaps he just needed to work with some different people. Which is exactly what he did, going to LA and collaborating with songwriter-producers Greg Kurstin, Andrew Wyatt and Dan Grech-Marguerat, demoing and recording new songs, some of which Liam played via Debbie's laptop for me when we were a bit drunk in the pub, miming the words and dancing as I listened through headphones giving them a thumbs-up.

The next morning, feeling groggy, we met at the production house with our flat whites to watch *Supersonic* together in their screening room, positioned one seat apart – hopeful, perhaps, that Noel would slip in between us.

It is hardly now a revolutionary position to describe *Supersonic* as a masterpiece music documentary. Collated from amazing home footage taken by band friends, family and associates, it traces the Oasis story in glorious detail from their youth in Burnage right up to stepping out of the choppers and on to the stage of Knebworth, all narrated by two long, off-screen interviews with Noel and Liam, as well as with Peggy and all the band's closest associates. The film, along with Liam's stratospheric solo career arc breathing new life into the Oasis catalogue, plays a key role as catalyst for the eventual Gallagher reunion, reminding one generation of what they had and another of what they were missing, whetting appetites for what might be again. It's a brilliant film. Perhaps you've seen it.

But you have never seen it sitting alone in a cinema with Liam Gallagher providing his own commentary, heckling his brother ('Get your story straight, lad!' 'Very convenient, mate!' and, mostly, 'Bollocks!'), as well as various other participants (mainly Bonehead), as it plays at full pelt on a huge screen in front of you. There's one moment when Noel is heard saying, 'Oasis's greatest strength was the relationship between me and Liam . . .' To which Liam stood and applauded next to me. But that clapping turned swiftly into V-flicking as Noel finished his sentence, '. . . But it's also what drove the band into the ground.' As the helicopter carrying the band hovers over Knebworth and the camera pans to Noel's face, Liam shouted, 'Shitting it!' The screen then captures Liam looking down at the site below, as the chopper swoops around. 'Loving it,' he declared proudly, shaking his fist at the screen.

When Liam is briefly pictured at the end of Knebworth sucking on a joint, he twisted around in his seat and said, 'I used to always smoke draw in the early days but as we got big I stopped before or during gigs. That was a very rare moment, there, smoking a spliff onstage. Must have been the last notes of the gig.'

Afterwards, as we stood dazed by the glare of the noon sun in the street, Liam revealed he had a couple of hours free before an appointment with his oldest brother, Paul. As if by magic, the Smugglers Tavern opposite us opened for the day. 'Fancy a pint and some lunch?' he wondered. We ordered two pints and a small bowl of fries to share.

I asked if watching *Supersonic* made him feel melancholic. 'Sad? Yeah, without a doubt. Sad, great and proud. We did some amazing things, didn't we? We were a great band.' It reminded him, too, he said, of the Noel he hadn't spoken to for a couple of years at that point. 'I miss the Noel in the film, that's the Noel I know. And I do love him. I don't sit at home crying into a picture of him, though, and I'm sure he doesn't of me either. But I'm an energy and I bet he misses that energy.'

We ordered more drinks, on the understanding that I had to let everyone know in the piece 'that we're back having refreshing pints for lunch after yesterday. We gotta let people know that we're still rocking it. There's got to be one legend people can rely on.'

There were quite a few things in *Supersonic* that he disagreed with, he said. For example, there was too much about his brutish dad, about him knocking Noel around when they were kids. 'It gets a bit sad, we needed the *EastEnders* drum beat in it. Listen, if our kid is alright with it, then I am. I know he's blood, but I have no urge to see [Dad] whatsoever.'

He also disputed the fact that West Ham fans were the cause of the disturbance on the ferry to Holland in February 1994. 'Don't remember that. Do remember being bopped by security. Guigsy had just been made redundant from BT and had his pay-off in £50 notes. Really it was because the security thought we kept buying drinks with forgeries. Someone's said "Fuck off" and it's kicked off. We spent twelve hours in the cell pissing in a bucket as we'd been drinking all day, watching the bucket slosh all over the place, tip-toeing on the mattress. I loved that. When did you last hear of a band getting in a scrape like that? The Benny Hill element has gone from rock 'n' roll.'

But there was one line, he admitted, from Noel that rang as

particularly true in the film: Noel's a cat and Liam's a dog. 'Without a doubt. He's arrogant, sticks his arse up, comes and goes as he pleases, stands apart, just surveying everyone. Loves being stroked. Total tart. Loves you when he wants. I only get took out on a lead. I'm not allowed on the sofa. I run around with the pack, barking, tongue hanging out. He's all aloof up there watching, licking himself and plotting. That's us alright.' Both brothers say in *Supersonic* that they believe in fate. What, I wondered as we stood swaying in the afternoon glare again a little later, did it have in store for them?

'I believe that Oasis will sail again and that it'll be glorious,' he said, suddenly very serious. 'Noel, let's do it because they want it. One year. A tour for a year. We'd smash it. My bags are still packed from my last tour, so I'm ready. In fact, I'm still packed from 1999 and I could wear that gear. I never unpack.'

This sounded very positive, but there was a hitch. 'I just don't know which house I've left my bags in and how quickly I can fetch them.'

As I emerged from my tube stop with the other commuters later, my phone vibrated with hundreds of notifications. What now? I checked my socials. My Twitter feed had a somewhat unusual 2,000 new followers and hundreds of messages. I followed the evidence.

In his cab on the way to collect his brother Paul from the dentist, a merry Liam had sent a simple message out to his million followers:

There's only 1 Ted Kessler!

Now that he'd finally learned my name, Liam was probably just making sure that he had a record of it. I felt like the luckiest girl at the prom.

The Liam Gallagher interview added an unheard-of 30 per cent uplift in sales to that issue of *Q*, a foretaste of how his solo career would deliver three UK number-one albums, two sold-out Knebworths and countless other accolades and milestones. From then on, the question my employers would most regularly ask me over the next four years was ‘when can you put Liam Gallagher on the cover again?’ with a monotonous, desperate repetition. As often as possible, as it turned out.

2020

'Don't Stop . . .'

STANDALONE DEMO

Like most people on Planet Earth in April 2020, Noel Gallagher was locked up indoors.

'I've had infinite time to kill lately so I thought I'd finally look and find out what was actually on the hundreds of faceless unmarked CDs I've got lying around at home,' he said. 'As fate would have it, I have stumbled across an old demo I thought had been lost forever . . . Hope everyone is staying safe and trying to ride out the lockdown with a minimum of fuss. You're welcome by the way.'

When he'd done his Reddit AMA (Ask Me Anything) five years earlier, Noel had been asked repeatedly about 'Don't Stop . . .' – or 'Bye Bye My Family', as fans were calling the bootleg version – and described it as 'a great song . . . I love it and when I finally release it, you're going to love it (fans, that is).'

He would re-record it as part of 2023's *Council Skies*, but in the meantime the demo did a fine job of cheering people up during the pandemic and starting some rumours about whether Oasis were getting back together, which obviously would never happen. **HM**

ACKNOWLEDGEMENTS

Thanks to . . .

Special Agent Becky Thomas of Lewinsohn Literary; Ingrid Connell, Melissa Bond, Jiri Greco and all at Pan Macmillan; Debbie Gwyther; Paul Stokes for generously giving us sight of his transcripts; everyone we've ever spoken to about Oasis; Jean, Jagger and Joey; beautiful Emily; the great Raymondo; Spud and his back-breakingly huge archive of Oasis ephemera; Café Boheme and the Coach & Horses.

These sources were invaluable . . .

Books: Simon Halfon, *Supersonic: The Complete, Authorized and Uncut Interviews* (Headline, 2021); John Harris, *The Last Party: Britpop, Blair and the Demise of English Rock* (Fourth Estate, 2003); Paolo Hewitt, *Getting High: The Adventures of Oasis* (Boxtree, 1997); Paul Mathur, *Take Me There: Oasis, the Story* (Bloomsbury, 1996); Tony McCarroll, *Oasis: The Truth* (John Blake, 2010).

Media: *The Oasis Podcast* and stopcryingyourheartout.co.uk were vital resources, both compiled with the devotion of true fans. The Live4ever forum and the *Behind the Curtain* podcast also provided good insight.

Publications: *The Guardian*; *Independent*; *Melody Maker*; *NME*; *Q*; *Select*; *Tribune*; *The Times*; *The Sunday Times*; plus assorted red-tops.

Pieces by Max Bell, James Brown, Keith Cameron, Carol Clerk, John Doran, Danny Eccleston, John Harris, Will Hodgkinson, Tim Jonze, Fergal Kinney, Paul Lester, Michael Odell, Sylvia Patterson, Andrew Perry, Alexis Petridis, John Robb, Paul Stokes, Phil Sutcliffe and Simon Williams were particularly helpful.

Thank you, for reading this far.

PICTURE CREDITS

p. 14 © James Fry via Getty Images
p. 20 © Kevin Cummins via Getty Images
p. 84 © Niels van Iperen via Getty Images
p. 148 © Jill Furmanovsky Archive
p. 162 © Jill Furmanovsky Archive
p. 202 © Dave Benett via Getty Images
p. 214 © Gareth Davies via Getty Images
p. 216 © Patrick Ford/Redferns via Getty Images
p. 244 © Ethan Miller via Getty Images
p. 272 © Dave Hogan via Getty Images
p. 276 © Mick Hutson/Redferns via Getty Images
p. 302 © Niki Nikolova/FilmMagic via Getty Images
p. 304 © JMEnternational/Redferns via Getty Images
p. 314 © Samir Hussein via Getty Images
p. 336 © Gie Knaeps via Getty Images
p. 355 © author's own

INDEX